Shidehara Kijuro
and
His Time

Shidehara Kijuro

and His Time

Okazaki Hisahiko

Translated by Noda Makito

Japan Publishing Industry Foundation for Culture

TRANSLATION NOTE

All Japanese names appearing in this book are written with surname first and given name last. In addition, all Japanese words and names have been romanized in accordance with the Hepburn system, and macrons have been applied to indicate long vowels wherever deemed appropriate.

Shidehara Kijuro and His Time
Okazaki Hisahiko. Translated by Noda Makito.

Published by
Japan Publishing Industry Foundation for Culture (JPIC)
2-2-30 Kanda-Jinbocho, Chiyoda-ku, Tokyo 101-0051, Japan

First English edition: March 2020

This book is the result of a collaborative effort between The Japan Institute of International Affairs (JIIA) and Japan Publishing Industry Foundation for Culture (JPIC).

Originally published in Japanese by PHP Institute, Inc. in 2003 under the title of *Shidehara Kijūrō to sono jidai*.

Jacket & cover design: Seno Hiroya

Printed in Japan
ISBN 978-4-86658-073-9
https://www.jpic.or.jp/

CONTENTS

CHAPTER 8
End of the Anglo-Japanese Alliance

CHAPTER 9
Peace and the Military

CHAPTER 13
Shidehara Diplomacy's Last Hurrah
—Shidehara Remained Unchanged in the Midst of Turmoil— 247

CHAPTER 14
Epilogue: The End of Shidehara Diplomacy
—Japan Is Deprived of a Priceless Diplomatic Asset— 269

CHAPTER

1

Diplomat of the New Age

— A Typical, Serious Bureaucrat in a Time of Peace —

A New Breed of Japanese Born in Meiji

Shidehara Kijūrō was born in 1872. His first overseas post as a diplomat was to the Japanese legation in Incheon, Korea. Having observed the words and deeds of this newly appointed diplomat, Consul Ishii Kikujirō asked Shidehara how old he was. Hearing the reply, Ishii exclaimed, "So you were born after the Meiji Restoration (of 1868). You are different from the other people. I have always suspected you were a new breed of Japanese." Although Ishii himself was born in 1866, only two years before the Meiji Restoration and was just six years older than Shidehara, this was such a time of politico-social turmoil that Ishii perceived a generation gap between Shidehara and himself.

How, though, was Shidehara different from his nominal cohorts? In a nutshell, he was a serious man born in a time of peace. One of Shidehara's colleagues from his days in London later reminisced:

> Japanese foreign service men in those days often affected an air of samurai machismo. When it came to mastering foreign languages, studying international law, or researching domestic and international situations, however, they were less than enthusiastic. . . . By contrast,

Shidehara never let up in his strenuous effort to acquire such learning. He paid particular attention to mastering English, spending long hours practicing it unbeknownst to others. And this made him the number-one master of the language among the many officials at the foreign ministry.

Also impressive was his quiet devotion to the study of not only the country he was assigned to but also economic conditions in Japan. . . Hardly any other diplomat was as diligent as Shidehara. Seeing him working so hard when others were far more lax, at first we regarded him as a mere omnivorous bookworm. Later, however, we realized that he had been silently showing us that it was not enough for diplomats in the new age to talk big and argue among themselves; that diplomats should work hard to learn how to govern a nation, provide succor to the people, and thus enhance Japan's wellbeing and prosperity. This is where Shidehara's greatness lies.

Certainly, one who applies himself to learning foreign languages and studying foreign countries will end up having a general grasp of the global situation, which will lead to a more accurate assessment of the power balance between Japan and the Western nations. He will notice the emptiness of such pompous and overblown slogans as saying Japan is destined to rule all of Asia.

The philosophy that developed out of these studies became the backbone of Shidehara's diplomacy for international cooperation, which later came to be known as Shidehara diplomacy. This diplomacy was not so much about Shidehara's personal convictions as it was about his accurate understanding of the international situation and clearer vision of the only way that Japan could survive in the world. Underlying this realistic and flexible way of thinking was Shidehara's upbringing in a non-samurai family in Osaka. People such as Shidehara remained a minority in the Japanese ruling class, not only in the early days when he was looked upon as a new breed but also throughout the period leading up to World War II. In today's context, however, Shidehara is just an ordinary smart bureaucrat, and it does not require any extra effort on the part of Japanese to understand his type. Thus I have decided that it would not make sense to delve into Shidehara's character by describing his childhood environment and upbringing at the same length as I did for Mutsu Munemitsu and

Komura Jutarō. Shidehara's social and family situations were such that they need little explication for today's readers.

Middle-Class Family Enthusiastic for Children's Education

The class system that prevailed when Shidehara was born marked him as born into a peasant family. While it is rumored that the Shidehara family was an old, established family in Kawachi, Osaka, the great flood of 1885 washed away any and all family records, leaving the family history in oblivion. What is known today is that Shidehara's grandfather made some money and became a landlord and wealthy farmer. Shidehara's father married into the Shidehara family. This man was so enthusiastic about his children's education that he was willing to sell half of the family's farmland to finance it. When relatives heard this, they criticized Shidehara's father as being presumptuous beyond his station as an adopted husband, perhaps indicating that the Shidehara family was not that rich after all. Yet thanks to the education his father provided, Shidehara, his older brother, and his two younger sisters all excelled in their studies. The brother earned a doctorate in letters, became an Oriental history scholar, and was later named president of Taihoku Imperial University in Taiwan. The older of the two sisters married a man who was then adopted into the family to carry on the family tradition, while the younger sister became the first female physician in Osaka. In today's terms, Shidehara's family was a moderately wealthy middle-class family, all of whose children got excellent educations and did well in their chosen fields.

If there is anything in Shidehara's life that differs from people's memories of the Shōwa era, it is the incomparably high status accorded graduates of Tokyo Imperial University in Shidehara's time. People of high rank or great wealth vied to see who could get their daughters married to graduates of Tokyo Imperial University, saying, "A Tokyo Imperial University graduate is worthy of my daughter!" Tokyo Imperial University graduates had their pick of jobs, too. The one exception was the Ministry of Foreign

Shidehara as a Tokyo Imperial University student

Affairs, which only employed those who passed the Foreign Service examination instituted at the time Mutsu Munemitsu was Foreign Minister, with the first examination held in 1894 when Shidehara was a junior at Tokyo Imperial University.

Although Shidehara wanted to become a diplomat, he suffered from a severe case of beriberi that prevented him from taking the Foreign Service examination. While his mentor encouraged him to consider other posts such as teacher at a high school in Sendai, Shidehara refused to apply for these jobs. In the end, he could no longer reject his mentor's recommendation and went to work for the Ministry of Agriculture and Commerce. Today, the examination for the Ministry of Economy, Trade and Industry, which succeeded the Ministry of Agriculture and Commerce, is one of the toughest to pass, but in those days the ministry seems to have willingly hired any graduate of Tokyo Imperial University. At the Ministry of Agriculture and Commerce, Shidehara proved himself quite useful due to his knowledge of law. After a while, Shidehara resigned from the ministry to concentrate on preparing for the Foreign Service examination, which he passed in 1896, immediately after the First Sino-Japanese War. He was assigned to Incheon, Korea, toward the end of the year. Shidehara was later the first Japanese foreign minister who entered the ministry by passing the Foreign Service examination. In this sense, too, he was a new-generation diplomat.

Meiji Man-Like Fortitude

While Shidehara's experiences as a young bureaucrat may not seem relevant to this study of Japan's modern diplomatic history, I find it important to point out that Shidehara married the youngest daughter of the Iwasaki family—the same Iwasaki family that founded the Mitsubishi zaibatsu. Shidehara's marriage made him the brother-in-law of Katō Takaaki.

Katō was a prodigy graduate of Kaisei Gakkō, as was Komura Jutarō. Kaisei Gakkō merged with Tokyo Medical School to form the University of Tokyo while the two were students there. Katō graduated at the head of his class but chose not to enter government service and instead joined the Mitsubishi zaibatsu, where he won recognition from founder Iwasaki Yatarō and eventually became his son-in-law. Subsequently, Katō was persuaded by Mutsu Munemitsu to join the foreign ministry, where he was put in charge of revising the unequal treaties with the Western powers and served as the Japanese minister (equivalent to today's Ambassador) to Britain until his appointment as minister for foreign affairs in 1900. While in London, Katō and his wife resided with Masako, his wife's stepsister, who attended a British school. The Katōs had their eye on Shidehara, who had been stationed in London, as Masako's marriage partner. With Katō Takaaki, three-time foreign minister and later prime minister as his brother-in-law and with the backing of the formidable Mitsubishi zaibatsu Shidehara managed to avoid hardship such as Mutsu's imprisonment or the poverty and alienation that afflicted Komura. He simply shot ahead on the road to success.

Given Shidehara's background, one may be forgiven for imagining he was a super-bright bureaucrat and a believer in not rocking the boat who was only interested in looking out for himself. Yet that would be a mistake, as he did have his share of the fortitude characteristic of Meiji men. Shidehara was the Japanese consul stationed in Busan, Korea, on the eve of the Russo-Japanese War. Looking out at the sea from the legation's second floor window, he saw a Japanese warship capture a Russian commercial vessel and take it out of the port. While he was wondering if the war had erupted at last, he received a letter of protest from the Russian consul

stationed in Busan. Since Shidehara had been on friendly terms with his Russian counterpart, he visited the latter directly instead of replying in writing. In his meeting with the Russian consul, Shidehara said, "I see war has already erupted between our countries. If that is indeed the case, diplomatic relations between us must already have been severed, making the exchange of official dispatches meaningless. I therefore cannot accept your letter of protest."

After Shidehara left the Russian legation, it occurred to him that the Russian consul most certainly would send a wire to his home country to report on this incident, which

The Shideharas, front row left to right: his wife Masako, his older son Michitarō, and his younger son Shigeo. Shidehara himself standing in the back.

could put Japanese vessels at risk of being sunk or captured by Russian cruisers anchored in Incheon. Shidehara decided, therefore, that the wire from the Russian legation had to be blocked at any cost. His memoir recalls that, "After pondering on how to accomplish it, I came up with an idea, although one of quite questionable morality." Shidehara summoned a Japanese policeman to the legation and asked him to undertake the following action in confidence:

> Go to the post office and threaten the staff there. Tell them not to accept the Russian legation's request to send a telegram. Mind you, this is an irregular operation and you may be dismissed from your post for it. Although I might be discharged myself, I shall do my utmost best to guarantee your livelihood.

The officer agreed to take the risk and left for the post office.

Sure enough, the Russian legation staff arrived in no time with a long telegram draft. When the police officer drew his sword and threatened to kill the post office clerk if he did not hand the telegram over, the clerk lost his presence of mind. Taking advantage of this, the police officer snatched the draft from the clerk's hands and tore it into pieces. After he returned to the Japanese legation, the police officer proudly told Shidehara, "I was just in time and it worked perfectly." When Shidehara replied, "Great, but I am afraid you will be dismissed," the officer said, "It felt so good, I don't care if I am."

Anticipating that the Russian mission would at any moment make a second attempt to send a wire, Shidehara mobilized a police squad to cut their telephone line, fully aware that doing this was "quite an outrageous act."

> Regardless of my motivation, my action was definitely not a commendable one, and I decided not to report it to the foreign ministry. Should my action be exposed, and should I be cross-examined, I knew that would be the end of my career. Fortunately, nothing like that ever happened. The statute of limitations has already passed, but I still have not told many people about my action.

It is quite like Shidehara to repeat how "outrageous" and "not commendable" this irregular operation was. And there is no sign in his memoir that he was particularly proud of himself. In fact, he appears to be ashamed of what he did. What was imperative for him at that time was to obstruct the Russian legation's attempt to send a report on the activities of the Japanese fleet in Busan, and he paid no heed to his job security in fulfilling the mission. Shidehara could disregard everything else in order to serve his country and, in this sense, he had something in common with Mutsu, who conspired to rebel against the government, and Komura, who intentionally leaked confidential information, both in the country's interest.

Calm Political Period under Prime Ministers Katsura and Saionji

It was when Shidehara was promoted to vice-minister for foreign affairs in 1915 that he assumed a position of some responsibility for formulating Japanese foreign policy. It is therefore worth pausing here to get an overview of the political situation in Japan in the late-Meiji to early-Taishō eras—the time during which Shidehara rose rapidly within the government bureaucracy. The Imperial Diet had been calm and uneventful during the Russo-Japanese War because even the opposition parties were fully supportive of the war effort. In a way, it may be said that parliamentary democracy under the Meiji Constitution was successfully managed without a suspension of the constitution or a coup d'état until the rise of militarism in the 1930s thanks to a continuation of crises, including the First Sino-Japanese War and the Russo-Japanese War.

In the late Meiji period, parliamentary politics in Japan enjoyed a period of relative stability called the Kei-En Era (Katsura-Saionji Era). This lasted until the passing of Emperor Meiji. Tokutomi Sohō, a Meiji-Shōwa journalist and historian, made the following observations on the period.

The decade between 1903 and 1912 can be called the reign of Prime Ministers Katsura and Saionji. When Katsura formed his cabinet, Saionji, as leader of the Seiyūkai (Friends of Constitutional Government) supported him in the House of Representatives. When it was Saionji's turn to form a government, Katsura assisted by mustering a majority in the House of Peers. It was always expected that the Katsura government would be followed by the Saionji government, which would be succeeded by the Katsura cabinet again. Thus, the center of the regime continuously sustained itself and nobody dared challenge it. Thus was a decade of domestic political peace maintained.

Although Saionji Kinmochi was the president of the Seiyūkai political party, he did not attempt to accomplish full-fledged party politics all at once. Every time he formed a cabinet, he appointed Hara Takeshi and one other Seiyūkai member to important posts. Yet other than these two posts, Saionji made it a rule to appoint the most qualified people to suitable posts, ignoring both party affiliation and *han* (feudal domain) background. Consequently, he succeeded in alleviating conservative worries about the emergence of party politics while at the same time muting criticism from party politicians who were apprehensive of interference from the *hanbatsu* (primarily people from the Satsuma, Chōshū, and other *han* that were instrumental in the coup d'état we call the Meiji Restoration and who stuck together in business and politics after that).

Saionji Kinmochi's Mischievous Boyhood

What kind of person was Saionji Kinmochi? Saionji survived the Meiji, Taishō, and Shōwa eras right up until 1940 as the last genrō (elder statesman). Hearing of Japan's signing of the Tripartite Pact with Germany and Italy in 1940, Saionji predicted Japan's future accurately, telling the women taking care of him, "Now perhaps you won't be able to die peacefully at home." Saionji passed away two months after this observation at the age of 94. He lived to witness the entire rise and fall of the Empire of Japan from the Meiji Restoration through the eve of the Pacific War. The Saionjis were court nobility. Among the 160 families of court nobles, the five with the highest status belonged to the Go-sekke (Five regent houses), which included the Konoe family that produced Konoe Atsumaro and his son Fumimaro, the 34th, 38th, and 39th prime ministers of Japan. These five houses were followed by the nine Kyu-seiga houses which included the Saionji family as well as the family of Sanjō Sanetomi, who was Daijō Daijin (Chancellor of the Realm) after the Meiji Restoration. In other words, the Saionji family was in the top 10 percent of the 160 families of court nobles. In his early childhood, Saionji Kinmochi was a mischievous and irrepressible boy, but his education by leading scholars converted him into a young prodigy and his brilliance became wellknown. At the time of the Meiji Restoration, Saionji, Iwakura Tomomi, Saigō Takamori, and Ōkubo Toshimichi were appointed San'yo (councilor). He was only nineteen at the time.

When confrontation between the Tokugawa shogunate and the Satsuma-Chōshū alliance became imminent, a proposal was submitted to the Imperial Court conference that this be treated as a private dispute between the Satsuma-Chōshū domains and the House of Tokugawa. This way, it was argued, the Imperial Court could maintain its outward neutrality and hence not be tainted should the Satsuma-Chōshū alliance be defeated. This was another manifestation of the traditional wisdom that had enabled the Imperial Court to survive for so long, and the majority of the conference participants were inclined to this position. Going against the mainstream, Saionji, who was the youngest participant attending the conference, objected, saying, "This battle will decide the fate of the nation. If the Imperial Court fails to take a clear stand and views it as a mere private dispute in order to avoid being associated with the outcome should the Satsuma-Chōshū forces lose, we will have forfeited a decisive chance."

Hearing this, Iwakura edged forward and shouted, "Well said, kid!" This shifted the discussion momentum and the conference ultimately decided to side with Satsuma and Chōshū. Backed by the authority of the Imperial Court, the Satsuma-Chōshū anti-Tokugawa forces won the Battle of Toba-Fushimi (1868) and marched east on the Tōkaidō road. At the age of twenty, Saionji was appointed commander of the San'indō pacifying force sent to extract pledges of renewed allegiance to the emperor from feudal lords in the San'in region. Next, he was appointed commander of the Hokuriku pacifying force, and after the completion of the Meiji Restoration, he was appointed Governor of Niigata. Saionji, however, had no intention of staying in Niigata. He came back to Tokyo without permission and studied at Kaisei Gakkō (living in a geisha house) while he prepared for studying abroad. He left for France toward the end of 1870.

It was 1871 by the time Saionji arrived in Paris, which was the heyday of the Paris Commune. For France, the decade of the 1870s was a period of transition in which the possibility for every conceivable political form coexisted. It was a period of vibrant political thought. Beginning with the Paris Commune, after which came Marxism-Leninism, the political thought that tyrannized the world and caused countless tragedies throughout the twentieth century, France was the arena where numerous factions competed, particularly the Legitimists led by Adolphe Thiers and Patrice de Mac Mahon and the Republicans under the leadership of Léon Michel Gambetta.

Saionji was there for all of this. While in Paris, Saionji associated with Gambetta and Georges Clemenceau, Prime Minister of France in 1906–09 and 1917–20, who was regarded as a radical, as well as with activists with socialistic inclinations. Saionji returned to Japan in 1880 and became president of the newly founded people's rights advocacy newspaper company Tōyō-Jiyū Shimbun-sha the following year. The year 1881 was the height of the Freedom and People's Rights Movement, with the Meiji government facing an existential crisis. For the government, it was utterly intolerable that Saionji, a court noble who was supposed to be defending the Imperial Family, should raise the banner of freedom and people's rights. Iwakura tried in vain to dissuade Saionji from his anti-government commentaries, but eventually it took an imperial edict by Emperor Meiji to get Saionji to resign from the newspaper. Although Saionji submitted a memorial to the emperor by way of refuting the edict, there was no response and he resigned the presidency of Tōyō-Jiyū Shimbun-sha before the end of March 1881.

Freedom and People's Rights Advocate but Not Anti-Government

This all happened when Saionji was thirty-three years old and it was, in fact, the last time this formerly brash boy did something that shocked the people around him. For the next sixty years, Saionji led a zen-like existence, taciturn but sophisticatedly refined, seeming to have risen above worldly affairs. But it was this Saionji, the last genrō, who occupied the central position in Japanese politics until the eve of the attack on Pearl Harbor. As such, understanding Saionji's personality and political philosophy is essential to understanding this side of modern Japanese politics. Liberalism was clearly at the heart of Saionji's political philosophy. In his nine years in Paris, he socialized with a number of socialists, including some who could have endangered his position. In his own congratulatory remarks on the inaugural issue of the *Tōyō-Jiyū Shimbun*, Saionji presented his thesis that all civilization, wealth, and power derive from freedom. This conviction came straight from his experiences in Paris. Even when he was forced by Imperial edict to resign the presidency of the Tōyō-Jiyū Shimbun-sha, Saionji still contended in his memorial to the emperor that it is natural to demand greater freedom in keeping with the advance of civilization and enlightenment.

When in 1898 he became education minister for the second time, Saionji even pondered drafting a second Imperial Rescript on Education (the first having been in 1890). Because traditional Japanese morals were a product of a time when society had a vertical structure, Saionji thought Japanese should be taught to respect each other on a totally horizontal footing as equals and to live and let live. Although he had already secured the Emperor Meiji's approval to draft a more liberal Imperial Rescript on Education for this purpose, Saionji never got to write it due to the resignation of the Itō Hirobumi cabinet, himself included. Had this second Imperial Rescript on Education actually been written, Japan's future might have been radically different. One major reason behind the decline of parliamentary democracy in pre–World War II Japan was the dearth of people after Mutsu Munemitsu and Hara Takashi championing democracy. Had the education envisioned in Saionji's liberal Imperial Rescript on Education been realized, generation after generation could have emerged with aspirations to the establishment of parliamentary democracy, and this could have prevented the decline of Taishō Democracy over a span of less than ten years.

Saionji did not advocate freedom and people's rights as an anti-government activist. For instance, he observed of the Paris Commune he encountered upon his arrival in France, "Rebels have established an illegitimate government headquartered in Paris and have tyrannized the country. The people's suffering is indeed beyond description." He concluded that the Japanese government should not immediately give important positions to people returning from overseas studies but should assign them small jobs, observe their proclivities, and "fire them if they advocate republicanism." While this might have been a natural response from a court noble who had just come out of feudalistic Japan, it appears that Saionji's wariness of the people's republicanism remained unchanged even after his stay in Paris—during which he must have learned the value of freedom and fully enjoyed it himself.

In his congratulatory remarks on the occasion of the inaugural issue of *Tōyō-Jiyū Shimbun*, Saionji insisted that, "because people are liable to go in the wrong direction, shouting 'Freedom, freedom!' they need to be guided in the right direction at an early stage." In his memorial to the emperor, too, Saionji stressed that the true purpose of the newspaper was to check and correct people's excesses under the banner of freedom. As a sophisticated court noble, Saionji was particularly averse to desperado-like, blustering conduct. In a speech as education minister, he said:

> Japanese must have a cheerful, delightful, and positive outlook. We must not be dominated by indignation, tragic heroism, or vehemence. Heroic tales of loyal retainers in the olden days were tales of exceptional times. According to those tales, even an unruly vassal could be called a loyal retainer if and when, facing an emergency, he sacrificed his life in front of his master. I would seriously question the validity of these tales in the context of today's education.

On the surface, Saionji's speech was a harsh criticism of the radical elements of the Freedom and People's Rights movement that had terrorized society with disturbances such as the Kabasan Incident of 1884. But this speech was more importantly a modern counter to the general Japanese disposition that had been carried over from feudal times through World War II. These personal preferences underlay Saionji's later trust in Shidehara as foreign minister. Regarding the emperor system, Saionji was a firm believer in the court nobles' role as guardians of the imperial family. When Saionji was ordered to do something by the emperor, therefore, he had to comply, as shown in his resignation from the *Tōyō-Jiyū Shimbun* as well as his actions when and after he retired from politics in 1913 during the early Taishō turmoil.

Saionji the Politician

In the political arena, Saionji remained unavaricious and unselfish, showing no interest whatsoever in power or money, as all historians unanimously point out. It was probably his indulgent upbringing that made him avoid anything that could be complicating. When he was asked to serve as president of the *Tōyō-Jiyū Shimbun* newspaper company, Saionji declined at first, saying, "Although it is good of you to recommend me as president, I am not cut out for painstakingly careful office work." More than an expression of false modesty, this was doubtless a genuine self-assessment. Saionji was always more interested in associating with writers, artists, the quick-witted, and the beautiful both in Japan and overseas. He was once heard to quip of Itō Hirobumi's Ōiso residence, "Politics is made for worldly men like the master of this house." Historian Kimura Ki authored the biography *Saionji Kinmochi-den*. What apparently impressed Kimura most about Saionji was that he never availed himself of the ample opportunities to finance his party's activities by collaborating with businessmen or engaging in graft during his stints as Prime Minister. Comparing Saionji with his contemporary politicians, Kimura lavished praise on Saionji for his integrity.

Saionji was a man of clear vision. Whenever he found someone he could trust to understand his ideals, he spared no pains in support of this person. It was Mutsu Munemitsu on whom Saionji placed the highest hopes. Saionji was appointed acting foreign minister when Mutsu took a leave of absence from the foreign ministership due to illness after the Triple Intervention of 1895, but Saionji followed Mutsu's instructions faithfully on all foreign ministry business. Deeply moved by Saionji's friendship, Mutsu on his sickbed told his family, "Only a true friend can be trusted to act so responsibly in another's stead." Upon hearing of Mutsu's death, Saionji became so disheartened that it was painful for people around him to watch. Dejected and crestfallen, he was heard to mutter, "Mutsu has passed away. It is unfortunate that all of those in the *hanbatsu* are such survivors. . . . Why are non-*hanbatsu* people so mortal?" After Mutsu's death, Saionji stood behind Itō to protect the constitutional government from the pressures of the *hanbatsu* and the military. After he became a genrō, Saionji helped Hara Takashi become prime minister: Hara is the one who accomplished parliamentary democracy in Japan. In his later years, Saionji unsuccessfully attempted to restrict military despotism; he passed away predicting the Empire's ruin.

Taishō Political Crisis

As if triggered by the passing of Emperor Meiji, Japanese politics underwent drastic change that made Meiji a remote memory. This was the Taishō

Political Crisis. When Emperor Meiji's demise became imminent, Prime Minister Saionji, contrary to the tradition of not announcing an imperial death for about a month, publicized the emperor's condition daily and shared this grief with the Japanese people. Then, when the Empreror died, he disregarded the wishes of Yamagata Aritomo, a Meiji-era elder statesman and President of the Privy Council, and others who insisted the Imperial funeral be financed by the government without Diet approval, Saionji passed the budget for the funeral at an extraordinary session of the Diet.

The Saionji cabinet was, however, forced to resign due to an unexpected turn of affairs toward the end of 1912. The greatest challenge facing the Saionji cabinet at that time was that of putting the nation's finances in order. More than a half of the 2.6 billion yen in government bonds issued to finance the Russo-Japanese War were floated overseas and accrued interest charges of more than 60 million yen annually. It was obvious the government would go bankrupt if the nation's trade deficit persisted. In an attempt to achieve a breakthrough with budget cuts, the Saionji cabinet instructed each ministry to reduce its annual budget by 8 to 15 percent off a normal year. While the other ministries complied, the army cut its budget a mere 3 percent and then insisted that the money it had saved with this 3 percent budget cut be used to finance the establishment of two additional divisions. When these divisions were actually established, however, it became obvious that the increased maintenance costs more than offset the army's budget cuts.

It was soon after the death of Emperor Meiji that Minister of War Uehara Yūsaku proposed the establishment of two additional divisions. Prime Minister Saionji quickly decided to reject the proposal, and many others at the cabinet meeting also opposed Uehara's proposal. Ten days after the cabinet meeting, Uehara tendered his resignation directly to Emperor Taishō, who had just recently succeeded the throne. It was unprecedented for a cabinet member to tender his resignation directly to the emperor rather than through the prime minister. Although Saionji must not have been pleased by this, he did not think much of it at the time. When a minister of war resigned, he thought, all he had to do was to appoint a new one. When Saionji asked Privy Council President Yamagata Aritomo to recommend Uehara's successor, however, Yamagata doggedly tried to persuade Saionji to settle the issue by compromising with the army and refused to recommend a new war minister. Faced with Yamagata's resistance, Saionji quietly resigned his prime ministership.

It had been rumored, perhaps correctly, that Yamagata was behind Uehara's conduct from the beginning. It was, after all, true that Uehara often visited Yamagata at his residence, Chinzan-sō, and it would not be unreasonable to think Uehara had been able to take this bold step of tendering his resignation directly to the emperor only because he had Yamagata's backing. Although Yamagata had long been apprehensive of Saionji's liberal inclinations, which he had intended to rein in sooner or later, he never imagined that Saionji would go as far as to resign. It appears Yamagata's plan to protect the army's interests by maneuvering Saionji to compromise went astray due to Saionji's adherence to principle and his indifference to power.

Katsura Tarō succeeded Saionji and formed the next cabinet (his third). In forming the cabinet, Katsura had to resort to rather high-handed maneuvering. When the navy, expressing opposition to the establishment of two additional army divisions, proved reluctant to recommend a candidate for minister, Katsura used an imperial edict to force Navy Minister Saitō Makoto to remain in office. Although Saionji, too, could have used an imperial edict himself instead of resigning, it was such an unprecedented maneuver that it had never occurred to him.

It is also noteworthy that Katsura appointed Ōura Kanetake his interior minister. Ōura was a former policeman from Satsuma with a well known aversion to political parties. This appointment appears indicative of Katsura's determination to roll back Saionji's liberal line. Public opinion was outraged at those moves by the military and the Katsura cabinet. As soon as the army's demand for two additional divisions was publicized, all of the major newspapers and magazines denounced the army's despotism and expressed their support for the Saionji cabinet. Organizations to protect parliamentary politics were launched among Seiyūkai and Kokumin-tō Diet members as well as within the Kōjunsha, an association of graduates of Keiō University, established by Fukuzawa Yukichi. At the Diet session at the beginning of 1913, Ozaki Yukio, who later came to be known as "the father of parliamentary government," denounced the Katsura cabinet, saying its act was "tantamount to an attempt to defeat its political enemy using the Imperial throne as its armor and imperial edicts as its bullets." Although Prime Minister Katsura responded that it was all the wish of the emperor and that his cabinet had nothing to do with it, nobody bought the argument that the Emperor Taishō, who had just succeeded to the throne, had issued the imperial edict on his own initiative.

The Seiyūkai and Kokumin-tō drafted a no-confidence motion against the Katsura cabinet. Passage of the motion appeared inevitable when an imperial edict was issued for Saionji, president of the Seiyūkai, to "settle the issue"—in other words, to make Seiyūkai withdraw the motion. Although Saionji must have been fully aware of Katsura's maneuverings behind the imperial edict, he simply said, "Now that an imperial order has been issued, I have no choice but to obey," and he would not listen to entreaties from other Seiyūkai members.

One of the basic philosophies of a traditional monarchy is that an order by the monarch must be obeyed unconditionally. For a violator of this philosophy to go scot free, even if the order he disobeys is an irrational one, would constitute a precedent undermining the authority of the monarchy and the foundation of its sanctity. Saionji, who regarded himself a guardian of the imperial family, could not possibly become the first to disobey an imperial order. From a pro-imperial historical view, Saionji's conduct is highly praiseworthy as the supreme expression of loyalty to the emperor. In retrospect, it may be said that, if Katsura dared to resort to such an underhanded measure, Saionji, for his part, could have appealed Katsura's misdeed to the emperor. For Saionji, however, such an appeal itself would have undermined the emperor's authority.

Saionji's efforts notwithstanding, a general meeting of the Seiyūkai Diet members unanimously decided to go ahead with the no-confidence motion against the Katsura cabinet. This was only natural. If Diet members had obeyed the imperial order, parliamentary democracy itself would have collapsed. Meanwhile, the movement to protect the constitutional government spread like wildfire. Mobs surrounded the Diet building and welcomed pro-constitution Diet members' arrival with applause, while members of the Katsura faction had to enter the building stealthily using the back gate. Not only the mounted police but, eventually, the military was mobilized

Saionji Kinmochi (photo courtesy of the Ministry of Foreign Affairs Diplomatic Archives)

to maintain order, and there were some among the mob who were killed or injured by the horses' hooves. Riots spread all over Japan in no time. There were cases of police stations and koban being set on fire. Taking the blame for his failure to carry out the imperial order, Saionji resigned the Seiyūkai presidency. He was made a genrō by edict of the emperor.

Curtain Opens on a New Era

Thus the Taishō era started in the midst of nationwide turmoil in support of constitutional government. Parliamentary democracy in Japan, after twists and turns caused by resistance from the *hanbatsu*, eventually blossomed in the form of Taishō Democracy in the 1910s and early1920s. This was the start of a new era. In fact, the rule that stipulated only generals and admirals on active duty could become war and naval ministers, the very rule that had proved fatal to the Saionji cabinet, was abolished by Yamamoto Gonbei immediately following the Katsura cabinet's resignation. After that generals and admirals in the first reserve and the second reserve, as well as retired generals/admirals, could serve as war and navy ministers. Opinion was divided at the cabinet meeting that ratified this modification and, as it turned out, the war minister held the decisive vote. Facing this situation, War Minister Kigoshi Yasutsuna resolutely voted for the modification, going against the wishes of the entire military, and then immediately tendered his resignation. To borrow social commentator Watanabe Shōichi's phrase, Kigoshi was indeed a man of great courage.

2

Beginning of an American Century

—Emerging Japan Encounters a Rising United States —

A Period of Transition in American History

In winning the Russo-Japanese War (1904-05), Japan became the strong-est nation in Asia, and it appeared the Japanese century was about to begin. In retrospect, we find that the twentieth century ended as an Amer-ican century with the United States dominating the globe, Asia included. Thousands of years from now, historians might summarize the history of Asia in the first half of the twentieth century simply as a period in which an emerging Japan unsuccessfully challenged a rising United States for global hegemony.

Such vicissitudes are nothing new in world history. Toward the end of the fourteenth century, for instance, the newly emerging Serbian empire was on the verge of dominating the Balkans when it clashed with another emerging power, the Ottoman Empire, which was expanding northward. With the expectations of all of European Christendom on its shoulders, the Serbian empire fought the Turks heroically. At one point, Paris was filled with excitement over reports of Serbia's victory. But Serbia was defeated in the end and disappeared from history's center stage. When two con-tending powers are emerging and in an expansionary period, high morale on both sides makes the confrontation fierce and heroic, as exemplified by the Russo-Japanese War. In the mid-twentieth century, Japan and the United States engaged one another throughout the Pacific region, fighting fierce battles such as the human race will probably never witness again.

Yet I have gotten too far ahead of myself. Coming back to the beginning of the twentieth century, it is worth examining when the American century began. Although 1898, the year of the Spanish-American War, is arguably a pivotal turning point in American history, the genesis of the US transition can be dated back to the 1880s. One factor was the disappearance of the Western frontier in North America. Construction of the trans-continental railways in the 1880s, starting with the Union Pacific Railroad (completed in 1869) followed by the Southern Pacific Railroad (1883), the Northern Pacific Railway (1883), the Canadian Pacific Railway (1888), and the Atchison, Topeka, and Santa Fe Railway (1888), meant the American west coast was no longer a frontier. More fundamental than the disappearance of the frontier was the rise and expansion of the United States' national power. By 1885, American manufacturing production capacity had overtaken Britain, which in earlier days had been called the "the workshop of the world." American production capability continued to grow by leaps and bounds, leaving other countries far behind.

In contrast, US military power remained unbelievably meager. The state of the military was attributable to the principle proclaimed by George Washington that the United States would not get involved in European politics, making it unnecessary for the United States to possess military power sufficient to vie with European powers. Also, the Monroe Doctrine, under which the United States rejected any European interference in the Americas, actually assumed protection by the British navy, allowing the United States to go without its own naval power. According to Henry Kissinger's *Diplomacy*, the US navy in 1880 was weaker than the Chilean, Brazilian, or Argentine navies. Although the US had an industrial capacity thirteen times Italy's, US naval power lagged behind its Italian counterpart.

Mahan's *The Influence of Sea Power upon History*

In the twentieth century, however, the United States rapidly became a great naval power. This happened because the United States grew rapidly and visibly stronger as a country. Kissinger attributes the growth of US naval power solely to the country's international influence, claiming that no country in history has failed to attempt to translate its growing national power into expanded international influence. Consistent with this, Kissinger has consistently argued that increased Japanese international influence inevitably led to an expanded Japanese military role. It was President Theodore Roosevelt who adopted the policy of expanding US naval power. Alfred Thayer Mahan provided the theoretical foundation for Roosevelt's policy. Princeton University's Margaret Sprout and her husband Harold pointed out in their *The Rise of American Naval Power* (1943) that no one else has ever had Mahan's level of direct and profound influence on naval power theory. Mahan's best-known work, *The Influence of Sea Power upon History* (1890), was promptly translated into Japanese, published as *Kaijō kenryoku shiron* (History of maritime power), and had a profound influence on Japanese naval policy. In his book, Mahan attempted to demonstrate that Britain's economic might, backed up by its naval power, was decisive in every European war from the mid-seventeenth through the eighteenth century, including the War of the Spanish Succession (1701–14), the Seven Years' War (1756–63), and the Napoleonic Wars (1803–15).

In retrospect, Mahan resorted to some fairly far-fetched arguments to make his points, a trait shared by practically all innovative thinkers. While Mahan's slighting of the role of the army had always been criticized, the thesis outlined in his book was enthusiastically received in Britain as praise for the British successes of the previous two centuries. *The Times* of London even compared Mahan's insights to Copernicus' accomplishments in astronomy. Mahan had the honor of being received in audience by Queen Victoria and receiving honorary doctorates from both the University of Oxford and the University of Cambridge in the space of a single week.

The gist of Mahan's thesis was that the foundation for the rise of national power was the expansion of foreign trade, which called for prominent merchant marine fleets fully protected by a powerful navy, as well as overseas transshipment ports and markets for manufactured products (i.e., overseas colonies). Mahan strongly argued that the United States, then devoid of a merchant marine fleet, a mighty navy, and overseas colonies, should strive to rectify these deficiencies. In essence, this was a recommendation that the United States take part in the global competition of imperialism. The most promising markets for the United States, Mahan asserted, were South America and China, and he put great store on the Panama Canal, Hawaii, and the Philippines as stepping stones for the United States.

Road to a Great Naval Power

As soon as *The Influence of Sea Power upon History* was published, Theodore Roosevelt praised the book highly in a book review and prided himself on having discovered Mahan. When Roosevelt became undersecretary of the navy under President William McKinley in 1897, he relied heavily on Mahan's advice. As Roosevelt rose to vice president and, eventually, president of the United States, he continued to stress the importance of becoming a great naval power, so much so that people remarked, "It is as if Mahan's sea-power theory has entered the White House in the guise of Roosevelt."

After Roosevelt became president in 1901, he succeeded in obtaining Congressional approval to build ten battleships by 1905. According to the 1903 naval plan, the US navy was to own 48 battleships by 1926. Assuming the US built two battleships every year, and assuming the life of a ship to be twenty-five years, the United States would have a powerful navy with 48 battleships and numerous support vessels. The United States obviously had far greater financial resources than Japan did. It was all Japan could do to build six battleships in preparation for the Russo-Japanese War, and even that was only possible by imposing heavy taxes on the Japanese people during the period of Gashin-Shōtan (persevering through hardship for the sake of revenge) period following the Triple Intervention and diverting almost all of the war reparations from Qing China to munitions.

Adding to the problem was the launch of the HMS *Dreadnought* in 1905. This British battleship was the product of numerous design innovations, including relocating the broadside guns to the center of the vessel, and it quickly became the prototype for subsequent modern battleships—all the way to the Imperial Japanese Navy's *Yamato* and *Musashi* battleships—making the types of battleship used in the Russo-Japanese War obsolete overnight. The HMS *Dreadnought*'s emergence forced all countries to reconsider their shipbuilding plans, as the only thing that mattered in the global competition was the number of *Dreadnought*-class vessels a country possessed. The HMS *Dreadnought* accelerated the battleship building race between Britain and Germany, which was later an important factor contributing to World War I. Given its greater economic strength, the United States quickly took the lead in this competition. and Japan, too, felt it was urgent it come up with plans to build warships far in excess of its national capability.

With warrior-like simple-mindedness, Mahan also shared the yellow peril argument that was on the rise in those days. Anticipating a world race for hegemony between the Eastern and Western civilizations, he believed that no country was more important than the United States as a buffer against Japan. Predicting early on that Hawaii would someday become a strategically critical outpost against the "waves of invading barbarians" from the East, Mahan argued for US control of Hawaii and for the United States to possess a great naval capability. The foreign policies of the three successive Republican administrations—McKinley, Roosevelt, and Taft—differed little from those of other imperialist powers. Although some anti-imperialistic elements did exist in the US Congress—a fact that distinguished the United States from other imperialist powers—the US governments under those three presidents overrode the opposition and carried out their imperialistic policies.

President Roosevelt's Imperialistic Policies

As I pointed out in *Komura Jutarō and His Time*, the United States annexed Hawaii through means that could hardly be called fair, and its annexation of the Philippines totally ignored the wishes of the local people. The independence movement in the Philippines, whose origin could be traced back to the French Revolution and the independence struggles in Latin America, already had a long history by the time of the Spanish-American War and was deeply rooted among the populace. As soon as the Spanish-American War erupted in 1898, the independence forces took control of the entire territory in no time, forcing the Spanish Army to retreat behind the city walls of Manila, where it was isolated with no water supply. The Spanish side was about to surrender when the American forces—the same white race as the Spanish—arrived in Manila. The

Spaniards viewed the arrival of the Americans as manna from heaven. In accordance with the protocol and manners shared among civilized countries, the Spanish side surrendered to the American troops after a pro forma exchange of fire, on the condition that the United States would not allow native independence activists to participate in the occupation.

Even though the native independence forces had been the main factor in the fall of Manila, they were denied entrance to Manila. In January 1899, the Filipinos declared the Malolos Republic's independence, but then had to do battle with US forces that fought to suppress them. The national independence day that is observed in the Philippines today commemorates the Malolos Republic's declaration of independence, not the day the country gained its independence from the United States after World War II. In the war with the US forces, Emilio Aguinaldo, president of the Malolos Republic, was always at the forefront of an attack, and the independence forces under his command followed him, convinced of his invincibility. During this four-year war, the American side mobilized some 130,000 troops, including 70,000 regular army soldiers, 20,000 of whom were killed or wounded. During this bloody war, the United States continued to justify its actions by denouncing the Filipinos as being too immature to govern themselves, a cliché often heard from imperialistic countries. When the independence forces requested Japan's assistance, Miyazaki Tōten and Inukai Tsuyoshi were instrumental in arranging for the dispatch of weapons and ammunition on the *Nunobiki Maru*, an old Mitsui & Co. ship. The ship sank in the East China Sea due to foul weather, failing to deliver any weapons and ammunition to the independence forces. It is said that Aguinaldo believed until he died that the sword Inukai sent to him was a gift from Emperor Meiji. When the Japanese Army entered Manila in the early days of the Pacific War, Aguinaldo and his wife welcomed them.

Artemio Ricarte, a general in the independence forces and known as the "Father of the Philippine Army," was imprisoned after the United States occupied the Philippines because he refused to pledge allegiance to the new colonial rulers. Ricarte subsequently took refuge in Japan. In 1941, he returned to the Philippines with the invading Japanese forces and collaborated with the Japanese forces to fight the Americans. Ricarte died in 1945, the year of Japan's defeat, while evading American and Filipino attacks in a mountain province.

The first paragraph of the 1905 Taft-Katsura Memorandum signed in

1905 states that pro-Russian elements in the United States had attempted to convince the Americans that Japan's victory in the Russo-Japanese War was a harbinger of a Japanese invasion of the Philippines. This should be understood in the above historical context. Although pan-Asianism never became an official policy of the Japanese government, that theme ran unbroken in Japanese thinking until 1945.

The way the United States handled Panama was far more outrageous. In 1901, the US government concluded a treaty with Britain by which the latter recognized the construction of a canal by the United States in Panama. Because the Panama region in those days was a territory of Colombia, the US government tried to gain control over the region by leasing it from the Colombian government. As soon as the US government learned that the Colombian parliament would not easily ratify the leasing agreement for Panama, it dispatched warships to Panama. Within two days of their arrival, the United States forced the local authorities to declare independence from Colombia. The US government then recognized Panama's independence the same day and was granted the rights to build the Panama Canal. The United States also obtained the right to administer the canal indefinitely. Compared with this manifestation of naked imperialism, Japan's establishment of Manchukuo in later years was far more legitimate and attentive to international public opinion.

US International Politics

Despite the existence of War Plan Orange, which outlined US military strategy for a possible war with Japan, and contrary to the conviction held by some postwar anti-American Japanese, the United States had not anticipated confrontation with Japan following the Russo-Japanese War. Edward Miller provides a detailed analysis of War Plan Orange in his book, *War Plan Orange: The U.S. Strategy to Defeat Japan, 1897–1945* (1991). The Roosevelt administration first started making war plans under War Plan Orange in 1903. War Plan Orange was originally one of a set of contingency war plans against various countries. Japan was not the only hypothetical enemy. For instance, there was also a Plan Black for Germany, a Plan Purple for Russia, a Plan Green for Mexico, and a Plan Red for Britain. Interim research reports for the Plan Orange were published in 1917, and the military strategy proposed under the Plan Orange was officially adopted by the US government in 1924. True, the recently established Joint Army-Navy Board had made preparations for a war with Japan in Hawaii and the Philippines without presidential sanction on the pretext of undertaking a military exercise in 1907. At the time, the issue of racial discrimination against Japanese had flared up in the United States and information about the differences of opinion between the president and the Joint Board were leaked to the press, infuriating the president.

President Roosevelt thought that, while he himself had not even dreamed of a confrontation with Japan, the Navy should be prepared for any contingency. US strategy vis-à-vis Japan was to let Japan attack the Philippines freely in the beginning and then to fight back when the powerful American navy was ready to strike. This strategy was basically the same as the US strategy in World War II.

It should also be recalled that the United States did not remain imperialistic throughout the whole of the twentieth century. Taft was soon followed by Wilson and Wilsonianism. Idealism was then followed by a revival of isolationism. Indeed, it was only after World War II that the United States overcame its isolationist tendencies to some extent and deployed its overwhelming might for non-territorial, non-colonial ends, including in Korea, Vietnam, and the Persian Gulf. During the twentieth century, countries all over the world shared the fate of being tossed around by this drastic change in US policy. When Japan recognized the independence of Manchukuo in 1932, it argued that it had acted similarly to what the United States had done in Panama, but by that time the United States had set off in a different direction with totally different values. Because international politics boils down to the differences in national power, the overwhelming might possessed by the United States made the twentieth century a period when American arguments prevailed.

US Discrimination against Japanese

The gravest misfortune that the immaturity of American politics in the early twentieth century wrought on US-Japan relations was in the area of race. The handling of this issue has long been a source of embarrassment for the United States. The final solution to this problem had to wait until the late 1960s, a full generation after the war with Japan, when the civil rights movement was in full swing. The movement to exclude Japanese from the United States had been preceded by similar moves against the Chinese. No sooner had California been annexed in 1848 and gold found there in 1849 than Chinese immigrants started to arrive in the United States. And no sooner had Chinese immigrants arrived than efforts to exclude them sprang up. The movement culminated in the passage of the Chinese Exclusion Act of 1882 by Congress, which restricted and basically prohibited immigration by Chinese people and people of Chinese descent until World War II. During this period Chinese immigrants, totally unprotected by anyone, were cruelly abused to the extent that American historians refer to this period as a huge blot on American history.

Japanese immigrants were able to make a more fortunate start. When Japanese immigrants started moving to the United States in the 1890s, they were favorably received because there was a shortage of laborers due to the Chinese Exclusion Act of 1882. The number of Japanese immigrants, which was only 2,000 in 1890, grew rapidly to more than 20,000 in 1900, partly because a number of Japanese moved to California after the annexation of Hawaii in 1898. The number eventually grew to more than 70,000 by 1910. Americans grew fearful of the Japanese immigrants. This was more a fear that the Japanese were more skillful laborers or better farmers than it was racial prejudice of the kind that poisoned the climate for Chinese immigrants. Political movements to restrict incoming Japanese immigrants, along with Chinese immigrants, started around 1901, accompanied by newspaper campaigns that fanned racial prejudice against Japanese immigrants. The first incident of racial prejudice against the Japanese that became a political issue between the two countries took place in 1906, one year after the conclusion of the Russo-Japanese War. This was triggered by the San Francisco education authority's attempt to relocate Japanese pupils to an elementary school for other Asian pupils. Although it was explained that the proposed relocation was due to a lack of classroom space aggravated by the 1906 San Francisco earthquake, the relocation was hardly justified when there were only about a hundred Japanese pupils. It was obvious that the proposal was motivated by an intention to subject the Japanese to discriminatory treatment based on race. This incident infuriated the Japanese public, particularly because Japan had donated more for earthquake victims than any other country had.

The Japanese government immediately lodged a strong protest with the US government. It should be noted, however, that the Japanese government's protest was not exactly based on a universal denouncement of racial prejudice. Although the Japanese government did protest racial prejudice itself, it was infuriated more by the fact that the United States was treating the Japanese people, who were citizens of a first-rank country, the same as inferior people such as the Chinese, thus insulting Japan. Although this seems a bit incongruous today when all nations are considered equal, the Japanese had long been given special status—e.g. classed as honorary whites in South Africa, which was the last country in the world to abolish its apartheid policies. The postwar historic view in Japan criticizes the contradiction that Japan committed by suppressing the Koreans while advocating racial equality in the League of Nations after World War I, but this argument is an example of trying to impose postwar values on prewar incidents without fully understanding their historical context.

The ill treatment of the Japanese pupils was also upsetting to Americans, particularly President Roosevelt. In his State of the Union address of December 1906, Roosevelt specifically referred to this incident and pointed out, "The friendship between the United States and Japan has been continuous since the time, over half a century ago, when Commodore Perry . . . opened the islands to western civilization. . . . During that fifty years the progress of the country in every walk in life has been a marvel to mankind, and she now stands as one of the greatest of civilized nations." Defending the rights of the Japanese, he declared, ". . . in the matter now before me affecting the Japanese everything that it is in my power to do will be done, and all of the forces, military and civil, of the United States which I may lawfully employ will be employed. . . , It is unthinkable that we should continue a policy under which a given locality may be allowed to commit a crime against a friendly nation." But because of jurisdictional complexities within the American constitutional system, not even the dauntless and decisive Roosevelt could rein in San Francisco's educational authority. In later years, French President Charles de Gaulle defined the United States as a country which brings complicated domestic affairs and childish emotion to the discussion of grave international problems. This observation was truly well said.

Japanese Immigrants Make Whites Wary

In the end, Japan agreed to settle the issue by concluding a gentleman's agreement with the United States under which Japan instituted self-imposed restrictions on emigration to the United States. According to the report from the Japanese Ambassador to the United States Aoki Shūzō, the US secretary of state had explained that the problem was that the Japanese laborers were better than the American laborers. If the situation were left unattended, the US government would be forced to enact a law restricting incoming Japanese laborers. The secretary of state pleaded for the Japanese government to stop granting passports to its laborers. In other words, the US government asked the Japanese government to self-restrict emigration so the US government would not have to pass a discriminatory law to protect the interests of American workers. President Roosevelt himself told Ambassador Aoki that it would be wise to limit the exchange of people between the United States and Japan to educated people, which view was shared by Japan's foreign ministry. Thus the Japanese foreign minister and the US ambassador to Japan won agreement within the Japanese government to voluntarily restrict labor emigration to the United States. Such was the gentlemen's agreement of 1907.

Yet this was not the end of the Japanese immigration issue. The Japanese farmers were diligent and competent. As the early Japanese settlers purchased farmland and became landowners, the white farmers became increasingly wary of the immigrants. Subsequently, the use of farmland by Japanese immigrants grew increasingly restricted under California's Alien Land Laws of 1913 and 1920. Each time, complicated domestic political considerations as well as jurisdictional issues between the federal and local governments surfaced, but that was par for the course in American politics. In any event, the end result was the passage of the exclusionary Immigration Act of 1924.

The American Fleet Visits Japan

The discriminatory US legislation notwithstanding, Japan remained restrained in its relations with the United States. In 1907, President Roosevelt planned a tour by the US naval fleet in the Pacific. In the United

States, the campaign to expel the Japanese in California was at its height. Across the Pacific, the Japanese media campaign against this American exclusionism was also at its height. And all of this coincided with talk by War Plan Orange officials of the possibility of a war between the United States and Japan. Even as President Roosevelt struggled to persuade the California state legislature to change its attitude toward Japan, he was also upset at the anti-American Japanese words and deeds. In order to underscore to the Japanese that his pro-Japanese conduct was not based on any fear of Japan, he decided to demonstrate that there was a white man's navy that was totally different from that Admiral Zinovy Rozhestvensky had commanded for Russia in 1905. The Pacific tour by the US naval fleet—nicknamed the Great White Fleet—was, in short, a show of force against Japan. The Senate Committee on Naval Affairs opposed Roosevelt's plan and tried to reject the budgetary proposal for the expedition. In the end, however, the president got his way by claiming that he would carry out the plan even if he had to use money already appropriated for other purposes.

The Great White Fleet of sixteen battleships, two armored cruisers, six destroyers, and eight transport ships sailed out through the Strait of Magellan and into the Pacific. This was the navy that Roosevelt had eagerly built as undersecretary of the navy. Aside from his policy-related show of force, Roosevelt was likely also looking for an opportunity to show off the imposing navy that he had built before his term as president expired a year and a half later.

The Great White Fleet's original itinerary only included visits to Australia and the Philippines. When Foreign Minister Komura Jutarō learned of this plan, he brought it to the attention of the cabinet, which decided to officially invite the American fleet to visit Japan. Pleased with the invitation, President Roosevelt issued a directive to the commander of the fleet saying, in paraphrase:

> I am confident the Japanese government will do its very best to express its utmost respect and friendship to the United States. I therefore request you do your very best to demonstrate the highest respect and friendship to all Japanese you and your crew come in contact with. I particularly urge you to make sure no US personnel violate any regulation whatsoever during your visit to Japan. Leave should be granted only to those whose good conduct is assured, and

every effort made to avoid giving the impression to your host nation that Americans are arrogant and uncouth.

The Japanese side did its best, with the public and private sectors cooperating to welcome the visitors. The emperor issued an invitation to the captains of all the vessels, which greatly pleased the United States and mitigated the strained atmosphere in US-Japan relations at that time.

James Bryce's Wisdom

Shidehara Kijūrō had been involved in the Japanese immigration issue all along. In 1912, at the age of 41, Shidehara was appointed counselor at the Japanese embassy in Washington, DC. In today's system, a counselor in the Japanese embassy in Washington is one of ten or so officials reporting to a few ministers, who in turn report to the ambassador. But in those days, a counselor actually counseled the ambassador and occupied the number-two position in the embassy. In January 1913, one year after Shidehara's appointment, a bill to ban foreign landownership was proposed to the California state legislature. Although ostensibly targeted at "aliens ineligible for citizenship," the bill's actual purpose was to ban Japanese immigrants from owning farmland. As such, the bill would have dealt a devastating blow to a majority of the Japanese immigrants, who were mainly engaged in agriculture. Secretary of State William Jennings Bryan was confident that he could easily persuade the California state legislature with his oratory. However, his dissuasion made no impact, and the bill was passed in May and went into force in August 1913. Shidehara made every effort to remedy the situation. He even considered, in consultation with the US government, contesting the bill's legality to the Supreme Court on the grounds that it violated the 1911 Treaty of Commerce and Navigation between the United States and Japan. Shidehara also proposed additional treaties between the two countries. None of his ideas proved feasible, however, and Shidehara had to abandon them.

Shidehara noted in his memoir that he learned a great deal during this period from James Bryce, British ambassador to the United States. Aside from being a diplomat, Ambassador Bryce was also an academic, jurist, historian, and liberal politician who had lectured at the University of

Oxford. He was a man of wisdom and the architect of the theoretical basis for the Anglo-American cooperation policy that has continued to this day. The construction of the Panama Canal was completed in 1914. In spite of the US promise in the bilateral treaty that American and British ships would be treated equally in using the canal, the US Congress proposed a bill that would exempt American ships from the toll while levying heavy fees on foreign vessels, including British vessels. The British government protested the bill in very strong terms, and Ambassador Bryce tried to block it by talking to the State Department as well as the president. In the end, though, the Senate passed the bill.

One Sunday after this incident, Shidehara dropped in on the British embassy during his walk, despite his hesitation at showing up without an appointment. Shidehara was shown into the ambassador's study by Mrs. Bryce. Shidehara sympathized with Ambassador Bryce by saying, "You protested strenuously, but Congress still passed the bill, didn't it?" Bryce calmly replied, "Yes, it did." When Shidehara then asked if Bryce intended to continue to protest, Bryce said, "No, I shall not protest any longer." Surprised and a little taken aback by Bryce's air of indifference, Shidehara said, "But the bill is a violation of the Anglo-American treaty, and it must be difficult to appease the British public." To this, the British ambassador calmly replied:

> If we continue to protest, the situation will inevitably develop into a war between our two countries. But it is British policy not to go to war with the United States no matter what. What good would it do to protest unless you are prepared to fight? We would just embarrass ourselves. Therefore, I will cease this futile protest and leave the matter as it is. We should not focus so much on petty honor or trivial interests that we lose sight of the big picture.

Democracy's Self-Corrective Power

Although Britain and the United States share the same language and are of the same race, their bilateral relations in the twentieth century did not emerge naturally. The relationship between the two countries has been developed on the basis of the accumulated convictions and judgments of wise men such as Bryce. When France sold the Louisiana Territory to the United States, doubling the size of the US territory all at once, Napoleon Bonaparte is reported to have remarked that the acquisition would ensure the United States is a major player internationally and thus creates a maritime rival that will sooner or later eclipse Britain. History shows how right Napoleon was. Since the early twentieth century, however, Britain has adopted the policy of making the United States not a rival but a partner, thus outwitting Napoleon.

During the conversation at the British embassy with Shidehara, Bryce asked Shidehara what he thought about the Japanese immigration issue and California's moves to exclude Japanese. When Shidehara replied, "Given the public pressure in Japan, we have no choice but to continue to protest," Bryce asked:

> Is Japan ready to risk war with the United States? If so, that would be a major mistake. This is not an issue worth fighting the United States over and risking Japan's future over, is it? If I were you, I would forget about it . . . American history is littered with examples of unjust treatment of foreign countries. Those wrongdoings, however, have usually been corrected at America's own initiative even without protests or request from foreigners. This has been the historic process, and all we need to do is to wait silently for America to self-correct. As far as this issue in California is concerned, I would advise Japan to take the same position as we do.

This is democracy's self-correcting power. Shidehara wrote in his memoir that he had listened to Bryce with respect and found his observation very convincing. Even more impressive, though, is that Shidehara was able to visit the British embassy unannounced and be warmly welcomed by Bryce. The welcome and the frank advice Bryce gave him, a mere counselor at the Japanese embassy, indicated Shidehara had gained the friendship and trust of this ambassador from a great nation who was also a world-class intellectual in his own right. This episode alone marks Shidehara as a diplomat supreme. Bryce obviously had a high regard for Shidehara's linguistic ability and other knowledge, and it is inconceivable he would have welcomed an ordinary Japanese diplomat the same way.

Nor is that the end of this story. Shidehara was appointed Japanese ambassador to the United States in 1919. During his tenure, the second California Alien Land Law of 1920 denied Japanese immigrants not only the right to possess farmland but even the right to lease it, the last resort for Japanese farmers. One day, when Shidehara visited the US Secretary of State, he bumped into Bryce who, having retired, was just visiting the United States. Shidehara congratulated Bryce, saying, "In less than two years of your prediction, the Panama Canal discriminatory toll was abolished, proving you were right." When Shidehara half-jokingly added that Bryce's prediction had yet to prove out as far as US treatment of Japanese immigrants was concerned, Bryce admonished him:

> Do you not recognize the permanency of a state's fate? Compared to the long life of a state, five years or ten years do not really matter. If you focus only on a small strife and aim for a quick gain, you will end up painting yourself into a corner. I wish you would have a little longer perspective on the future of your country and not lose sight of the big picture.

Shidehara reminisced that he felt as if he had been admonished by his grandfather. Bryce's prediction about the Japanese immigrants almost came true around 1931, ten years later. Yet just as it appeared the Department of State was considering rescinding the anti-Japanese measures, the Manchurian Incident erupted, doing major damage to Japan's reputation and killing the possibility of repealing the discriminatory measures.

In retrospect, Shidehara seems to have been fated to be appointed to important posts dealing with the immigration issue every time it became a thorny topic in US-Japan relations. In 1912, Shidehara was appointed counselor at the Japanese embassy in Washington, DC, one year prior to the enactment of the California Alien Land Law of 1913; he was appointed Japanese ambassador to the United States in 1919, one year before the second California Alien Land Law; and his appointment as foreign minister was in 1924, the very year the Immigration Act of 1924 went into force. Although Shidehara did not succeed in blocking passage of anti-Japanese laws on any of those occasions, the situations were so treacherous that

US-Japan relations would have ended up far worse had it not been for him. Shidehara did his very best every step of the way to prevent a crisis in the bilateral relationship.

During his tenure as Japanese ambassador, Shidehara made a point of meeting weekly with Roland Morris, former US ambassador to Japan, to discuss the Japanese immigration issue. Secretary of State Bainbridge Colby willingly cooperated with this attempt to improve mutual understanding between Japan and the United States. Shidehara and Morris met more than twenty times, and the record of their discussions became a comprehensive document that extensively covers all the issues related to the immigration issue; it is a must-read for anyone who wishes to study this problem. Morris became a close family friend of the Shideharas. Hoping to nullify the Californian law, Morris and Shidehara even attempted to draft a treaty, because a treaty would constitutionally take precedence over state law. Unfortunately, Morris and Shidehara were forced to abort the idea of a treaty when Republican President Warren Harding took over the White House and Colby resigned as secretary of state. In his memoir, Shidehara laments, "[Our dialogue] played only a temporary role mitigating and restraining our respective publics." Still, it is undeniable that these twenty-plus meetings did play a role in the maintenance of friendly US-Japan relations.

US-Japan Friendship Supported by the Strenuous Efforts of a Few

The Immigration Act of 1924 rejected any immigration to the United States from Japan. Since the Act was so obviously and intentionally anti-Japanese, the Japanese public was furious. The angry public mood delivered a devastating blow to advocates of international cooperation and pro-American views within Japan, which had only just begun to exercise some influence under the Treaty of Versailles regime.

Partly because he was encouraged by the US secretary of state to protest the bill, Japanese Ambassador to the United States Hanihara Masanao argued that the passage of the Immigration Act would have grave consequences for US-Japan relations. But Senate Foreign Relations Committee chair Henry Cabot Lodge labeled Hanihara's comment, "a veiled threat" to the United States, thus helping the bill get passed.

Even the most persistent pro-American advocate, Kiyosawa Kiyoshi, who knew the United States better than anybody else, lamented:

A giant struck someone full in the presence of others. The one who was struck protested the unjustifiable and violent conduct. However, the giant struck the victim again, this time even harder, saying he did not like the way the victim protested. . . . Such is the US attitude toward Japan.

Other pro-American dignitaries, including Nitobe Inazō and Shibusawa Eiichi, also expressed their sorrow and indignation. Some even committed suicide in protest of the Immigration Act.

His earlier comment notwithstanding, Kiyosawa one year later emphasized the importance of friendship between Japan and the United States, saying, "While it is justifiable to denounce the wrongdoing of the United States, is it fair to deny its ten virtues in denouncing a single flaw?" Shidehara also remained calm. On July 1, 1924, when he delivered his first Diet policy speech as foreign minister, he stated his convictions about international cooperation. In this speech, Shidehara discussed the immigration issue impartially and objectively from the viewpoints of both Japan and the United States, drawing fully upon the knowledge and experience he had accumulated. While he acknowledged the United States was within its rights to restrict immigration and refrained from unilaterally denouncing the United States, he noted that Japan would continue to protest the discriminatory treatment as running counter to all sense of justice and fairness as well as being an affront to international courtesy. Noting that the US government and the American media were sympathetic to Japan, Shidehara assured Diet members that the issue was still in play and declared, "I shall do everything within my capacity to prompt a satisfactory settlement of this issue and thus to eternalize the friendship between Japan and the United States." This was a declaration of his decision to wait quietly for the settlement, relying on the fairness of American public opinion, as James Bryce had advised.

Friendly relations with the United States were supported by the strenuous efforts of only a few such as Shidehara and Kiyosawa. And even these efforts tended to be criticized by the public as weak-kneed diplomacy. It was inevitable that the racial discrimination measures would erode the respect and trust that Japanese had felt toward the United States since Commodore Perry's time. This was particularly so among ordinary people. While there were other causes for the pan-Asianism and anti-Americanism in Japan in the 1930s, it is undeniable that American racial discrimination was a persuasive argument justifying such views. Before long, public opinion in Japan rushed to support calls for independence and self-reliance, further isolating the pro-Anglo-American advocates. Once that happened, it was impossible for a single pillar to support a great hall already on the verge of collapse.

CHAPTER

3

Chaos on the Continent

—Clumsy Handling of the Twenty-One Demands—

Views on China after the Xinhai Revolution

Asia opened the twentieth century with the Xinhai Revolution of 1911.
Yet because the revolution in China is still going on, it is not easy to write
the history of China since the Xinhai Revolution. The leftist historical
view in postwar Japan is that the establishment of Communist China in
1949 was the grand finale of the Chinese revolution, and categorizes anything that contributed to the rise of Communist China as righteous and any
obstruction as evil. If the Communist regime in China remains stable and
guarantees the welfare of its people throughout the twenty-first century,
this reading will be vindicated. After all, history is only concerned with
outcomes. It is true that tens of million Chinese died in the Great Leap
Forward and the Cultural Revolution, many of whom doubtless perished
cursing the Communist regime. The regime itself, however, survived and
subsequently showed tremendous growth potential under Deng Xiaoping's leadership. Nevertheless, objectively speaking, it is impossible
to be overly optimistic about China's future. After all, even the mighty
Soviet Union, the mother of all Communist regimes, collapsed. Because
China is an empire sharing the same Marx-Leninist ideology and is a
society characterized by multi-ethnicity, there is no guarantee that what

happened to the Soviet Union will not be repeated in China.

Should China share the Soviet Union's fate, we would have to answer a number of nagging questions: Would it not have been better for China to have adopted a more democratic regime that reflected Kan Yuwei's constitutional democracy argument or Song Jiaoren's advocacy of a cabinet system, proposed immediately before and after the Xinhai Revolution? Instead there was one-party domination by the Kuomintang, followed by the Chinese Communist Party. Was the democratic model a realistic possibility? Was it appropriate to aim for a greater China including Tibet, Xinjiang, Mongolia, Manchuria, and Taiwan—the reincarnation of the Great Qing Empire—as the goal of nationalism instead of building a nation-state of ethnic Chinese?

Because the outcome of the Communist revolution has not yet reached its end stage, the proper approach to Chinese history must be to confine oneself to the objective facts as seen from many angles rather than to declare any one set of "facts" proof of the success or failure of the revolution. It remains a historical fact, however, that Japan's policies toward China in the Taishō and early Shōwa eras failed, and an objective and dispassionate examination of why they failed is in order.

Sun Yat-sen, the Unyielding Revolutionary

The Qing Dynasty was overthrown following the Xinhai Revolution in 1911, the same year that Komura Jutarō passed away and only one year before the passing of Emperor Meiji. The convergence of these events clearly marked the end of one era and the beginning of a new one. While space does not allow a full explication of the complicated details of the dynasty's collapse, broadly speaking, I attribute it to the trend of the times and to the revolutionary campaigns by Sun Yatsen and his fellow activists taking advantage of those trends.

China already had decades of history trying to modernize by trial and error

Sun Yat-sen (photo courtesy of Kyodo News)

starting with the Opium Wars, followed by events such as the Meiji Restoration (1868), the Sino-French War (1884–85), the First Sino-Japanese War (1894–95), and the Boxer Rebellion (1900). But the event that most inspired all Asian nations, especially China, was the surprising Japanese victory in the Russo-Japanese War (1904–05), which showed that even a tiny Asian nation could modernize and stand shoulder to shoulder with the Western powers. Revolutionary fever in China intensified immediately after that war. When the Guangxu emperor was succeeded by the infant Xuantong emperor, the Qing court tried to weather the revolutionary storm by promoting Yuan Shikai. Yet because Yuan was an ambitious man whose ulterior motive was to topple the Qing court and take power himself, he actually accelerated the end of the 268 years of rule by the Qing Dynasty. When Sun Yat-sen established an interim government in Nanjing in 1911, Yuan decided not to subjugate it by force but to try to contain it by inducing Sun Yat-sen's side to accept a compromise, taking advantage of the interim government's financial straits. At the same time, Yuan persuaded the emperor to step down by stressing the changes in the people's thinking, saying that the monarchy had lost the mandate of heaven and that the mandate of the people was for a republican system, thus making it impossible to maintain the dynasty. This was followed by the Second Revolution (1913) and the Third Revolution (1926-28), in a never-ending drama of scheming and counteractions by revolutionaries and provincial tycoons. Much of this was Yuan's doing, but there is no denying that the revolutionary force around Sun Yat-sen was always the chief engine of change in China at that time.

Sun Yat-sen was not from the elite class. Nor was he an impoverished peasant, judging from his mastery in reading the Four Books and the Five Chinese Classics by the age of twelve. He came from a Guandong farming village facing Zhujiang Bay that had sent many villagers overseas as migrant workers. Among them was Sun Mei, Yat-sen's brother, who migrated to Hawaii when he was seventeen years old. Having started as a laborer in a sugarcane field, Sun Mei, who was twelve years older than Yat-sen, worked hard and quickly built a fortune. Yat-sen himself migrated to Hawaii when he was fourteen to live with his older brother and enrolled in the junior high school for British children in Honolulu. When he graduated at the age of seventeen, he won a runner-up award in English grammar that was presented by the Hawaiian King. It appears that people in the Sun family, including not only Yat-sen himself but also his father and brother, were extraordinarily diligent workers.

According to Sun Yat-sen's memoir, it was during the Sino-French War, when he was sixteen years old, that he first aspired to revolution and decided to dedicate his life to the revolutionary movement while earning his livelihood as a physician. Accordingly, he graduated from a medical school in Hong Kong with a doctorate at the age of twenty-seven and went into private practice. Two years later, he sent a memorandum to Li Hung-chang proposing measures to enhance the state's prosperity and defense.

In the same year (1894), Sun Yat-sen founded the Revive China Society in Hawaii, an organization to promote China's independence and nationalism. In 1895, he plotted the first armed uprising to capture Guandong, which ended in failure, forcing him to flee to Japan. He plotted a total of ten more armed uprisings in his lifetime. Only his eleventh uprising—the Wunchang Uprising, which paved the way for the Xinhai Revolution—was successful. Such tenacity and determination are unheard of even among other revolutionaries. Even more amazing was the revolutionary energy in China in those days. China produced one activist after another despite high death tolls resulting from oppression and poor planning.

Japan as a Base of Operations for Chinese Revolutionaries

Sun Yat-sen spent eight of his sixteen years abroad in Japan. Japan was then a base of operations not only for Sun Yat-sen but for many other Chinese revolutionaries as well. They preferred to use Japan as their operational base not only because it was close to China but also because they found many sympathizers and supporters among the Japanese. Central among those sympathizers were Miyazaki Tōten and Inukai Tsuyoshi, whom Miyazaki revered. Miyazaki had an eccentric aspect of traditional Japanese thinking and, in that sense, he can be a good frame of reference for understanding one of the traits of the Meiji Japanese. Miyazaki's father was a country samurai from Kumamoto. He repeatedly patted the infant Tōten on the head and said, "You will be a hero. You will be a general some day." When Tōten touched money one day, his father reprimanded him saying that handling money was beneath him. His mother also repeatedly told Tōten that the greatest shame for a man is to die in his bed.

Strongly influenced by his father, Tōten's eldest brother, Hachirō, grew up to be a master swordsman and died as a member of Saigō Takamori's rebel force advocating freedom and people's rights during the Satsuma Rebellion. Even as a young child, Tōten was repeatedly told by his relatives and village elders to be like his oldest brother. According to Tōten's autobiography *Sanjūsan-nen no yume* (The 33-year dream), he took it for granted the freedom and people's rights movement was a good thing without knowing much about it. He was also convinced, according to this book, that any government official was, by definition, a thief or a villain and that rebellion and mutiny were the calling of great heroes. Tōten's second-oldest brother, Tamizō, became a social activist, while Yazō, the third oldest, dreamed of governing China. It was Yazō who got Tōten interested in China. Yazō aspired to restore the rights of the yellow race against the white race's abuses of power, and he believed this would take a hero. So he decided to go to China, seek out a hero, and offer his services. When he could find no hero, he decided to become the hero he sought. Although this was a juvenile fantasy, it was typical of the kind of idealistic thinking that appealed to Meiji youth.

Among desperados in Japan in those days, it was fashionable to talk about "bringing all of China under one's rule." Thus, a popular song of the time was:

I am going to China and so should you.
I am done with being confined to tiny Japan,
When a massive China lies beyond the waves,
With 400 million people awaiting our arrival . . .

It's over ten years since I left my motherland
And I am now a famed Manchurian warlord
Commanding some five thousand brave men
Marching down from the Asian highlands.

Legend has it the lyrics were written by Miyazaki Tōten, but this may well be apocryphal. In any event, thousands of Japanese were swayed by the atmosphere of the times as seen in this song and moved to China to become *tairiku rōnin* (Japanese adventurers/political activists in mainland China). While some of them collaborated with the Japanese military to promote the Japanese government's policies there, many struck out on their own and contributed to the turmoil. Not all *tairiku rōnin* were ne'er do wells. Arao Sei, a graduate of the Imperial Japanese Army Academy, and Yamanaka Minetarō, who had enrolled in the Army War College, both resigned from the military and gave up the bright futures that were promised them to join the revolutionary movements in China.

Miyazaki Tōten's Philosophy

When Miyazaki landed in China at the age of twenty-two, he was invited to use the Sino-Japan Trade Institute run by Arao Sei as his base in China. Miyazaki, however, thought Arao's group "a bunch of people advocating the conquest of China" and politely declined the offer. The postwar historical view in Japan attributes this action by Miyazaki to the incompatibility between the kind of China management Arao and other expansionists advocated and the Christian philanthropy-based Pan-Asianism Miyazaki and others advocated. While there may be some truth to this, it could not have been a fundamental problem for either Miyazaki or Arao, since imperialism had not yet been deemed evil and the concept of nationalism had not been firmly established. Accordingly, we should think of Miyazaki's walkaway as being more attributable to the difference in temperament between his free and uninhibited nature and Arao's militaristic stoicism. In fact, the only reference in Miyazaki's autobiography critical of Arao's group was limited to the line quoted above characterizing Arao's group as advocating the conquest of China. In reference to subsequent relations with *tairiku rōnin*, Miyazaki declared, "Never once in more than twenty years did I have an emotional clash with them or was there a chill in our relations."

Relying on Emerging Japan to Achieve the China Dream

It was in 1897 that Miyazaki first met Sun Yat-sen. No sooner had Sun Yat-sen arrived in Yokohama in August than Miyazaki, who had long wished to meet this famed Chinese, sought a meeting. The two hit it off immediately. Thus began Sun Yat-sen's revolutionary activities using Japan as a base of operations. Sun Yat-sen was not the only Chinese revolutionary who chose Japan as his base of operations. While the first group of Chinese students who arrived in Japan in 1896, immediately after the First Sino-Japanese War, numbered only twelve, this number expanded rapidly to some 12,000 by 1906, one year after the end of the Russo-Japanese War. Nor were students the only visitors from China. In 1898, Kang Youwei and Liang Qichao sought asylum in Japan after the abortive Hundred Days' Reform. Zhang Binglin, who was reputed to be the greatest scholar in China at the time, also fled to Japan, where in 1902 he attempted to organize a movement to revere the Ming Dynasty and overthrow the Qing Dynasty. Huang Xing, the army commander-in-chief and chief of the general staff of the Republic of China under Provisional President Sun Yat-sen at the time of the Xinhai Revolution, also sought asylum in Japan after the abortive coup attempt. While in Japan, Huang Xing met Sun Yat-sen in person for the first time. It was Miyazaki who made the introduction. Other Chinese expatriates in Japan included Song Jiaoren, who was the primary advocate of parliamentary democracy during the Xinhai Revolution and who was later assassinated by Yuan Shikai, as well as Wang Jingwei, who drafted the oath of office for Sun Yat-sen as provisional president of the Republic of China and who served as Sun's right-hand man until his death.

In July 1905, those Chinese in Japan convened an organizational meeting of the Tongmenghui (Chinese Revolutionary Alliance). Taking part were some seventy Chinese students as well as Miyazaki Tōten and Uchida Ryōhei, founder of the Black Dragon Society, a prominent paramilitary, ultranationalist group in Japan. This meeting decided that the Alliance would adopt the political platform "Expel the Tatar barbarians and revive Zhonghua, establish a republic, and distribute land equally among the people." Equal distribution of land was a slogan derived from Sun Yat-sen's philosophy of equality and social revolution. Some at the meeting started off opposing this philosophy, but Sun eventually talked them around.

Thus a united front of the revolutionary forces was established with Sun Yat-sen's Revive China Society, Huang Xing's Huaxinghui, and Zhang Binglin's Guangfuhui as its nucleus. Sun Yat-sen said of this development:

When the Chinese Revolutionary Alliance was formed in Tokyo in the fall of 1905 by outstanding individuals from all over China, I became convinced, for the first time, that the Chinese revolution would indeed be possible during my lifetime.

As history shows, Sun's conviction was well-founded: the Xinhai Revolution succeeded.

Japan's Aggressive Expansion to Manchuria

It is no exaggeration to say that Japan made concerted efforts after the death of Itō Hirobumi to pursue a policy of aggressive expansion into Manchuria both diplomatically and militarily, with only minor strategic or tactical differences among the approaches. Japan's policy to consolidate its power base in Manchuria was more or less successful. As a result of the rise of nationalistic sentiments among Asians after the Russo-Japanese War, a campaign arose in Qing to reverse the concessions it had been forced to grant the Western powers after the First Sino-Japanese War. The Qing counted on support from the United States to accomplish this goal.

Itō had long foreseen this danger. In a letter to Foreign Minister Hayashi Tadasu written two years before his assassination, Itō predicted:

If Japan continues to pursue self-serving policies, it will not only provoke resistance among the Chinese but will also give third countries chances to stir up trouble. This could result in another war between Japan and Qing, who belong to the same race. This would only please the anti-Japanese forces. The general trend worldwide has been toward isolating Japan. If mishandled, this trend will bring down disaster on us. I therefore remain deeply apprehensive about the future of our empire.

Itō's prediction came true thirty years later in the form of the Manchurian Incident. But this time, it was the United States' turn to be isolated as all the other Western powers sided with Japan against the Chinese push to recover the concessions it lost at the nadir of Chinese power after the First Sino-Japanese War. When William Taft succeeded Theodore Roosevelt as president of the United States in 1909, his Secretary of State, Philander Knox, proposed internationalizing the management of the Southern Manchurian Railway—that is, allowing the Qing to buy back the railway, which had been divided between Japan and Russia, with funds provided by the Western powers and putting the railway under the joint management of the Western powers. But the other Western powers, including Britain, cold-shouldered this proposal, which never came to fruition. Moreover, this proposal prompted rapprochement between Japan and Russia as both countries were suspicious of US intentions. The United States was instrumental in forming a four-country consortium with Britain, France, and Germany, and excluding Japan and Russia, to provide financing for the Qing. Given the realities in the Far East, however, Japanese and Russian participation was found to be essential, at which point the United States withdrew from the consortium on the grounds that the conditions for the loans impinged upon Qing sovereignty. Loans to the Qing then ended up being provided by the five imperialist nations, which well reflected the reality of international politics in the Far East.

Meanwhile, Japan and Russia were steadily solidifying the foundations for establishing their special spheres of interest in Manchuria. There was one difficult issue that was constantly on the minds of everyone concerned: the expiration of the term of the lease on the Liaodong Peninsula in 1923. This peninsula had been ceded to Japan after the First Sino-Japanese War, only to be returned to the Qing through the Triple Intervention. After that, Russia obtained its leasehold, which was passed on to Japan after the Russo-Japanese War. Because Japan had already made the peninsula a stronghold for its continental operations, similar to Hong Kong under the British, nobody in Japan intended to return it to China. Thus the phrase "fundamental settlement of the Manchurian issue," which frequently appears in various Japanese documents of the time, was code for the extension of this leasehold.

This was the situation when the Xinhai Revolution took place. Those in Japan who wanted Japan to have a greater presence on the continent grew excited. Since the end of the Ming Dynasty, Manchuria had been the territory of the Manchu people. Now that the Qing Empire, the dynasty of the Manchu people, had collapsed, there was no longer any reason for Manchuria to be controlled by Han Chinese. Mongolia, which also had been under the control of the Qing Empire, declared independence immediately following the Xinhai Revolution, and after many twists and turns became the Mongolian People's Republic with the help of the Soviet Union. Taking advantage of this revolution, Kawashima Naniwa, one of the *tairiku rōnin* who had been on friendly terms with members of the Qing royal family, attempted to establish an independent Manchurian-Mongolian kingdom by helping Prince Su to the throne and encouraging the king of Kalaqin in eastern Inner Mongolia to rise up in arms. This was later to be called the First Manchuria-Mongolia Independence Movement. All the army officers working on policy issues at that time advocated aggressive advances into Manchuria. Yamagata Aritomo was part of this, insisting on the dispatch of two divisions to Manchuria. In Moscow, Ambassador Motono Ichirō was on the verge of proposing a plan to divide Manchuria with Russia.

But the second Saionji government refused to dispatch troops to Manchuria. This was partly due to Navy opposition, particularly by its leading figure, Yamamoto Gonbei. Yamamoto was such a staunch believer in the primary role of the navy in defending the island empire that, even on the eve of the Russo-Japanese War, he claimed, "Losing Korea is not a problem. It is enough if we can defend the home territory of the Japanese Empire." Yamamoto maintained that Japan had to consult and coordinate with Britain on everything and that it was out of the question for Japan to act on its own in agreements with Russia. Excessively quick-footed and expeditious diplomacy, Yamamoto contended, might do Japan more harm than good. His view on national strategy was based on Japan's need to cooperate with the Anglo-Saxon world, i.e., Japan had nothing to fear so long as it collaborated with Britain, the master of the seven seas. Prime Minister Saionji, who remained a lifetime advocate of cooperation with Britain and the United States, doubtless agreed with Yamamoto.

On the other hand, the Japanese Army and the aggressive elements in the foreign ministry thought Japan had missed a golden opportunity to advance into Manchuria. Dissatisfaction over this oversight later culminated in the form of Twenty-One Demands, and the Army's resentment of the Saionji cabinet, which only listened to the Navy, became one of the seeds of the subsequent Taishō Political Crisis.

A second Manchuria-Mongolia independence movement erupted in 1915 when Kawashima again used Prince Su as a figurehead and plotted an uprising of the Mongolian cavalry in Inner Mongolia. Since the Japanese government had already given up on the ailing Yuan government, it secretly supported the anti-Yuan activities in Manchuria and gave tacit approval to this bid for independence. The Japanese government, however, changed its policies upon Yuan's sudden death and dissuaded local independence activists, including the Mongolian cavalry which had already started advancing southeastward, from taking further action. Thus ended the second Manchuria-Mongolia independence movement, and the frustration that accumulated as a result of these the two abortive attempts was a factor fueling the later Manchurian Incident.

Twenty-One Greedy Demands

While all of this was happening in the Far East, World War I erupted in Europe in 1914. From Japan's perspective, this meant that the European powers, whose reactions always had to be taken into account whenever Japan attempted to do anything on the Chinese continent, could no longer afford to pay attention to Far Eastern affairs. This in turn meant, as Yamagata Aritomo put it, "Resourceful though Yuan Shikai might be, he is out of policy options," and "it is a great chance for Japan to firm up its China policy, shake off past negligence, and devise new policies." Other Meiji elders more or less shared this view. The Army, for its part, proposed specific demands to be made of China. At the top of the list of demands was, needless to say, the extension of the leasehold on the Liaodong Peninsula. This was followed by demands for each and every concession on the Army wish list, including succession to the German concessions in Shandong Province. The last two items on the Army's list read:

China must ask for Japan's guidance in military development and weapon manufacturing.

China must consult with Japan when it intends to cede or lease concessions to foreign countries.

These two demands would make China a Japanese protectorate and echoed the process during the annexation of Korea. Objectively speaking, these demands were asking too much. Some people argued that it was not even necessary to demand the extension of the leasehold on the Liaodong

Peninsula. Uchida Kōsai, foreign minister at the time of the Xinhai Revolution, for instance, said,

> Nobody, not even Britain, expects Japan to return the Liaodong Peninsula. Therefore, there is no need to hasten the extension of the leasehold or to offer compensation for it. If China demands its return, Japan should simply ignore the demand. Just like the British have refused to withdraw from Weihaiwei, this is something that China will have to bear until it becomes powerful enough to demand the return of its concessions.

The Army and other aggressive elements in Japan, however, did not think extending the leaseholds on the Liaodong and Shandong Peninsulas was enough. Their primary goal in issuing the demands was to put the Chinese continent effectively under Japanese suzerainty. It was Director-General Koike Chōzō of the Ministry of Foreign Affairs Bureau of Policy Affairs who was the central figure in drafting the demands that were issued. Koike was an active advocate of Japanese advances into China as well as a highly competent schemer. Foreign Minister Katō Takaaki, who was not very familiar with China affairs, often relied on Koike's congenial relations with the Army whenever coordination with the Army became necessary. Although some within the ministry, including Hirota Kōki, opposed these high-handed demands, the proposal was drafted by foreign ministry officials on the basis of the Army demands, was adopted without modification, and became the official demands to China. This was unlike the conventional foreign policy making process in Japan, which would have first taken the ideas of the Meiji elders into consideration, in that it was the middle-echelon military people and bureaucrats who were the chief protagonists this time. This fit nicely with Katō's "let the foreign ministry make foreign policy," motto in eliminating the influence of the Meiji elders. In a way, this can thus be regarded as an example of a power struggle obscuring grand strategy.

In the drafting process, the foreign ministry partially moderated the Army's controversial demands (noted above), and integrated them into what it called a wish-list Group 5. But because this Group 5 included "wishes" that would severely intrude on foreign interests—such as those related to weapons procurement and railway concessions—it made the

The portion of the Twenty-One Demands dealing with Shandong (photo courtesy of the Ministry of Foreign Affairs Diplomatic Archives)

whole of the Twenty-One Demands extremely controversial. When the Japanese government secretly showed these demands to Britain, it omitted Group 5, ostensibly because this was a group of mere "wishes" and not demands. The truth was more likely that the Japanese side did not want to notify Britain about those wishes until they became fait accompli, as they would certainly invite British intervention. In fact, because these requests would have sharply affected British interests in China if approved, the British government immediately condemned the Japanese government. Although the requests of China were to be kept confidential, they were quickly leaked by the British side, infuriated the Chinese people, and provoked a nationwide anti-Japanese movement. In the end, the Chinese gave in to the demands after the Japanese government sent an ultimatum, excluding Group 5 from the list due to strong opposition from Britain and the United States.

Sun Yat-sen and Chiang Kai-shek claimed that meeting the Twenty-One Demands was the quid pro quo for Japan's support of Yuan Shikai's imperial rule. It was true that Prime Minister Ōkuma Shigenobu had known Yuan for quite some time and had frequent contact with him. Immediately after China accepted the Twenty-One Demands, Ōkuma announced, "Monarchy is a necessity in a country like China, and there is no more appropriate monarch than Yuan Shikai." Ōkuma also published an informal opinion that Japan would not meddle in China's polity unless it affected Japan's interests. It is believed that it was actually the Chinese side that asked the Japanese government to issue an ultimatum to convince the Chinese people of the inevitability of accepting the Twenty-One Demands. But all of these were technicalities that can be found in any negotiations, and they are thus irrelevant to the essence of the matter, even if they are all true.

The real problem was the folly of demanding such important concessions from China, in effect making it a Japanese quasi-colony. This is what drew censure worldwide, and calling the demands "wishes" without being determined to follow through on them with action in no way mitigated the situation. The Japanese government's conduct only isolated Japan internationally and infuriated the Chinese. It was so foolish a move that the day the demands were presented became remembered by the Chinese people as a day of national humiliation.

Prime Minister Ōkuma and Foreign Minister Katō were responsible for this mishandling. If it had been Itō Hirobumi, Mutsu Munemitsu, or Shidehara Kijūrō, they would have restrained the military and excluded Group 5 from the beginning. Komura Jutarō, by contrast, would have insisted on much tougher measures, including the use of military force to gain Chinese acceptance of the demands, even if the military would have hesitated. In short, everything was half-hearted, and it was this same sleep-walking bureaucratic attitude of just going through the paperwork motions without rigorously pursuing the discussion to its logical conclusion, already prevalent in the Japanese government at that time, that was the genesis of all of Japan's numerous blunders culminating in World War II.

Ōkuma's personality also played a part. He had a tendency to accept any and all requests that came to him. He prided himself on his flexibility, but he rarely delivered anything except rhetorical justifications. Knowing the Army's request was unreasonable, the foreign ministry officials decided to compromise by including it as "the Japanese government's wish" instead of demands, so as to tone it down without causing the Army to lose face. The ultimatum, which was absolutely uncalled for even as a half-hearted request, may have been an effort, at least in part, to project a hard-line stance in anticipation of an election.

Hara Takashi's speech denouncing the Ōkuma cabinet delivered at the Imperial Diet attacked precisely those points. He said:

> While the great turmoil in Europe prevents the European powers from meddling in Oriental affairs, all of them doubtless think that Japan is seeking to take advantage of this vacuum to realize its colonial ambitions. The Ōkuma cabinet's clumsy and intimidating conduct can only have deepened Western suspicions of Japan and provoked antipathy toward Japan among Chinese officials and people alike. Japan's supremacy in Manchuria and Mongolia have long been recognized by China as well as the Western powers. Japan's acquisition of the Shandong Peninsula from Germany is also viewed as an inevitable result of the war. Extension of the leasehold on those two territories could have been accomplished over a cup of tea if Japan had sincerely pursued friendship with China without stirring up the international community. This disgraceful diplomatic bungling by the Ōkuma cabinet is most deplorable. This incident has not only provoked hostility toward Japan in China, which should be Japan's friendly neighbor, but also caused misunderstanding of Japan among the Western powers with which Japan must maintain close relations.

Similar criticism of the Ōkuma government was also heard in the Diet from Inukai Tsuyoshi, who found it outrageous that Japan should issue an ultimatum to the Chinese, who value honor above all. Ishibashi Tanzan, who later advocated the "small-Japan policy" including abandoning both Manchuria and Korea, denounced the mishandling by the Ōkuma cabinet as follows.

If this were only about the concessions in South Manchuria, the

Chinese side would not have made an issue out of it because this was already a fait accompli. By adding an additional nineteen demands, the Ōkuma cabinet made Japan's control over the Liaodong Peninsula and the South Manchuria Railway points of contention, which they had not been before.

Was Japan Able to Restore Trust?

Imperialism was the norm at the time, and even Hara and Inukai were imperialists. Therefore, no one dreamed Japan would return the Liaodong Peninsula to China. But there was a certain moderation to be maintained even in imperialistic policies. As impossible as it may seem to people now, it was eminently possible for a country to pursue its imperialistic goals without overly damaging its friendly relations with others if it took a moderate attitude. It was still possible for Japan to restore friendly relations with China even after the Twenty-One Demands. In fact, Sun Yatsen never gave up on Japan.

When Feng Yuxiang, a follower of Sun Yat-sen's Three Principles of the People, temporarily conquered Beijing in 1924, Sun Yat-sen moved from Guandong to Shanghai, where he was enthusiastically welcomed. Although he declared that he would immediately go to Beijing, he headed for Kobe first to meet with his Japanese friends. His lecture was attended by an overflow crowd. In this lecture, Sun Yat-sen advocated Greater Asianism (or Pan-Asianism), saying,

> Oriental civilization is the rule of Right; Occidental civilization is the rule of Might. The rule of Right respects benevolence and virtue, while the rule of Might only respects force and utilitarianism. The rule of Right always influences people with justice and reason, while the rule of Might always oppresses people with brute force and military measures. . . . Japan today has become acquainted with the Western civilization of the rule of Might, but retains the characteristics of the Oriental civilization of the rule of Right. Now the question remains whether Japan will be the hawk of the Western civilization of the rule of Might or the tower of strength of the Orient.

Since Sun said, "the question remains," it was not yet too late for Japan. Subsequently, Sun sailed to Beijing, where he was again received with utmost enthusiasm. By that time, however, he had already become terminally ill with liver cancer; and he died soon after his triumphant return to Beijing. Thus, the Kobe lecture became Sun's last appeal to the Japanese people, his dying wish to Japan. In a sentimental interpretation, Sun's speech was advising Japan to part from its past imperialistic attitudes, return the concessions to China, and repent of the country's past misdeeds. But the true purpose of his last visit to Japan was rather limited. In a press conference in Moji en route to Kobe, he announced that the purpose of his visit to Japan was "to request Japan's support for China's effort to abolish its unequal treaties." On his death bed, upon the pleading of Wang Jingwei, Soong Tze-wen, Sun Fo, and K'ung Hsiang-hsi, Sun Yat-sen delivered his dying message to Wang. The message concluded with the wish that the national assembly be convened and the unequal treaties be abrogated as soon as possible.

In Chinese rhetoric, philosophy is just an introductory remark. What really matters is the specific request that follows. Sun Yat-sen held the view that the utmost priority for the new government was to abrogate the unequal treaties with the foreign powers. This seems only natural when one recalls the forty-five years of painstaking efforts that Japan had to make in order to revise its own unequal treaties. What Sun sought was Japan's help and support in tackling this difficult task. Some may argue that the Japanese lease of territories was itself an unequal treaty, but it was utterly inconceivable that the demand Japan abandon all of its concessions on the continent—an echo of which was to be found years later in the Hull Note on the eve of the Pacific War—was in Sun's mind. As a matter of fact, Sun remained flexible as far as Japan's concessions in Manchuria were concerned.

While it is futile to ask "what if?" about history, if Japan had taken the lead in abolishing unequal treaties with China, recognized China's tariff autonomy, and induced other powers to follow suit, just as the United States and Mexico had done with Mutsu a quarter of a century earlier, that would have allowed Japan to easily regain the trust it had lost with the Twenty-One Demands. Even that was difficult for the Japanese government, however. The utmost priority for Japan in defense of its national interest was to steadfastly maintain the Anglo-Japanese Alliance and it was therefore impossible for Japan to take a unilateral measure that would affect British trade interests. Because Japanese advocates of international cooperation put their priority on the partnership with Britain; and the expansionists, for their part, were fully occupied plotting the imperial development of the Asian continent, it was difficult to fulfill the desires of the Chinese nationalists, represented by Sun Yat-sen and pro-Japanese groups.

CHAPTER

4

The Era of the Anglo-Japanese Alliance

—The British Gentleman a Model for the Japanese—

Where Did Shidehara's Conviction Come From?

Shidehara Kijūrō was appointed Vice Minister for Foreign Affairs in October 1915. He was still at the Japanese embassy in the Netherlands when the Twenty-One Demands were imposed on China in January. A Japanese minister in those days was equivalent to an ambassador by today's standards. Even though Japan began to exchange ambassadors with the major powers after winning the Russo-Japanese War, the head of the Japanese diplomatic mission to the Netherlands, a minor power in Europe at this point, was still a minister. After Shidehara learned of the Twenty-One Demands, he was seen deep in thought for several days. Subsequently, he wrote a private letter to Foreign Minister Katō Takaaki offering his opinion that Japan should refrain from such high-handed conduct. Although this private letter is nowhere to be found among official documents, Tani Masayuki, who worked under Shidehara in the Netherlands and later became foreign minister himself, had the following memory of this incident: "Because I was just a raw beginner and had no understanding of what diplomacy was all about at the time, I did not see anything wrong with the Twenty-One Demands. I secretly thought it was only natural for Japan."

This was actually the conventional wisdom in Japan at the time, with the exception of a few outstanding intellectuals. Japanese newspapers unanimously supported the government's action, and even Yoshino Sakuzō, who later became the ideological leader of the Taishō Democracy, said, "Now that things have come so far, we have no choice but to send this ultimatum to China." Tani, however, also reminisced, ". . . but the Twenty-One Demands became the direct cause for a series of anti-Japanese movements in China, making relations with China an unsalvageable crisis. Seeing the diplomatic prediction of Minister Shidehara come to pass, . . . I could not but admire his keen insight." Shidehara was consistently firm in his foreign policy convictions and did not hesitate to say what he thought even if it went against the mainstream. Unlike Komura Jutarō's expansionist aggressiveness, Shidehara's stance was always moderate. It is not that difficult to persist with a hard-line argument. It is particularly easy to arm your argument with a theoretical foundation and arouse public support and sympathy when advocating nationalism or imperialist expansion. Maintaining a moderate stance, however, is not easy. Being a centerist does not constitute a conviction; when the general trend shifts to the right, the center also naturally shifts. This is what happened to most Japanese politicians in the 1930s. It requires an unshakable, moderate frame of mind to hold firm convictions unaffected by the trends of the time.

Where, then, did Shidehara's conviction come from? Recalling his upbringing and career, it is obvious that it did not come from any extraordinary circumstances. Rather, he acquired his convictions through endless study and insight. Although Shidehara, a diligent student until the end, kept full diaries and compiled massive amounts of materials in his notebooks, everything was destroyed in the fires after the Great Kantō Earthquake and during the Pacific War. What remains is only the oral account that Shidehara offered the *Yomiuri Shimbun* newspaper after World War II. Shidehara's close association with first-rate individuals from Britain and the United States shines through this record. This association was possible because of his high intellectual standard obtained through serious study in English and of political and diplomatic thought in the Anglo-Saxon world. Influenced by those first-class figures, Shidehara learned the Anglo-Saxon world and its political views, which became the pillars of his conviction and remained unshakable until the end.

A Typical British Gentleman

History inevitably trails facts. The British Empire in those days was the global hegemon that ruled the seven seas. It was only natural for people to attribute British hegemony to the British political system and national character. In the era of the Anglo-Japanese Alliance, worship of Britain was not a mere worldview for the Japanese; it could even be one's outlook on life. Now, few people remember beyond the militaristic days before and during World War II, and the Anglo-Japanese Alliance era has been nearly forgotten. While it is hard to imagine today, the British gentleman was universally perceived as an ideal to be admired and emulated, not only during the Anglo-Japanese Alliance days but throughout the days of the Taishō Democracy. This view lingered until the late 1950s. In the mid-1960s, when Japan was enjoying spectacular economic growth and the British economy was stagnant, conservative commentator Fukuda Tsuneari commented, "Strange, isn't it, that the Japanese worship of Britain has vanished without a trace?"

Unlike the "democracy of the masses" in the United States, British democracy was, from the beginning, a representative democracy of the chosen—in other words, it was "government by gentlemen," which fit well with the situation in Japan, where parliamentary government by local dignitaries had been maintained since the first general election in 1890. Shidehara was indeed a Japanese British gentleman, and he modeled himself on the British gentleman throughout his life. Before being appointed Japanese minister to the Netherlands, Shidehara was a counselor at the Japanese embassy in London. He later reminisced about Sir Edward Grey, then the British foreign secretary, whom Shidehara referred to as "a typical British gentleman indeed."

> Whenever I visited him for information, his reply was always on the mark, never missing the point. He told me everything, even classified information. As soon as he had said what he could, however, he stopped talking and became silent. He never said anything that was not relevant.

Having recognized his interlocutor as a gentleman, Grey would not hesitate to disclose everything at his disposal and would not waste words on unnecessary comments. This was indeed conduct becoming a typical British gentleman. Shidehara also reminisces:

Sir Edward Grey (photo courtesy of Kyodo News)

> Although the Grey family was an old family with a long history and a sizable fortune, Grey sold all his stocks and bonds when he was appointed foreign secretary. Because the position of foreign secretary carries access to confidential information, someone in that position may be suspected of taking advantage of this information for personal gain if he owns stocks and bonds, even if he has no such intent. Sir Edward wanted to avoid this.

"Refrain from doing anything that might incur suspicion" must have been what drove Grey to dispose of his holdings. Compared to the average Japanese politician today, the British gentleman's attitude in those days was superior.

> In those days, every country tried to decipher other countries' coded telegrams. When foreign office officials brought decoded messages to Grey, however, he paid them no notice, saying, "Please discard these somewhere." Grey once said that reliance on decoded messages could even misguide, and one should not decide policy on the basis of information obtained through such despicable means.

In short, it was the spirit of fair play.

Respect for the British Diplomatic Sense

Shidehara also once spoke of the following episode which demonstrated the diplomatic sense of ordinary British citizens and the British diplomatic stance toward the United States in those days. In the early 1910s, Mexico was experiencing a rise of nationalistic movements to take back concessions that the country had lost to foreign powers. In the course of one outburst, the British manager of an oilfield was murdered. When Shidehara met Grey after this incident, Grey was visibly indignant, saying,

> While nothing can be done about the dead person, we decided to dispatch naval ships to Mexico to protect British residents. But the United States declared it would not countenance this deployment because it would go against the Monroe Doctrine and insult the United States. When we changed our policy and instead requested the US protect our nationals in Mexico, the United States turned us down, saying it would not be responsible for the protection of British lives and property. American insolence is truly despicable.

When Grey was questioned in Parliamentary that evening whether he had known of the incident, he answered in the affirmative and said he would take no concrete action to protect British residents in Mexico. Anticipating a great fury among the British public, Shidehara was surprised to find the newspapers praise Grey the next morning. The gist of the newspapers was that "it took someone like Grey to respond that way." A newspaper reporter whom Shidehara approached for an explanation said, "It is only natural. After all, do you think we should go to war with the United States over such a trifle?" Shidehara reminisced:

> This is an example of the common sense that ordinary British people shared, which is far beyond the Japanese imagination. It must be so easy to be a foreign secretary in such a country. I cannot but be envious, thinking I would have been killed multiple times if I had given a similar reply in the Imperial Diet.

Ishii Kikujirō, a Japanese diplomat six years Shidehara's senior, identified Grey and Viscount Castlereagh as the two most outstanding diplomats in Britain in his *Gaikō yoroku* (Diplomatic commentaries), writing:

> They were both honest and candid. They were not endowed with such oratory as to cover up their wrongdoings with a wealth of wit,

nor were their views flighty. Their thinking was based on common sense and was always on the mark. After all, down-to-earth common sense prevails in diplomacy. It is this common sense that distinguished British diplomats and ordinary people from the others.

British Common Sense and Japanese Anglophilia

The Imperial Japanese Navy sent numerous outstanding officers to the British naval college, which generously taught them shipbuilding technology, creating a generation of staunch Anglophiles in the Japanese Navy. This Anglophile attitude was not confined to the navy. Francis Stewart Gilderoy Piggott, a British army officer who participated in the grand military exercise in Kyushu in 1911, recorded that almost all of the Japanese officers he came into contact with were pro-British, some of them emphatically so. Children in some schools sang both *Kimigayo*, the Japanese national anthem, and *God Save the King*. The Anglophilia in Japan in those days was far and away greater than today's Americophilia.

Another example of the Japanese identification with the British can be found in the classic, though not widely known, masterpiece on the theory of war, *Sensō yoron* (On war, published in 1925), written by Lieutenant General Murakami Keisaku, who was later the commanding general of the 3rd Army in Manchuria at the time of Japan's defeat. Murakami was a brilliant military officer who died in 1948 while in a prisoner of war camp in Siberia. In his book, Murakami referred to mystic notions in politics and assessed that the Germans had "a concept that they are the superior race specially chosen by God to reform the world and it is their mission to conquer the world and spread German culture," while Russia's Bolsheviks "dreamed of a world revolution." Murakami argued, "these notions are difficult to understand for pragmatic people such as the Japanese and British," grouping the Japanese with the British. It was only fifteen years after this season of Anglophilia that Japan raised the banner of *Hakkō Ichiu* ("All the world under one roof") and started advancing toward war against the Anglo-Saxon world. Yet as the above episodes and quotes indicate, the Japanese during the Anglo-Japanese Alliance and the Taishō Democracy had very common-sensical perceptions quite different from those of the Japanese in the Shōwa era and later.

While there is an abundance of testimony to the state of Anglophilia in Japan in those days, let me introduce an anecdote that appeared in *Jiyū to kiritsu* (Freedom and discipline), the memoir of Ikeda Kiyoshi, even though it is unrelated to international politics. Ikeda spent his youth in a British public school and attended the University of Cambridge during the Taishō Democracy days. Ikeda heard this story about a game of cricket from an old college waiter.

There once was a cricket player who was about to break a centuries-old record. He kept on hitting steadily in that particular game and he was only one run short of the record

. . . when all the players on the defending team rushed back to the pavilion. In other words, the opposing team abandoned playing defense. Nobody had the heart to catch the ball or bowl him out. The bowler, the only one remaining on the field, looked up at the sky and took a deep breath before pitching what was to become the ball of destiny.

Because there were no defenders on the field to catch even a weak pop-fly, the great record was as good as established. The next moment, the batsman took a couple of steps leftward and swung the bat, deliberately missing the ball.

The ball struck the wicket. The batsman was out. He took off his cap with his right hand and bowed lightly before walking toward the pavilion.

Finally, the umpire came to his senses and dismissed the batsman, as if he were about to cry. This was followed by thunderous applause . . .

"Oh, what a fool!"

"So long as such fools exist, our empire is . . ."

Although it was not at all a warm day, grey-haired men hastily took out their striped handkerchiefs to wipe "sweat" off their eyes and slapped their knees.

Although some might question whether it was really cricket for the defenders to abandon their positions, this episode as a whole reminds us of the degree of Anglophilia among the Japanese in those days—the idea, that is, that "we must emulate the British example because their conduct is admirable beyond imagining."

Shidehara Kijūrō, an Ideal Bureaucrat

While serving as the Japanese embassy counselor in Washington, DC, Shidehara learned a lot from British Ambassador James Bryce, just as he had from Foreign Secretary Grey in London. It is amazing that Shidehara was able to make the acquaintance of such first-rate people during his brief stays in the two cities. It is not how long people know each other that determines the quality of the relationship. Particularly for a diplomat whose term of appointment is always limited, everything depends on whether he is recognized at the first meeting as someone worth talking with. Among members of diplomatic missions, whose number was still limited in those days, it was critical for any newly appointed diplomat to be recognized as somebody. From this perspective, Shidehara must have been equipped with enough education and intelligence to convince Anglo-Saxon gentlemen that he was worth knowing.

In September 1912, Shidehara was posted to Washington, DC. He was then transferred to London in late 1913 at Ambassador Inoue Katsunosuke's strong request that he be appointed counselor at the Embassy there. In no time, however, Shidehara was appointed envoy extraordinary and minister plenipotentiary to the Netherlands in June 1914. While this appointment nullified Inoue's effort, it was a great promotion for Shidehara, and Ambassador Inoue approved the transfer with a sigh of disappointment. But again in almost no time, Shidehara was asked to assist Ishii Kikujirō, who became the foreign minister in the Ōkuma cabinet. Shidehara returned to Japan and was appointed vice-minister for foreign affairs in October 1915—from which time he served five foreign ministers over the next four years: Ishii, Terauchi Masatake, Motono Ichirō, Gotō Shimpei, and Uchida Kōsai. Among these five was a political rival of Katō Takaaki, Shidehara's brother-in-law. Against all speculation that this person would not allow Shidehara to remain in such a key position, in fact all four foreign ministers requested he stay on as vice-minister.

This phenomenon is attributable to the fact that most foreign ministers in those days were a few ranks lower than the Meiji elders and the prime ministers, while vice foreign minister was an even lower administrative post that was not a political consideration. But according to *Shidehara Kijūrō* published by the Shidehara Peace Foundation, "Amazingly, Shidehara was completely trusted by all the foreign ministers he served, all of whom entrusted the ministerial business to him." The same biography continues:

> How did Shidehara win such complete trust? . . . It may boil down to Shidehara's steadfast adherence to reasonable arguments, abstention from any unreasonable conduct, his vast knowledge of past practices and present conditions, and his capacity to process ministerial business with the efficiency of a legal professional. These qualities made him extremely reliable.

Shidehara appears to have been an ideal bureaucrat in peacetime. He was indeed a diplomat par excellence for Japan when its security was perfectly protected by the Anglo-Japanese Alliance. Nevertheless, Shidehara did not remain confined to the role of good bureaucrat in peacetime. Once he was appointed foreign minister, he dauntlessly devoted himself to the cause of international cooperation. Wei Zhang, the great Tang statesman famous for his poem that contains the lines of "I am won by heart/Let someone else talk about merit and honor," once advised Emperor Taizong that he should "encourage his subordinates to become good retainers and never tame them to be loyal retainers." What Wei meant was that he wished to be called a good retainer by collaborating with the emperor to help the country prosper. While those retainers who were punished with death after remonstrating the emperor, which resulted in the fall of the empire, were praised as historical loyal retainers, Wei did not wish to become one.

Shidehara was a good retainer in peacetime, but he also became a loyal retainer later during the turbulent times. Had people such as Shidehara been the majority at the heart of the Japanese government, Japan's subsequent course would have been quite different. Unfortunately, there were not many like him. Because the governments in which Shidehara served as vice foreign minister, from the Ōkuma cabinet through the Terauchi Masatake cabinet to the Hara Takashi cabinet, were prelude to the Taishō Democracy, the next section is devoted to a brief description of the changes in domestic politics during this period.

Times Trend toward Parliamentary Democracy

No sooner had the Taishō era begun after the demise of Emperor Meiji, than the Taishō Political Crisis started. The Saionji cabinet, which had refused to fund two additional Army divisions, was forced to resign due to Army non-cooperation, while the subsequent Katsura cabinet, which had been formed by overcoming the Navy's opposition with an Imperial edict, was also forced to resign by the Movement to Protect Constitutional Government. It would have been Saionji Kinmochi's turn to form a government, but he had announced his resignation from the presidency of the Seiyūkai political party by way of taking responsibility for his failure to persuade his own party to accept the Imperial edict to block submission of the no-confidence motion against the Katsura cabinet. This marked the end of what was called the Kei-En (Katsura-Saionji) era, which had stabilized domestic politics in Japan since the Russo-Japanese War, and the beginning of the Taishō political turmoil.

In subsequent years, Japan had to go through many twists and turns before it finally established a parliamentary democracy. Politics, after all, is an accumulation of who said and did what why. Accurately describing Japanese politics in those days would therefore require tracing all of these words and deeds, which would be an endless endeavor and, more importantly, could cloud our vision of the big picture. Instead, I shall attempt to portray the history relevant to the main flow of events by introducing several episodes and personalities that affected the events.

The most prominent flow was the trend toward parliamentary democracy and party politics, whose roots had been firmly embedded in constituencies all over Japan since the Freedom and People's Rights Movement raged. Although the governments dominated by *hanbatsu* at first tried to counter the welling up of party politics by establishing a pro-government political party, it soon found that the political parties were not so fragile as to be affected by this tactic. And when Itō Hirobumi himself became the president of the Seiyūkai, which was established around former members of the Jiyū-tō (Liberal Party), political parties became recognized as a part of the political process. No longer were political parties seen as a bunch of disloyal rabble-rousers. Subsequently, the Seiyūkai continued to grow more powerful. In terms of the number of affiliated Diet members, it was comparable to today's Liberal Democratic Party, which has long monopolized postwar Japanese governments and which has its roots in the Seiyūkai.

One factor that blocked this shift toward party politics from becoming as powerful as they are in our postwar parliamentary democracy was the power of the military, the bureaucrats, and the *hanbatsu* led by Yamagata Aritomo. The power of these three forces overtly and covertly restrained Itō, who was much more flexible even though he himself had come from a *hanbatsu*. Particularly significant was the rule enacted by the second Yamagata cabinet that stipulated that only generals and admirals on active duty could become war and naval ministers. As the movement for the defense of the constitution grew more powerful during the Katsura administration, the rule was revised in 1913 by the Yamamoto cabinet to also allow admirals and generals on reserve duty to assume ministerial posts. Because the military remained formidable, however, no one who was not on active duty ever became war or naval minister even after the revision, and the rule reverted to its original form after the February 26 Incident in 1936.

According to Meiji-Shōwa journalist and military commentator Itō Masanori, this rule ". . . allowed the military to gain an invincible position in Japanese politics and protect its privileged position for nearly half a century until Japan's defeat in 1945." With this rule, the military controlled the fate of each cabinet by appointing or not appointing ministers of war and navy to a new cabinet. The political parties were not, however, totally devoid of counter-measures, having the final say on any budget questions.

The Meiji Constitution was decisively different from the Prussian Constitution on this point. The Prussian Constitution did not have a provision on what to do if a government budget proposal were rejected by the parliament. Bismarck insisted that the decision be left to royal prerogative when there was no constitutional provision, taking advantage of the oversight to administer budgets for military expansion on his own. Although German legal experts had advised Japan to adopt this Bismarckian parliamentary management style in drafting the Meiji Constitution, Itō Hirobumi and Inoue Kowashi rejected this advice and decided that the same budget as the previous year would be implemented when a government budget proposal did not pass parliament. As a result, it became impossible for the Japanese government to implement new policies when the Diet opposed a budget proposal. This became a serious constraint for such a fast-growing country as prewar Japan.

The military budget was indeed the biggest problem. After the end of the Russo-Japanese War, the Imperial Army requested additional divisions in preparation for the Russian retaliation. The Army also needed extra forces to suppress the anti-Japanese movement by Korean insurgents on the peninsula. The Imperial Navy, for its part, had an urgent need to modernize its battleships in light of the commissioning of the HMS *Dreadnought* the year following the Russo-Japanese War and was about to launch a large-scale battleship building plan. The timing also coincided with the worsening of relations with the United States, which had already started building a grand fleet. Thus, the naval balance with the United States was a covert consideration behind the Imperial Navy's plan. How to respond to these demands from the military was the greatest issue for Japanese politics in the early Taishō era, and the Taishō Political Crisis had its genesis in the Army's demand for additional divisions.

When the Yamamoto cabinet stepped down due to the Siemens scandal of 1914, Kiyoura Keigo received an Imperial mandate to form a new cabinet. But because the Navy would not recommend a minister of navy unless its battleship building plans were approved, the Kiyoura cabinet was stillborn. The Ōkuma cabinet, which ended up succeeding the Yamamoto cabinet, was a peculiar intermediate government. The *hanbatsu*'s intent was to deal a blow to the Seiyūkai, the strong political party that had annoyed one *hanbatsu* cabinet after another since the Taishō Political Crisis. Given the history of conflict between the Jiyū-tō, a precursor of Seiyūkai, and the Kaishin-tō (Constitutional Reform Party), the *hanbatsu* people singled out anti-Seiyūkai Ōkuma as the next prime minister. Kindly put, Ōkuma was a flexible man with a big stomach; more bluntly, he was an unprincipled braggart. Facing election, Ōkuma was said to "preach the virtues of abstinence at a temperance meeting in the morning and make a long speech on the merits of *sake* at the brewers' association in the evening." He accepted the nomination, promising the military all the expansions they were demanding, and attempted to integrate all non-Seiyūkai forces, whether in the government party or in the opposition parties.

Ōkuma was popular among the Japanese people. He still retained his image as having been the first party-government prime minister and, due to his cooperative attitude toward newspaper reporters in the fifteen years while he had been out of government, he was also well liked by the media. Most of all, the mood of the times—the trend that eventually culminated in parliamentary democracy—was behind Ōkuma's popularity. The Japanese people were frustrated by the way the *hanbatsu* had monopolized government by forming affiliated cabinets one after another, even though the Seiyūkai had already become mature enough to be the government party by that time. This mood and Ōkuma's popularity were, however, taken advantage of by the *hanbatsu* to hurt the Seiyūkai.

In the general election under the Ōkuma government, all the *hanbatsu* got together to win. Under the leadership of Interior Minister Ōura Kanetake, the police freely interfered in the election. Major businesses were mobilized to raise unprecedented levels of campaign funds, making the election an epochal money election. It was an ominous prelude to the future corruption of party politics. As a result, the Seiyūkai lost heavily, losing eighty seats and becoming the number-two party for the first time in its history.

Hara Takashi, Successor to Mutsu Munemitsu's Will

Hara Takashi became president of the Seiyūkai at Saionji Kinmochi's recommendation immediately before the formation of the Ōkuma cabinet. As such, Hara had to cope with an unprecedented crisis within the party. Coming from the Nanbu *han*, a domain in northern Honshu that had sided with the anti-Imperial government northern alliance during the Boshin War, Hara had experienced the hardship of a domain that became an enemy of the emperor. After spending a difficult youth, he became a newspaper reporter, realizing he could not expect a bright future in government under the *hanbatsu*-dominated system. Winning the confidence of Inoue Kaoru while working as a reporter, however, Hara entered the government. Since he worked under Mutsu Munemitsu as a secretary at the Ministry of

Hara Takashi (photo courtesy of the Ministry of Foreign Affairs Diplomatic Archives)

Agriculture and Commerce, Hara enjoyed Mutsu's patronage and Mutsu appointed him to a variety of important posts in the Foreign Ministry.

It is no easy task to understand Hara's political philosophy. For one thing, Hara was a cool-headed realist who was not aroused or driven by any ideology or political philosophy. After serving as vice foreign minister and Japanese minister to Korea, Hara became president of the *Ōsaka Mainichi Shimbun* newspaper company. He published a critical essay, "*Gaikō shisō*" (Diplomatic philosophy) in 1900, around the time he participated in the establishment of the Rikken-Seiyūkai party. In this essay, Hara wrote:

> Although it is said that a philosophy is essential for diplomacy, it is no use crying such vague slogans as "protection of Chinese integrity" or "division of China." Diplomatic philosophy is, in my opinion, nothing but common sense.
>
> . For instance, a treaty takes a partner and it cannot be determined by Japan's wishes alone. While every independent country is supposed to have equal rights, in actuality, some countries are stronger than others. One should not recklessly wage war even against a single opponent, and it is impossible for any nation to fight against multiple opponents at the same time. It is the people who understand these simple things who can be said to possess a diplomatic philosophy.

This brief quote wonderfully summarizes the essence of diplomacy, and it was commendable of Hara to speak so candidly on his reliance on realism and common sense. Had all Japanese shared Hara's degree of common sense, Japan would not have confronted China with the Twenty-One Demands paying no heed to the reactions on the receiving end, nor would it have dreamed of confronting several countries at the same time militarily, including the United States and Britain, either of which alone was much more powerful than Japan.

Another reason Hara's philosophy is difficult to understand is Hara's preoccupation with seizing power as his political goal. To achieve this goal, Hara needed to edge closer to the *hanbatsu*-dominated power center so that he could keep it off guard, and it was safer not to say anything uncalled for about party politics or democracy. On this point, Hara was decisively different from Mutsu, who would not compromise even an inch and repeatedly tendered his resignation, "standing his ground with sword drawn even if he had to confront a million enemies." But it was this Mutsu that Hara most deeply admired and respected.

Meiji journalist Sakazaki Sakan reports that Mutsu left the following farewell message on his deathbed.

> My true wish has been to revise the unequal treaties with Western powers and complete constitutional democracy in Japan. While I managed to accomplish the former, I have not come even midway regarding the latter. This will bother me even after my death.

Sakazaki interpreted this farewell message as Mutsu's declaration that his sole goal in politics was to establish democracy in the form of party cabinets. It is beyond doubt that the goal for Hara, who succeeded Mutsu, was also to consolidate party politics in Japan.

There were moments when Hara himself spoke of this goal. Although he concealed his convictions with extremely careful wording on formal occasions such as during speeches to the Diet, he revealed his true intents in his eulogy for Itō Hirobumi, assassinated by a Korean extremist. There he said:

> Looking at global trends, the season has already passed for cunning politicians to exercise autocracy in the guise of constitutional government. There is no way that Japan can go back. No politician in Japan today can engage in politics ignoring political parties, and there is an abundance of recent incidents proving that politics moves only with the power of political parties. I am convinced that political parties will continue to develop and Japan will accomplish genuine constitutional government. While we all deeply grieve the passing of Prince Itō, only the politically ignorant would say his death shakes up and changes our party. Our country will continue to develop further and further on the foundation that Prince Itō has left us.

Curtain Rises on Party Politics

Although the Ōkuma cabinet succeeded in delivering a serious blow to the Seiyūkai, Ōkuma himself soon fell out of favor due to the fiasco of the Twenty-One Demands and the corruption scandal involving Interior Minister Ōura. But it was only natural for the Ōkuma cabinet, which had temporarily enjoyed tremendous popularity at the outset, to lose favor as time went on. The cabinet was able to sustain a certain level of popular support for quite some time, however, perhaps due to the wartime boom triggered by World War I.

From the vantage point of the *hanbatsu* and the military, the Ōkuma cabinet was no longer useful once they had gotten their long-sought two additional army divisions. Hence, they had no need or desire to protect the already unpopular Ōkuma. Upon the resignation of the Ōkuma cabinet, Yamagata recommended General Terauchi Masaki, whom he regarded as his direct disciple, form a cabinet. Although it would be another supra-party cabinet supported by the *hanbatsu*, no pro-constitution movement erupted against the cabinet's formation this time. The public had already become too weary of politics. Meanwhile, the Seiyūkai under Hara's leadership was willing to cooperate with the Terauchi cabinet and, in the subsequent general election, it succeeded in winning back the Diet seats it had lost during the Ōkuma regime and regained its position as the top party.

After a while, Terauchi resigned for health reasons, the rest of the cabinet also resigning with him. While the cabinet did suffer from the 1918 Rice Riots triggered by post–World War I inflation, the real cause of the resignations is believed to be the cooling of relations and subsequent estrangement between Yamagata and Terauchi. Although the general trend appeared to favor the emergence of a party government, Hara remained cautious. Fully aware that he had no chance to form a government without Yamagata's endorsement, Hara went out of his way to appease Yamagata, to the extent that, at one point, Yamagata declared that he and Hara were in complete accord politically. Nevertheless, Yamagata missed no opportunity to remind Hara that he did not share Hara's belief in party government.

Thus Hara was heard to say, "We cannot hope to form a party government so long as Yamagata lives. Or perhaps Yamagata may allow me to form a cabinet after he has exhausted all means to obstruct the birth of a party government." Unable to identify an appropriate successor to the government after Terauchi stepped down, Yamagata again recommended Saionji to the emperor to head the next cabinet. But Saionji adamantly refused this suggestion and, instead, recommended Hara to Yamagata.

While he would never have recommended Hara on his own, Yamagata grudgingly endorsed Saionji's recommendation, provided Saionji take full responsibility for the results. Thus was the Hara cabinet born.

Except for the ministers of war and navy, the Hara cabinet was composed solely of Seiyūkai members or sympathizers. Thus was the first full-fledged party government born thirty-seven years after the establishment of the Jiyū-tō in 1881 and twenty years since the premature and short-lived Ōkuma-Itagaki cabinets of 1898. It was, indeed, a curtain raiser for a new era of politics in Japan. This new era soon evolved into Taishō Democracy via the second movement to protect constitutional government in 1923, which allowed Shidehara to pursue his own foreign policy free of hindrances.

CHAPTER

5

The Anglo-Japanese Alliance at a Crossroads

—*How Japan Missed the Chance to Strengthen the Alliance*—

A Turning Point in History

World War I (1914–18) transformed the world. The Hapsburg, Hohen-
zollern, and Romanov monarchies all fell in ruins, while the econo-
mies and manpower of victorious Britain and France were thoroughly
exhausted. Consequently, the prosperity and glory of nineteenth-century
Europe, which had presented a model for Japan since the country opened
its doors, became things of the past. Instead, the United States emerged as
the strongest power in the world. Russia became the global headquarters
of Communism, which was to plague the world for seventy years. Nationalism rose like a flood tide in China. The stage for the major twentieth
century trends was set during World War I.

It would have been impossible for any country at the time—much
less for Japan, which had just become a world power as the result of the
Russo-Japanese War—to understand this massive transformation and
accurately assess its impact. Moreover, because Japan was not directly
involved in the war in Europe, it had not been faced with the need to seriously assess the international situation. From Japan's perspective, World
War I had the effect of temporarily eliminating the threat of Russian retaliation that had haunted Japan since the Russo-Japanese War. In addition,

because the Western powers could no longer afford to pay that much attention to East Asia and were unable to contain Japan militarily, Japan no longer had to seriously consider the Western reactions before it did anything. In the economic realm, Japan did not have to make any special effort: there was automatic demand for Japanese products in international markets that Europe could no longer supply. Orders for military-related equipment poured in from European countries, giving Japan an unprecedented export boom.

When World War I erupted in 1914, Japan was struggling to find ways to repay the 2 billion yen debt it had accumulated from the Russo-Japanese War. By 1920, Japan was a creditor country with 27.7 billion yen to lend. As Inoue Kaoru pointed out, World War I was a godsend for Taishō Japan. In retrospect, however, Japan's future ruin also had its origins in this period when Japan did not have to pay serious consideration to the international situation and other countries' interests. The power vacuum in the Far East lingered for another ten to fifteen years; it was 1926 when Chiang Kai-shek launched the Northern Expedition in China and 1932 when the Soviet Union completed its first Five-Year Plan. Meanwhile, the United States remained isolationist throughout the post–World War I years. This prolonged power vacuum allowed Japan to remain unaware of the potential risk in the East Asian environment. The flip side of the godsend was a curse that later ruined the Empire. Japan's foreign policy during World War I, particularly its stance vis-à-vis participation in the war, was closely related to the later dissolution of the Anglo-Japanese Alliance. The circumstances were a great turning point pushing Japan into isolation in the international community.

British and American Intentions for Micronesia

First, let us look back on how Japan decided on its role in World War I. It was on August 1 and 2, 1914, that Germany and Russia declared war on each other. France and Britain joined shortly thereafter. This left Japan, Britain's ally, to decide whether to join the war. In the very early stages, Britain was not interested in having Japan take part in the war. There was no knowing how extensive the war would be and, while Britain had to devote itself to the crisis in Europe, it did not wish to damage its economic interests in China by causing a stir in the Far East. Even after Japan's help was needed to keep German naval vessels from jeopardizing British merchant ships in the Pacific, Britain remained reluctant to ask for Japan's cooperation and instead requested Japan restrict its range of activities.

Many historians attribute Britain's attitude to its suspicion of Japan. In a sense, this view is accurate. At stake were the Micronesian islands that Germany had controlled. Although the sun never set on the British Empire and Britannia ruled the waves, Britain had no stronghold in the North Pacific. The German-controlled islands extending north from New Guinea, were Australian and New Zealand hinterlands, and Britain was naturally concerned about them. Had Japan not joined the war between Britain and Germany, Britain would have considered seizing these territories. The Micronesian islands are situated in a position that would enable them to block the sea routes used by American vessels connecting Hawaii, Guam, and the Philippines. As early as August 18, naval strategist Alfred Mahan warned that a Japanese occupation of the Micronesian islands could have a grave impact on British-American relations, as well as on Australia and New Zealand. His supporters in the US Congress submitted a resolution that the United States should not countenance even the slightest change in the status of the Pacific islands. Britain was naturally attentive to the US attitude. As history shows, it was the US stance that later decided the outcome of the Great War.

On the other hand, Britain's top leaders did not consider obstructing Japan from seizing Jiaozhou Bay, the German stronghold in the Far East. While British Foreign Secretary Edward Grey told Japanese Ambassador Inoue Katsunosuke on August 9 that Japan should refrain from taking any military action until so requested by the British government, he added, "Let there be no misunderstanding. The British government has no objection to Japan's taking Jiaozhou Bay should there be war between Japan and Germany, or to Japan's continuing to occupy the bay after the war." In other words, Grey said, "Britain is reluctant about Japan's participation in the war, but not because it does not wish Jiaozhou Bay to be held by Japan." In retrospect, Grey implied that it was the Micronesian islands that Britain was really worried about.

Prior to Grey's conversation with Inoue, Sir William Conyngham Greene, British Ambassador to Japan, had on August 7 requested the Japanese government search out and destroy German cruisers in the

Pacific under instructions from his home office. But Japan could not take military action against Germany without declaring war on the country. At the August 8 cabinet meeting, which lasted until dawn, Foreign Minister Katō Takaaki strongly argued that Japan should join the fray, "believing in the final victory of Britain" and "to show our friendship for an ally and raise Japan's status in the international community by driving Germany from the Orient." This position was approved by the Cabinet. The Cabinet conveyed its decision to the elder statesmen as a fait accompli, without prior consultation, seriously alienating Yamagata Aritomo and other elders. This was then the reason for the elder statesmen's aloof attitude later toward the Twenty-One Demands. Hearing of the Japanese government's decision, the British government requested Japan delay its participation in the war or limit its operations in exchange for the withdrawal of the request submitted by Ambassador Greene. Because Foreign Minister Katō rejected this request, saying it was already too late for Japan to delay its participation, the British government had no choice but to approve Japan's decision.

Samurai-Like Conduct by the Battlecruiser *Ibuki*

Japan appeared to have forced itself into the war, but as the war loomed much larger than anyone's expectations, cornering Britain in a critical situation, Britain really could not afford to be concerned about the reactions of the United States and Australia to Japan's actions. The reactions of those two countries became of only secondary importance to Britain as the rampant presence of German naval vessels became a serious threat to British trade routes throughout Asia and the Pacific, making it difficult for Australia to dispatch troops to Europe. Preoccupied with the situation in European waters, the British navy could not possibly send warships to the Pacific. After a while, it was feared the German fleet had operational bases in the Marshall and Caroline Islands, making it imperative Britain's ally, the Japanese fleet, destroy and occupy those German bases. Urged by necessity, public opinion in Australia and the United States also changed. When the Japanese fleet entered the Australian port of Fremantle to guard the transport of some 30,000 Australia/New Zealand troops, it was reported in Japan that, "Cheers filled the city and it appeared that all of their past fears of Japan had vanished. Now they rely on us completely."

In the course of escort operations, the Japanese fleet encountered the German light cruiser, SMS *Emden*, a menace in the Indian Ocean that had sunk numerous British merchant ships. Although the Japanese battlecruiser *Ibuki* was the most powerful vessel in the escort fleet, it never left the convoy to confront the *Emden*. Instead, it let the Australian ship *Sydney* have the honor of being the first Australian naval ship to sink a German ship. This gesture by the *Ibuki* was so highly regarded in Australia that the "samurai-like conduct of the *Ibuki*" has been praised every time a Japanese training squadron visits Australia. After the German Pacific fleet was annihilated, all the British ships returned to the European front, leaving safety in the Pacific to the Imperial Japanese Navy.

Cautious about Japanese Troop Deployment

On August 15, 1914, Japan issued an ultimatum to Germany with a time limit of seven days instead of the conventional forty-eight hours, a gesture made to emphasize that Japan was not recklessly looking for war. The ultimatum included two demands:
1. either withdraw or disarm all German naval vessels in the Far East and
2. turn Jiaozhou Bay over to Japan so that it can be returned to China.

Although British Foreign Secretary Grey had suggested Britain would not oppose Japan's occupying Jiaozhou Bay, the Japanese government decided to announce its intention to return the bay to China. This was meant to underscore that Japan had no territorial ambitions. Judging from the British attitude at the beginning of the war, it was quite clear to Japan that its future action might rouse suspicions among the Western powers. Also, there was a need to forestall German moves to negotiate a compromise with China, since Germany was apparently unable to defend Jiaozhou Bay for long.

Japan, however, had no intention of unconditionally returning Jiaozhou Bay to China after seizing it from the Germans. The British minister to China at that time was pro-Chinese, and he insisted Japan guarantee it would return the bay to China. When the Japanese government sounded out British Foreign Secretary Grey one more time through Ambassador

Inoue, it was reconfirmed that Britain had no objection to Japan's continued occupation of Jiaozhou Bay. The British embassy in Tokyo also conveyed Grey's intention to the Japanese foreign ministry. Foreign Minister Katō told the British ambassador, "We cannot guarantee the return of the bay to China. But when we return the bay, we will have to attach appropriate conditions including those on concessions in South Manchuria," with which the British diplomat expressed his agreement. Foreign Minister Katō announced in the Imperial Diet that December, "Now that Germany has rejected our ultimatum, Japan's actions vis-à-vis Germany or China will no longer be restricted by our previous announcements."

Because Germany failed to reply to Japan's ultimatum by the deadline of noon on August 23, 1914, Japan declared war on Germany and raided Qingdao. Since Germans were surrounded by stronger Japanese forces, the outcome was self-evident from the beginning. Nevertheless, the Germans put up a good fight and surrendered after a month. With the capture of Qingdao and the occupation of the North Pacific islands, Japan more or less accomplished its strategic goals in the Asia-Pacific region. The issue, then, was how much further Japan should continue to cooperate with Britain. Meanwhile, pressure on Japan to join the European battlefront was mounting as the situation there became increasingly dire. As far as the navy was concerned, it was only one month into the war when British Foreign Secretary Grey requested Japan dispatch battlecruisers to counter German cruisers in the Mediterranean. Japanese battlecruisers were then the most advanced vessels with combat readiness that even Britain envied. In response, Foreign Minister Katō turned the British request down on the grounds that the Japanese navy had not been designed to operate in such a remote area and, besides, all of its vessels were employed in operations in Qingdao and the Pacific, leaving none to spare.

In November, when the operations in Qingdao were completed, British Navy Secretary Winston Churchill requested Japan dispatch a fleet to Europe. While Prime Minister Ōkuma Shigenobu bragged that Japan would be able to dispatch this or that many ships for this or that political concession, both the elder statesmen and the Imperial Navy remained cautious. Also in play was an element of resentment of Britain, which had earlier sought to limit the range of Japanese naval operations. Toward the end of 1916, Germany further reinforced its operations to disrupt sea traffic, using submarines and other means. This increased the pressure on the

The destroyer *Sakaki* hit by a torpedo in anti-submarine operations against Germany in the Mediterranean.

allied powers, which prompted Britain to again request the Japanese fleet be dispatched. Although pros and cons were discussed within the Japanese government, it was obvious that Japan no longer had the option of turning down the British request. The Japanese government decided to send twelve destroyers, headed by the antiquated cruiser *Akashi*, on the condition that Britain support Japan's position regarding the Shangdong Peninsula and the Micronesian islands in future peace negotiations.

The Japanese fleet sent to the Mediterranean did its job with typical Japanese diligence and enhanced Japan's reputation. But the United States, which joined the war after Japan did, sent an incomparably massive force of 64 destroyers and 77 submarine chasers to carry out the same anti-submarine mission as the Japanese fleet. Compared to this show of strength by the Americans, Japan's contribution was relegated to the "of interest to specialists" level. Subsequently, the British government requested the dispatch of Japanese battlecruisers or the loan of some for use by the British Navy. Similar requests from France and Italy followed. The Imperial Japanese Navy turned them all down.

The Imperial Army never sent troops to Europe. One month into the war, Russia requested the dispatch of three Army divisions. Later, Britain asked for reinforcements from Japan in November in order to cope with the shortage of forces caused by Turkey's participation as a German ally. When German troops closed in on Paris in 1917, just as the Russian troops were withdrawing from the front, the city's plight was critical. France and

Britain strongly requested Japan dispatch its troops. Even US Secretary of State Robert Lansing suggested the Imperial Japanese Army dispatch troops to Europe.

There were some in the Japanese government too who advocated the dispatch. In response to the Russian request at the very early stage of the war, Ambassador to Russia Motono Ichirō advised Tokyo that Japan should accept the request "in order to have Japan carry as much weight as possible when it comes time to conclude the peace agreement." Major General Ugaki Kazushige, who was a member of the Imperial Japanese Army General Staff Office at that time, expressed his wish that Japan dispatch large numbers of troops to Europe in the hope that the war preparations and subsequent conduct of the Japanese troops would elevate the national spirit, help solve all the problems in the Far East, and buttress Japan's influence in European affairs. In other words, Ugaki saw it as a golden opportunity for Japan to act as a full member of the international community, even though sending troops might overstretch Japan. In the end, however, Japan rejected all requests for army troops.

A War between Whites

One of the reasons Japan remained reluctant to dispatch naval vessels and refused to send army troops to Europe was that it interpreted the terms of the Anglo-Japanese Alliance as not obliging Japan to provide ground or sea forces in this case. Backing this, the preambles of both the second Anglo-Japanese Alliance (1905) and the third Anglo-Japanese Alliance (1911) stated that the alliance was intended to maintain peace in East Asia and India. The first and second articles of both treaties stipulated that the two countries must consult one another and join the war when the territories or special interests of either country in said region are violated. To be sure, it was stated that the Alliance obligation would also apply to wars originating in conflicts in regions outside Asia and that the treaties did not limit the geographical area in which Japan was obliged to help Britain to Asia. Further complicating this, once Japanese naval vessels had been dispatched to the Mediterranean, it was not logical to claim the army was somehow not obliged to dispatch troops. Nevertheless, the general interpretation in Japan was that, judging from the aim of the Anglo-Japanese Alliance, the area to which Japan was obliged to dispatch military forces was limited to Asia and the dispatch of troops all the way to Europe was outside the scope of the treaty. In the cabinet meeting that decided Japan would join the war, there was no talk of "obligations stipulated by the Anglo-Japanese Alliance." Instead, the discussion was of "friendship for an ally."

Underlying the Japanese reluctance to join the war was the perception that World War I was essentially a European war of not much concern to Japan. When Japan decided to join the war, Yamagata Aritomo, believing that an alliance of the white nations would inevitably emerge and confront the yellow nations after World War I, objected to Japan's participation in the war, saying, "This white war could end at any moment. What would Japan's position be when it does?" This racial view—that although Britain was Japan's ally, it was after all a white country—was not at all absurd or overstated in those days. In fact, the German government used the newspaper of a neutral third country to criticize Japan's participation in the war, saying, "It is suicidal for Europe to invite a different race to a war in Europe. Those who insist on Japan's relief will be held responsible for the future oppression Japan inflicts on Christiandom." In the United States, the anti-Japanese Hearst-affiliated newspapers editorialized:

> Future confrontation with Japan is unavoidable. Japan's dispatch of troops to Europe not only endangers the United States but also imperils the existence of the entire white race. Dispatch of Japanese troops to Europe will allow Asians to slaughter Caucasians, weaken the white man's military capabilities, and eventually allow Asians to annihilate Caucasians.

The Japanese leadership appears to have thought at some level that Japan should conserve its strength when there was no knowing which "white country" would become hostile to Japan in the future.

Considerations for the Future Military Balance

Ozaki Yukio spoke in the Diet to express his opposition to Japan's participating in the war:

The more naval forces we dispatch to Europe, the less powerful the Imperial Navy becomes. Meanwhile, Japan's ally can preserve its own naval power because of the relief from Japan. We must seriously consider how the naval balance will be reflected in future diplomacy.

Ozaki's speech was received with applause. A more concrete issue was the naval balance between Japan and the United States. Although Alfred Mahan, who had warned of Japan's designs on the Micronesian islands at the start of World War I, passed away in December, his idea of a grand American navy lived on after his death. In December 1915, President Woodrow Wilson announced his wish to build the US Navy into a force that was "equal to the most powerful navy." In 1916 the US Congress passed a bill to build "a navy second to none"—the Naval Act of 1916 calling for building 185 ships, including ten battleships.

Its meager government finances no match for the United States, Japan in 1916 was only able to build the super-dreadnoughts *Fusō* and *Yamashiro*, which were comparable to their US counterparts, and four battlecruisers, such as the *Kongō* and *Hiei*. At the time, the Imperial Japanese Navy battlecruisers were said to be the best in the world, and it was those battlecruisers that Britain was anxious to invite to European waters. The *Kongō*, with a displacement of 27,500 tons, maximum speed of 27.5 knots, and eight 36-inch guns, was the largest naval ship in the battleship and battlecruiser category in the world in terms of displacement and main armament. When Britain requested the dispatch of naval vessels in 1917, the Imperial Japanese Navy General Staff argued, "If we accept this request, we will have to dispatch even the *Kongō* and *Hiei*. We must not recklessly send our battleships, the mainstay of our nation's defense, to dangerous waters."

In other words, "What might happen to the military balance that would protect Japan if we offered such treasures as the *Kongō* and *Hiei*?" Consequently, the Imperial Navy decided to keep these state-of-the-art ships for the defense of Japan and instead dispatch destroyers to the Mediterranean under the command of a single, old cruiser so that the Japanese destroyers would not be put under foreign command.

In the case of the army, the logistics were another difficult issue. In October 1917, the Imperial Army compiled a study on dispatching

Japanese troops to Europe. This study concluded that it would require 0.3 million tons of vessels to transport one army division to Europe, meaning it would take twelve to thirteen million tons to transport 40 divisions—an utterly impossible proposition. The argument that it would be to Japan's advantage to dispatch troops to tip the military balance in Europe and defeat Germany was a valid one in that Germany would in all likelihood advance to the Far East if it won the war, but the study argued that Japan had also to consider whether the allied powers would support Japan's position in the subsequent peace negotiations in gratitude or whether they would look down on a Japan exhausted by the dispatch of its troops to Europe. In this, the study went so far as to predict that the Western world would be all the more suspicious and envious of Japan if the dispatch of Japanese troops ended up deciding the outcome of the three-year war.

The focus of the discussion was on whether Japan should dispatch sufficient force to decide the outcome of the war, and the possible postwar consequences if it did. Curiously, the notion that dispatching Japanese troops, no matter how few, might strengthen the alliance was completely missing from the study. It appears that there was no sense in the minds of the study group that, as in the case of friendship, any chance to enhance an alliance must not be missed.

In the end, the Japanese government issued instructions to Ambassador Chinda Sutemi, who explained at the Paris Conference of the Allied Powers in November why it was impossible for Japan to dispatch army troops. The reasons included:

1. The Japanese army was not structured in terms of organization and equipment to be sent on expeditions.
2. It would take at least 20 army divisions to make a difference, and Japan was not capable of transporting such a large number of troops.
3. It would be difficult to gain the public support needed to mount the first overseas expedition for Japanese troops in history.
4. Nor would the Japanese people support a smaller-scale dispatch, given the unlikelihood of visible results.

It is noteworthy that the Japanese delegation made a highly unusual reference to the need for the support of the Japanese people. This reference could be interpreted as a nod to the current of history.

Britain's Disappointment

The Japanese press argued even more strongly against the deployment. Although the British government went to the trouble of dispatching the famously pro-Japanese Robert Scott to Japan, he caused quite a stir when he contributed an article entitled "Are You Really Samurai?" to the August issue of the monthly *Shin-Tōyō*, in which he criticized Japan for being self-centered when the Americans had set aside their self-interest and were fully engaged in the war. In the ocean of resentment among the Japanese, the September issue of the monthly *Taiyō* prepared feature articles on this issue. Suzuki Makoto argued in his article "The Nonsense of Dispatching Japanese Troops to Europe" that Japan would be like a slave if obligations arising from alliances kept increasing endlessly. Ōba Kakō contributed "An Irrational Argument Found in *Shin-Tōyō*," in which he said, "I was amazed by the cowardness of Britain's request for the dispatch of Japanese troops. This shows that we cannot rely on the Anglo-Japanese Alliance as a lifeline." The October and November issues of *Taiyō* also carried articles opposing the dispatch of Japanese troops to Europe. While those arguments distorted the facts and were not exactly sophisticated, they reflected the xenophobic nationalism, populism, and anti-government sentiments prevalent among the general public in Japan at the time.

The Japanese attitudes disappointed Britain immensely. Captain Edward H. Rymer, the military attaché to the British Embassy in Tokyo, sent a report entitled "The Present Situation of Japan" to his home government. In this report, Rymer said:

> Japanese politicians claim that the alliance between Japan and the UK is "the Keystone" of Japanese diplomacy. But Japanese basic rules for this war are, first of all, pursuing the most economical benefit, and next considering international relations after the war. That is not to cause strong anti-Japanese feelings in Germany. Thus, support for the allies would be made minimally These two rules control every activity by Japan. Although pro-German feelings are too much, it is because Japanese leading academics, doctors, and lawyers learned from Germany and Japanese military was modeled on the German military.

It is true that many Japanese were pro-German. Mizuno Hironori, a liberal military expert who later championed criticism of the military clique, praised the good fight put up by the light cruiser the SMS *Emden* as the manifestation of the "virile German spirit" and "paragon of navy men" and argued that Germany-Austria had already 70 percent won the war. In 1917, the Ministry of Education translated the German propaganda "Germany and the World War" and distributed it to schools; the British government protested. Rymer continued:

Every Japanese is an absolute Japanophile—an egoist who thinks about only himself and has no feeling of sacrificing himself for other countries. Japan does not accept the request of dispatching fleets because dispatch would affect trading and lose benefit. Dispatch is against the first rule that is to pursue the maximum benefit. Japanese are not interested in us pointing out that Japan is not an undeveloped country in East Asia but has a lot of responsibilities as a member of the western camp. If we strongly suggest how Britain should support Japan, what Japan should do as an ally, and that Japan should have an obligation as an ally, Japan would desert us. If Britain concedes and begs for their support, the wise Japanese would become complacent inwardly with doing well or the ignorant Japanese would simply increase his confidence and escalate his demand . . . Japan was spellbound by money and blinded by the dream of being the leader in the Pacific.

This reminds us of foreign criticisms of Japan's unwillingness to join the military campaign during the 1991 Gulf War and the denunciations by some American experts of the one-sided nature of the current US-Japan alliance.

Another thing that Britain was unhappy about with Japan was its attitude toward Indian independence activists who had sought refuge in Japan. Newspapers carried editorials sympathetic to these activists, while such private citizens as Inukai Tsuyoshi and Tōyama Mitsuru openly extended them cooperation with the tacit approval of the Japanese government. It was a time when nobody in Japan knew which side would win the war or how the Caucasian countries would deal with Asia after the war. That said, from the second treaty on, the Anglo-Japanese Alliance was mainly to mutually protect Japan's interests in Korea and British interests in India. Considering how furious Japan would be if Britain supported Korea's independence, Britain's indignation with the Japanese conduct was understandable. In 1916, the British General Staff office issued a document which reflected the British displeasure with Japan's support of the Indian independence movement, and this document was circulated within the British government.

Anglo-Japanese Alliance but a Wisp of Paper

The British foreign office was also deeply disappointed with Japan's attitude. At the time of the Twenty-One Demands, Foreign Minister Grey said, "I was disappointed by the Japanese government, particularly Foreign Minister Katō," while Vice-Minister Nicholson commented, "I have no faith in the Anglo-Japanese Alliance at all. Japan only tries to draw the maximum benefit with the minimum risk and burden-sharing." British Ambassador Green also wrote to a friend, "I do not think it necessary to tell you how disappointed Britain was with its ally Japan when we had our hands full with the war." The Memorandum on Anglo-Japanese Relations that was circulated at the 1917 Imperial Conference of the British Empire was a comprehensive summary of British views on this issue. As the relative position of the British overseas territories improved with British power war-worn, the Imperial Conference became the most important forum to determine the empire's diplomatic strategy. The later abrogation of the Anglo-Japanese Alliance also reflected the discussion at this conference.

Although the Memorandum's conclusion was harsh on Japan, its analysis was extremely fair and objective, reflecting the high intellectual standard of the British foreign office. While space does not allow introducing the memorandum in its entirety, the document is a source of inexhaustible interest. First, the memorandum stated that it was understandable that Japan take it as an insult when Britain attempted to restrict the Imperial Japanese Navy's area of activities. It also noted that Britain's interference in Japan's Twenty-One Demands must have appeared to Japan as though Britain were obstructing a legitimate Japanese right and something that Britain itself had done elsewhere. The document showed understanding of Japan's indignation. Then, the memorandum emphasized Japan's uncooperative attitude toward the war in Europe and pointed out that Japan totally lacked any understanding that, for Britain, the fate of the country was at stake in this war even though, unlike the Russo-Japanese War, it might not be a critical war for Japan.

As the memorandum declares:

> It has been said that Japan has to expand. That is true. However, why doesn't Japan develop Korea, Taiwan, Manchuria, and Sakhalin? These districts should absorb the increasing population of Japan. Regarding resources, Japan's political aims in part involve the fall of the British Empire so that there is no common purpose of co-operation between Japan and Britain. If we cannot approve of such Japanese ambition, we must determine that the time will come to stop Japanese ambition by military force. The Alliance between Japan and Britain is built on sand.

Among the foundational fragilities the memorandum cited were:
1. While the territorial integrity of China and the open-door principle are important for Britain, they are nuisances for Japan.
2. Japan's cooperation in the defense of India is de facto inconceivable.
3. In case of war between Japan and the United States, Britain is exempted from the obligation to assist Japan even though this conflict would threaten Japan's very existence.

The Memorandum went on to say that the Anglo-Japanese Alliance is a doomed effort to connect two ethnically and temperamentally adversarial countries. Backing that, it characterized Japanese as inherently aggressive patriots who wish to take the leadership in the restoration of the yellow race, a goal made more attainable by Japan's victory in the Russo-Japanese War. Japan has, it contended, been under strong German influence, so much so that one is justified in calling it the Prussia of the Far East. The Anglo-Japanese Alliance's days were clearly numbered unless Japan could reverse these perceptions and prove its worth as an ally.

Nevertheless, Britain Remained Open-Minded

Although it is no use pondering history's what-ifs, the ravages of World War II were so atrocious that one cannot help but wonder what could have been done to avoid them. In other words, what could and should have been done to avoid the collapse of the Anglo-Japanese Alliance and thus to avoid Japan's international isolation? While the British memorandum implied in its analytical section that Japan and Britain were incompatible, it in fact presented several feasible options, which reflected British realism: One of the scenarios postulated Japan's pursuing Prussia-like realpolitik and threatening India or the United States, in which case war would be inevitable and Britain is advised to prepare before it is too late. Another scenario had Britain choosing to pursue a reconciliatory policy toward Japan, which would require some concessions on Britain's part. There are, it said, sensible people with international perspectives in Japan and they may be able to draw upon the lessons of history and liberal thinking to curtail the country's blind imperialism. Even so, it concluded, Britain should not forget its German experience and should not let down its guard.

In other words, all Japan had to do was to become a moderate and respectable member of the international community. The memorandum did not demand that Japan abolish all of its expansionistic ambition. Because it was a time of imperialism and expansionism for all countries, Japan was entitled to pursue moderate expansionism that was compatible with other countries. More to the point, Japan could stay expansionistic as long as it did not harm British interests. Britain was not opposing Japan's occupation of Manchuria and Mongolia. Reviewing what Japan should have and should not have done before World War II, many Japanese would say, "If only Japan had stopped in Manchuria. . . ." While this is a historical view that would certainly be criticized today for not having departed from the imperialist model, it was nevertheless an accurate observation in light of the British attitude as seen in the memorandum.

Britain was indeed open-minded. The memorandum noted that Foreign Secretary Grey considered the British interest in China would be the easiest sacrifice to be made if Britain had to sacrifice something when the Japanese expansion did not stop in Manchuria. And the conclusion of the memorandum reflected this view. The memorandum went so far as to say that Britain would be prepared to make some concessions even on its interests in mainland China, so long as such action could inspire and energize the internationalists and the moderates in Japan. In other words, the memorandum seemed to be saying that Britain was willing to compromise if that would help people like Shidehara come to power in Japan.

Symbolic Meaning of the Dispatch of Japanese Troops

Specifically, what exactly went wrong for Anglo-Japanese relations? First, the Twenty-One Demands were a disaster. Britain was not opposing the extension of Japan's lease in Manchuria, and China seemed to have no choice but to accede. Against that background, the actions that dealt a decisive blow to Japan's image were:

1. Prime Minister Ōkuma's unprincipled and irresponsible adoption of the Group 5 wish-list demands, which were tantamount to wanting to make China a Japanese protectorate, just to appease hard-liners in Japan even though he had no intention of following through on them.
2. The stop-gap foreign policy of Foreign Minister Katō, who decided not to notify Japan's ally, Britain, of the Group 5 wish list since the demands there were mere "wishes."
3. The rudeness of the Japanese government in issuing an ultimatum to China.

If only those areas had been handled more diplomatically—more moderately—criticism of Japan's expansionism, which was the under-lying basis of the above memorandum, could have been avoided. Even after the Twenty-One Demands were communicated to China, Japan was still not without the means to repair the damage done. Japan still could have dispatched Imperial Army troops to the Western Front and fought side by side with the British and French troops against the Germans. And this should have been done before the United States joined the war. It was immensely important that Japan, a British ally, dispatch its troops ahead of the United States. At this point, Japan could have sent as many troops as its transport capability allowed. In light of the total 240,000 troops from the eleven army divisions that Japan was able to muster at the time of the Siberian Intervention (1918–22), it would not have been impossible for Japan to send two or three divisions to the Western Front during the war. Dispatching a small number of troops would have been sufficient. During the Vietnam War, Thailand and Korea sent two divisions each, while the Philippines staffed a field hospital as a token of support for the United States. As a result, Korea became seen as America's most reliable ally, which contributed greatly to improving the issue of Korean migration to the United States—an issue that Japan and China have not been able to settle for almost a century. During the Gulf War, Korea sent some twenty pilots, which got more praise from the United States than Japan's financial contribution of over 1 trillion yen.

Considering that the pros and cons of abrogating the Anglo-Japanese Alliance were almost evenly matched in the Commonwealth countries in later years, there is a good possibility Japan could have tipped the balance in favor of continuing the alliance had it dispatched troops to Europe and strengthened mutual trust with Britain. Was it really possible to maintain the Alliance? What would the international environment have looked like had this been done? These are some of the questions that will be addressed in a later chapter on the Alliance. In any event, the twenty years of the Anglo-Japanese Alliance provided Japan with the most favorable international environment in the stormy hundred years since Commodore Perry's arrival in Uraga. The joint naval powers of Britain and Japan were invincible, and the security of the Japanese archipelago was 100 percent protected in this age predating air power. Moreover, Japan also benefitted from the markets and resources of the British Empire. When people enjoy peace and prosperity, they are naturally apt to seek freedom. Under the protection of the international environment, the movement for freedom and people's rights in Japan finally accomplished its goal with the establishment of parliamentary politics. However, during World War I Japan missed a chance to put the Anglo-Japanese Alliance on a perpetual footing.

CHAPTER

6

The Russian Revolution
and the Siberian Intervention

—Repercussions of the Revolution Reach Japan—

Communism as a Philosophy of Hatred

With the revolutions in Eastern Europe (1989) and the end of Communist
rule in the Soviet Union (1991), the October 1917 Russian Revolution of
seventy years earlier became a thing of the remote past. Socialist ideas had
already been fading for nearly ten years before the fall of the Berlin Wall.
After the birth of the liberal-conservative Margaret Thatcher government
in the United Kingdom, the Western country where the socialist tradition
had been most influential, anti-socialist thinking became the mainstream
among industrialized countries with privatization and deregulation. In
Southeast Asia and Latin America, Communist guerrilla activities lost
steam and democratization became the trend of the times, coupled with
economic growth and the emergence of the middle class. Communist fervor was also lost even within the socialist camp. According to Zbigniew
Brzezinski's *The Grand Failure: The Birth and Death of Communism in
the Twentieth Century,* the thirtieth anniversary conference of the *World
Marxist Review,* the only surviving successor to the Comintern, was
a painfully desolate affair that was almost completely ignored by the
world's mass media. This was in contrast to the first and second World
Congresses of the Comintern in 1919 and 1920, which were full of hope

for the victory of Communism despite the destitution all around them.

Communism in Russia collapsed as if it were an abandoned house. This is not the place to explore the reasons for Communism's failure. Here, it is more useful to analyze why Communism so completely succeeded in fascinating people and menacing the world throughout the twentieth century. Because these are historical facts that will inevitably be forgotten by post–Cold War generations, they need to be documented for the historical record. Communist leaders explained everything in terms of class struggle, even to the uneducated, and persuaded the people that a utopia awaited on the other side of the proletarian revolution. Particularly enticing for the oppressed was the Communists' justification of violence toward and persecution of the former privileged class. A revolutionary song sung during the Taishō era went:

Evil hands of insatiably greedy capitalists
Have long deprived laborers of the fruits of their works . . .

This was the versification of Marx's exploitation theory. The song continues:

If you hate capitalists
You must also avenge yourselves on capitalists' children
Rape rich women and their daughters
And pour molten lead on them

This reflected the psychological background of the later massacres of the former ruling class by the Soviet and Chinese Communist parties and Cambodia's Pol Pot government.

It was only natural for the former ruling class to become fearful and apprehensive of Communism as they were now the targets of the Communists' class-based hatred. During the inter–World War period, this became one of the causes of the rise of fascism among middle-class citizens. After World War II, the same fear and wariness led to the emergence of the Cold War, which lasted for half a century. When Hendrick Sneevliet (Maring), a Comintern representative, asked Sun Yat-sen to share his revolutionary philosophy in 1921, Sun answered, "I aspire for revolution because of my love of the people," quoting the Chinese tradition since the time of Emperors Yao and Shun. Hearing this, Maring commented to Sun's aide,

"A revolution out of love for the human race can never be accomplished. Therefore, we will pursue a revolution to avenge ourselves on the ruling class." It was this philosophy of hatred in Communism that gave birth to many tragedies of the twentieth century. Brzezinski further explains that Communism not only provided an outlet for the oppressed people's unhappiness and justification for their hatred but also offered intellectuals a means by which they could intellectually understand human history, politics, and economics. Those who adopted Communism's view were able to be self-confident, having no doubt that they were right.

In "The Sources of Soviet Conduct," which provided the US government with theoretical foundation for its containment policy during the Cold War, George Kennan, writing as X, explained that Marxist theory had appealed to the Russian people who had been oppressed by the tyranny of the Tsar. But the influence of Marxist theory was by no means confined to Russia; it spread worldwide from Europe all the way to Algeria, India, China, Korea, and Japan, creating a strong Marxist–indoctrinated generation up to the 1960s. The Korean philosopher/statesman Yu Ji Nho once said:

If the true nature of Communism had not been revealed during the Korean War, the Republic of Korea would have become a Communist country. Almost all Korean intellectuals were Communists throughout the Japanese occupation and after World War II. And those who were not were haunted by their not having become Communists due to their fortunes, social status, or, simply, lack of courage.

Diffusion of Ideological Anxiety

The socialist movement had started in Japan by the end of the Russo-Japanese War. Soviet historians regarded the anti-government movements in Russia during the Russo-Japanese War as prelude to the Russian Revolution, and these movements began to influence the entire world, including Japan. In 1911, the High Treason Incident, a socialist-anarchist plot to assassinate Emperor Meiji, was revealed, leading to the execution of twelve people, including Kōtoku Shūsui. While the socialist movement was stymied by the harsh government crackdown, the February

Revolution and the October Revolution in Russia in 1917 re-energized Japanese revolutionaries. Yamakawa Hitoshi, one of the founding members of the Japan Communist Party in 1922, reminisced:

> They say workers in London hugged each other and shed tears of joy upon hearing of the Russian Revolution. It was the same in Japan. Although I was asked to speak at one meeting on the Russian Revolution, I remember being too emotional and tearful to say anything.

Because of these developments, Prime Minister Terauchi Masatake became apprehensive about the trend to praise the democratic philosophy, which was particularly popular among journalists, and pushed for loyalty and patriotism to be instilled in the people as a countermeasure. Hara Takashi, who was to form his cabinet that autumn, had a much more insightful reaction than Terauchi's. He, too, expressed concern over the future rise of democracy, as did bureaucrats such as Terauchi, but what distinguished him from the bureaucrats was that, as he himself said, his method was not to try to suppress the movement but to provide outlets for it to prevent catastrophe.

At the time, the Japanese translation of "democracy" was not yet fixed as "*min-shu-shugi*," as it is today. Since "*min-shu*" meant the people were master, it could be seen as a challenge to Imperial rule. Even Yoshino Sakuzō, a Taishō Democracy champion, used the term "*min-pon shugi*" (meaning the people are central) instead of "*min-shu-shugi*." Therefore, when Terauchi and Hara referred to "*min-shu-shugi*," they probably had vaguely in mind a system in which the ordinary people were sovereign. It was while fear of the Russian Revolution was still fresh in many minds that the Rice Riots of 1918 erupted. This series of riots was sparked by impoverished housewives, who had been suffering from the sharp rise in rice prices and demanded lower prices from the rice retailers. Because newspapers exaggerated these incidents, they spread all over Japan and developed into a major national disturbance, including assaults on the houses of the nouveau riche. Reading documents on this incident, one is struck more by the discipline demonstrated by the Japanese people. To be sure, the mob did resort to classical methods of direct appeal and intimidation, banging on doors and smashing paper windows, to buy rice at a reasonable price, but when they took the rice from the rice retailers, they paid for it at the price that had it had sold for before the sharp hikes. There was hardly any misbehavior such as looting under the cover of confusion, which is rampant in riots in other countries.

This was, of course, an incident that was totally unrelated to the socialist movement, but the Terauchi cabinet resigned one day after the riots were settled, ostensibly for health reasons. The direct cause of Terauchi's resignation was believed to be his estrangement from Yamagata Aritomo. According to *Hara Takashi-den* (Biography of Hara Takashi) by Maeda Renzan, when Hara was asked why he thought Yamagata had approved his appointment to succeed Terauchi as prime minister, he nonchalantly replied, "Because of the rice riots." Hara further said, "Had the Seiyūkai instigated the mob, Yamagata could have been killed." Hearing this, Maeda became convinced that Yamagata, while putting up a bold front, must have realized that nothing less than full-parliamentary democracy in the form of party politics could calm the popular unrest. The Rice Riots of 1918 erupted the year after the Russian Revolution, when the red revolution was still vivid in people's minds. To explain the situation in the simplistic style of *Chunqiu*, an ancient Chinese history, it was the historical trend generated by the Russian Revolution that gave birth to the Hara cabinet.

Needless to say, the foundations for the formation of the first party government in Japan under Prime Minister Hara rested upon his strenuous efforts to placate Yamagata and gain Saionji's cooperation. When Yamagata asked Saionji to form a government, Saionji, while declining, obtained Yamagata's pledge that he would not oppose a Hara cabinet and recommended Hara to Emperor Meiji. Saionji thus succeeded in achieving his and the late Mutsu Munemitsu's political ideal in the form of the first stable party government in Japan. These and other political bargains were undeniably supported by the current of the times, a current that no longer allowed the continuation of a supra-party government that ignored the people's wishes. Establishing party government was already the natural course of events, if only Yamagata's resistance could be eliminated.

Russo-Japanese Agreement and the Fall of Tsarist Russia

It is an already forgotten fact of history that Japan concluded an alliance with Tsarist Russia on the eve of the Tsar's fall. This alliance was mainly at Russia's request as the war in Europe became fiercer. Although both Foreign Minister Katō Takaaki and Ishii Kikujirō, who succeeded Katō, were reluctant to conclude the alliance on the grounds that it might weaken the Anglo-Japanese Alliance, Yamagata and others strongly supported the idea. In the end, the alliance was concluded in 1916, one year before the Russian Revolution.

Japanese leaders had mixed feelings about entrusting foreign policy to the foreign ministry. This was partly attributable to the arbitrary actions by Foreign Minister Katō when Japan joined World War I (1914) and the diplomatic mishandling of the Twenty-One Demands (1915), but there was also resentment of Katō's announcement that he would "take foreign policy back from the elder statesmen and put it into the hands of the foreign minister."

In June 1917, a provisional advisory council on foreign policy was established under the Terauchi cabinet to promote nonpartisan diplomacy. This council included the prime minister, foreign minister, minister of war, and minister of navy from the cabinet; three members of the Privy Council; as well as Hara Takashi, president of the Seiyūkai, and Inukai Tsuyoshi, president of the Kokumin-tō, from the political parties. Katō was president of the Kenseikai (Constitutional Association), but he did not participate in the council because it ran against the slogan, "Foreign policy in the hands of the foreign ministry" that he himself championed. Officials at the foreign ministry were naturally displeased with this advisory council, which remained active for five years until 1922. Obata Yūkichi, the Director-General of the Policy Affairs Bureau at the foreign ministry, reminisces:

> With the establishment of the provisional advisory council on foreign policy, foreign policy authority left the foreign ministry, which became a mere office to handle clerical work. Important foreign policy decisions made by the Terauchi cabinet, including the Nishihara Loans, the Sino-Japanese Military Treaty, and the Siberian Intervention, were all first deliberated and their outlines decided in the council, after which the foreign ministry was instructed to carry out specific measures.

At the time, Shidehara Kijūrō was vice minister for foreign affairs, but he exercised no influence over this development. According to the memoir of a foreign ministry official, however, "For such a staunch believer in the militarist hierarchy as Terauchi, vice ministers or directors general at the foreign ministry were mere clerical officials and their views not considered." Thus Shidehara diplomacy did not materialize until his later appointment as foreign minister.

The Russo-Japanese Agreement concluded in 1907 consisted of an open agreement and a confidential agreement. The most important point about the agreement was the pledge to fight together when either's recognized territories or special interests in China were violated by a third-party country and to restrain from making separate peaces. As such, the agreement was unmistakably an alliance treaty. Germany was the hypothetical adversary during the agreement negotiations, and the agreement was intended to defeat the German forces if they returned to China. When the Soviet government was established, all the secret treaties concluded by Tsarist Russia were opened, including the Russo-Japanese Agreement. This agreement was exposed by the daily *Izvestia* in its December 19, 1917, issue with a note attached saying that the referenced third-party countries were Britain and the United States. When this agreement was exposed, the Japanese Embassy in Moscow put out a statement to the effect that "Japan's position vis-à-vis Britain is unambiguous." Since no similar announcement was made about the United States, Japan's statement fed US State Department suspicions. There was no evidence that Japan had been specifically conscious of the United States when the agreement was concluded. Yoshimura Michio, a historian who has attempted to make impartial observations of history by citing various viewpoints, concludes:

> In short, although Russia and Japan initially considered Germany and the United States their major targets, when they concluded the Russo-Japanese Alliance, they chose Germany as the common hypothetical enemy because it would be least controversial in the context of the international situation at that time. But it would be reasonable, in actuality, to see the alliance as targeted at any third-party country that could violate the interests of the two countries in China in the future.

I think this was a fair judgment.

In any event, had Tsarist Russia not collapsed and had this treaty lived on, the common target of the alliance would naturally have been the United States, given the subsequent developments in international relations. Meanwhile the conflict of interest with Britain might somehow have been resolved. And if Tsarist Russia had remained on the battlefront until the Paris Peace Conference of 1919, Japan would have had a powerful supporter in its pursuit of the Shandong Peninsula during the conference, given the Russian government's earlier announcement to a newspaper that "It would be only natural for Japan to expect from China what we expect from Galicia and Constantinople, because Japan has been fighting the same war." Also, had friction arisen between Britain and Russia over the issue of the division of Turkey, Japan would have sided with Russia, which could have led to a confrontation with Britain and the United States under the Russo-Japan alliance.

Yet Tsarist Russia collapsed, and so did Japan's option that Yamagata and others had envisioned. But Japan's decision to adopt a policy line that steered Japan away from cooperation with Britain and the United States further cooled the Anglo-Japanese alliance and increased suspicions of Japan in the United States. The collapse of Tsarist Russia, on the other hand, also appeared to have offered Japan a new chance. Since the Xinhai Revolution, there was no central power in China, and Japan had been able to act freely as it wished. Now, another power vacuum was born in Siberia.

British, French, and US Intentions

History's assessment that Japan's participation in the Siberian Intervention (1918–22) was a complete failure seems to be indisputable. It did not take the left-wing historical view of the post–World War II world to establish this perception. Japan's participation had already been judged a failure. Wasting 1 billion yen and 3,500 lives, Japan did not gain one bit of territory out of this intervention. Instead, it only heightened American suspicions of Japan and provoked Russian antipathy, forcing the Japanese troops to withdraw empty-handed.

This withdrawal coincided with the period of Taishō party politics and freedom of speech. Criticism of the government rose among the Japanese people and this popular sentiment in turn adversely affected military morale, leaving a bad aftertaste similar to that felt in the United States after the withdrawal from Vietnam in the early 1970s. While it is easy today to cite the errors the Japanese government made at that time, some of the difficulties that government leaders faced were understandable. Most of all, there was no knowing which side would win World War I or whether the revolution in Russia would be successful. This uncertainty made Britain, France, and the United States adjust their policies as time went along. Within Japan, the intentions of elder statesmen, political parties, the foreign ministry, and the military were not unified and the reasons for the deployment to Siberia also changed from day to day. Having witnessed the October Revolution in 1917, France and Britain sounded Japan out as early as December on whether it would dispatch troops to Siberia. The initial mission of the Japanese troops was to prevent the massive war supplies the United States had sent Russia and stored in Vladivostok from being transferred to the Germans by the Bolshevik government, whose position remained unclear. Britain even informed Japan that, the situation permitting, it would give tacit approval to Japan's taking control of Amur Krai and the Trans-Siberian Railway. This was a typical British effort to reward military action with material gain.

British and French proposals were discussed within the provisional advisory council on foreign policy. While Foreign Minister Motono Ichirō consistently remained a strong advocate of sending Japanese troops, the council majority maintained a cautious attitude. They remained cautious because, most of all, the United States did not appear to be very enthusiastic about joining the Siberian Intervention. Japan did not wish to offend American public opinion, nor was it prepared to single-handedly bear the financial burden of the troop deployment in the event the United States decided not to join the intervention. In March 1918, William Barrett, policy advisor to President Woodrow Wilson, called Japan's deployment to Siberia "a Japanese invasion" and warned, "Unless the United States openly protests the dispatch, its moral standing in the world will be damaged." Influenced by Barrett's warning, President Wilson sent a message to the allied powers stating, "When intervention is needed, Japan might be the only country that can effectively carry it out. However, such would provoke suspicions of Japan's territorial ambitions and arouse tremendous resentment toward Japan among the Russians." He further expressed sympathy for the Russian Revolution, saying, "Despite all the miseries and misfortunes the Russian Revolution has created, the US government is most sympathetic." This is an indication that the Russian Revolution was not necessarily seen in a negative light at first by Western intellectuals.

In February, prior to these announcements and messages, the British war office expressed its support for Japan's dispatch of troops to Siberia but added the following observation.

> With this intervention, Japan will expand its influence at the expense of Britain, France, and the United States. However, Japan will not obtain any substantial gain from this. It is obvious from the experiences in Korea and Taiwan that Japan is not capable of ruling foreign nationals.

In other words, the British war office was saying the Western powers should let Japan do as it wished since nothing major would come of it. This was a manifestation of the British pragmatism that paid no heed to the rights and wrongs of intervention or invasion.

Decision to Send Troops to Siberia

Meanwhile, the situation in Siberia continued to change on a daily basis. Law and order was lost to the point that troops occasionally had to be mobilized to protect foreign settlers. After the central government was overthrown by the Bolsheviks, anti-Bolshevik local governments were established one after another in various locations in Siberia, motivating the Western powers to dispatch troops in support of those anti-radical forces. Particularly when German prisoners-of-war decided to side with the Bolsheviks, the argument to intervene so as to protect the common interests became stronger within the allied powers. When the Soviet regime concluded a peace treaty with Germany in March 1918, ensuring the withdrawal of the Russian troops from the Eastern Front, Britain and France became increasingly concerned with the military need to put more pressure on Germany in an attempt to keep it from moving its troops to the Western Front. At this point, the United States was obliged to go along with the British position.

In Japan, the Imperial Japanese Army General Staff Office had been enthusiastic about dispatching troops to Siberia all along. In preparation for the dispatch, Japan negotiated the Sino-Japanese Military Treaty intended to stipulate China's cooperation when Japanese troops were deployed to prevent German forces from conquering Siberia. This gave the Japanese troops freedom of movement in Manchuria to prepare for deployment around the Russo-Manchurian border. The deployment was treated separately from the US-Japan joint dispatch of troops that was presumed to be centered around Vladivostok. While Chiang Kai-shek's memoir criticized this treaty for having given Japanese troops a free hand within Chinese territory, Duan Qirui, Premier of the Republic of China at that time, told the Japanese minister to China, "Now, we can freely dispose of the territories east of the Urals between China and Japan."

Then an incident occurred which enabled Japan and the United States to decide to dispatch troops to Siberia. As soon as World War I erupted, Czechoslovakians organized a militia and joined the war on the Russian side, hoping to obtain independence from the Austro-Hungary Empire. After the Russian Revolution, the Czechoslovakian militia decided to return to Europe via Siberia, with the endorsement of the revolutionary government, in order to join the Western Front. Because the militia collaborated with local anti-radical forces on their way east, however, the Soviet government denounced the Czechoslovakians as a counter-revolutionary force. If an anti-Bolshevik government could be established in Siberia, this government could be expected to resume the war with Germany. The Czechoslovakian forces, which it was hoped would be the nucleus of this anti-Bolshevik government, launched a coup d'état on June 29 in Vladivostok and overthrew the local Bolshevik government. Czechoslovakia's independence and participation in the war against Germany were enough to provoke sentimental support among the Americans. Thus the US government finally decided to intervene militarily with Japan on July 6. Although it was agreed that the United States would dispatch 8,000 troops and Japan 12,000, Japan unilaterally decided to move an additional 60,000 troops from Manchuria, making the total expedition 72,000 strong. But in the Vladivostok city assembly election held prior to the dispatch of the US and Japanese troops, the Bolsheviks gained an absolute majority, showing that it was hopeless for Japan to expect public support in Siberia.

In any event, the joint US-Japanese force, in cooperation with local counter-revolutionary forces, drove the Red Army out and secured strategic points along the Trans-Siberian Railway one after another. By September, they had almost conquered all of East Siberia. At this point, Prime Minister Hara and War Minister Tanaka Giichi decided to withdraw some of the Japanese troops starting in October. Even after this partial withdrawal, however, there were still some 50,000 Japanese troops in Siberia, which the United States protested. The US government's protest can be summarized as follows.

> There is no provision in the US-Japan agreement that justifies the continued presence of the massive Japanese force in Siberia. Nor does it appear the Japanese decision is based on military necessity, either. Such monopolistic control by Japan can only provoke suspicion. It also goes against the objectives of the US dispatch of its troops.

It was a strong protest expressed without mincing. This US protest seems to have been based more on its official slogan at the time it joined the war—self-determination and no territorial cession—than on any sense of rivalry with Japan. When the war ended in November 1918, the objective of expelling German forces from Siberia no longer existed. The Hara cabinet implemented the second troop withdrawal in early 1919, reducing the total number of Japanese troops remaining to 24,000.

It might have been natural for some in the Japanese government to harbor a wish to retain at least some influence in Eastern Siberia now that Japan had dispatched its troops and put the region under its control. This wish was particularly strong among the upper echelons of the Imperial Japanese Army General Staff Office and the Ministry of Foreign Affairs. When Foreign Minister Uchida Kōsai spoke in the Imperial Diet in March 1919, he said, "The Imperial Japanese Army having occupied the territory and assumed responsibility for maintaining public order, it cannot withdraw without a convincing reason." Thus the purpose of Japan's deployment shifted from eliminating German influences in Siberia to maintaining public order in the region. Nevertheless, public order in Siberia was even then slipping out of Japan's control. Many of the provisional governments, established as a result of the US-Japanese control of Siberia were moderately socialist regimes that had gained local support on their own. Former Tsarist elements, however, staged a coup against these provisional governments and established the Kolchak government instead. Administratively incompetent, this government established by former military personnel accomplished nothing but internal power struggles. Since it stigmatized all who opposed it as Bolsheviks and massacred them, the Kolchak government quickly lost popular support.

The Bolsheviks, for their part, resisted the Kolchak government fiercely with strikes, sabotage, and partisan activities. At one point, the Trans-Siberian Railway was destroyed in forty places, which exhausted the Japanese troops who were defending the railway. As the Kolchak forces weakened, the Bolshevik forces began their eastbound advance over the Ural Mountains in August and conquered Omsk, the stronghold of the Kolchak government, in November. Of the 800,000 Kolchak troops, only 20,000 were able to reach Lake Baikal. In January 1920, even Irkutsk fell to the Bolsheviks. As a result, the Far Eastern Republic was established in Russia's Far East, only to be absorbed into the Soviet Union two years later. Forced to choose among dispatching reinforcements, withdrawing troops altogether, or defending only Vladivostok, the Japanese government consulted the US government. However, the United States remained indecisive and Japan received no response. Then, all of a sudden, in January 1920, the US government unilaterally announced it was withdrawing its troops from Siberia. Upon hearing this, Ambassador Shidehara Kijūrō, who had been stationed in Washington, DC, since November of the previous year, lodged a protest with Secretary of State Lansing and, as a result, obtained a free hand for Japan.

Shidehara explained his understanding of this abrupt US announcement at a colloquium on foreign policy organized by the *Asahi Shimbun* newspaper in 1932:

I do not believe that the United States intended to out-maneuver Japan. There had been widespread criticism in the United States against the continued presence of American soldiers in Siberia even though the Great War had already ended. Anticipating a Congressional resolution denouncing the continued deployment of US troops, the US government most likely made that announcement so that it could say that US troops had already been ordered to withdraw from Siberia.

This is no doubt what happened. When it comes to domestic politics, the United States pays no heed to other countries. Shidehara went on to say:

> Here, I tried to be logical, saying the Siberian Intervention was a joint effort proposed by the United States in which Japan agreed to participate. How could the United States have the gall to unilaterally withdraw its troops? Once districts had already been allotted to each force in Siberia, a unilateral withdrawal of US troops could endanger the Japanese troops. To this, the US side straightforwardly expressed its regret. At that point, I followed up with "If the US decision cannot be taken back, we understand that the United States would not complain if, in the future, Japan might make a unilateral decision, either to send reinforcements to Siberia or to withdraw our troops." The US side acknowledged our position and agreed to record the agreement in a memorandum. While I thought this would enable Japan to voluntarily withdraw its troops with honor, the government in Tokyo interpreted it totally the other way around. (laughter) The home government sent me a message saying, "You did very much the right thing. We will send more troops to Siberia."

Sharpness of Shidehara Diplomacy and Its Pros and Cons

There is much that can be said about Shidehara's handling of the situation, but I give him full marks as a diplomat. One of the essences of diplomatic negotiations is to draw out the maximum concessions from the other party while retaining as much freedom of action as possible. Taking advantage of the procedural error that the United States had committed—the failure to consult with Japan in advance due to purely domestic reasons—Shidehara succeeded in obtaining a US endorsement of Japan's freedom of action in Siberia. This was a diplomatic victory. The free hand that Shidehara secured for the Japanese troops proved particularly effective when it became domestically difficult for Japan to withdraw its troops because of the massacre of Japanese diplomats and residents in Nikolayevsk in 1920.

That said, Shidehara made two critical errors of long-term national strategy. First, he should have known how his telegram would be received by the government. Given his experience as vice minister for foreign affairs, he must have been fully aware of the attitudes of the Japanese military and hard-liners within the provisional advisory council on foreign policy. Shidehara's explanation that the Japanese government completely misunderstood his intentions sounds disingenuous.

Second, Shidehara seems to have failed to inform the Japanese government sufficiently on the situation in the United States. The United States is not represented by the State Department alone. Public opinion and Congress are also US voices, and it should not have been that difficult for Shidehara to imagine that the American public and Congress would most certainly feel betrayed if the Japanese troops continued to stay in Siberia. On top of securing a free hand for Japanese actions from the State Department, Shidehara should have warned Tokyo of the likely US reaction to a continued Japanese troop presence and of the resulting isolation of Japan in the international community. With this, he should have recommended an early withdrawal.

It appears Shidehara was determined to devote himself to diplomacy designated for foreign ministry officials, leaving the country's grand strategy to politics. This pattern was repeated later at the time of the abrogation of the Anglo-Japanese Alliance. He did not exhibit the courage to warn of the danger of a continued Japanese military presence in Siberia. Perhaps the times no longer needed a diplomat to be a statesman; perhaps a diplomat need only be a competent clerk. Although Shidehara worked to do what he believed in when he became foreign minister, he was determined to stay strictly in his role as a bureaucrat when he was a lower official. That was Shidehara.

A Strategy Based on Maintaining Good Relations with the US

Foreign Minister Uchida Kōsai demonstrated the same lack of political conviction. When he was called back from the ambassadorship in Moscow, Uchida said it would be outrageous to dispatch Japanese troops to Siberia because "appealing to the hearts of the Russian people, the radicals have already swept the entire country, and nobody can resist them." After he became foreign minister, however, he changed course completely and insisted on a continued Japanese troop presence to maintain public order. When he was questioned about the seeming disparity in the Diet, Uchida had to fend off the question, saying he could not be responsible for the comment because he had not read the newspaper article that carried it. Compared to their Meiji forebearers, it is obvious that Shidehara and Uchida lacked conviction. Nevertheless, blaming them for their lack of foresight might be too harsh. This was a time when nobody could foresee what would happen next. In contrast, it was obviously in the national interest to counter the Russian threat and revise the Meiji-era unequal treaties. These were matters of grave national concern for which people were willing to sacrifice themselves.

In the case of the Siberian Intervention, however, it was not at all clear what would be in Japan's national interest. If the anti-Bolshevik regime in Siberia had prevailed with local support, it might have been good for Japan's security because the future of the Bolshevik government was clear to none at the time. In the most extreme terms, if the future of the Bolshevik government had been clear and the birth of the cold-blooded Stalinist regime—which betrayed the Western intellectuals' expectations of socialism and later violated the neutrality treaty with Japan toward the end of World War II, bringing unspeakable misery to the Japanese in Sakhalin and Manchuria—had been foreseen, it could be argued that Japan should have never let go of Eastern Siberia, no matter what. But nobody knew what was coming. It was a time when predicting the future was extremely difficult. When the national interest is unclear, people tend to pay more attention to such small things as clever diplomatic techniques unrelated to the country's grand strategy. Praise for Shidehara's preventing Japan from shamelessly following the US lead in withdrawing its troops was one manifestation of this tendency.

Unpredictable as the future might have been, there was a grand strategy that Japan had to defend no matter what. At the risk of being criticized for using hindsight, I would say that the grand strategy ought to have been the establishment and maintenance of good relations with the United States. In that connection, I am amazed at how completely consistent Hara's insight was. In the early stages of deliberating the dispatch of troops to Siberia, two foreign ministers in the Terauchi cabinets, Motono Ichirō and later Gotō Shimpei, were both active advocates of the dispatch, while the majority of the cabinet had no definite opinion. In that atmosphere, it was Hara, the extra-government member of the provisional advisory council on foreign policy representing political parties, who consistently spoke up urging caution and blocked the deployment. In this at least, the council played the role that it had been expected to play. After the United States subsequently made the bold decision that led to the joint US-Japan dispatch of troops, Hara announced at the advisory council, "Since this will be the starting point of future US-Japan collaboration, we should stay as much in step as possible." By that time, Prime Minister Terauchi himself, who was pressured by the military, requested troops be dispatched not only to relieve the Czechoslovakian forces but also to enhance Japan's broader interest. But Hara continued to adamantly insist on limiting Japan's action to enhanced collaboration with the United States, and this stance was adopted by the council. Nevertheless, Terauchi later made a unilateral announcement, against the consensus of the advisory council, which expanded the objective of the troop deployment beyond cooperation with the United States.

One of the first missions of the Hara cabinet when it succeeded the Terauchi government was to deal with the aftermath of the troop dispatch. Hara decided on a partial withdrawal from Siberia, saying, "It will not matter if public order deteriorates somewhat when our troops withdraw. In fact, that may work to mitigate the criticism of Japan for having dispatched a massive force." It was Hara's pragmatic wisdom that, if the situation became unstable after the withdrawal, that would justify Japan's having dispatched so many troops. When the fall of the Kolchak government prompted the Imperial Army to insist on sending reinforcements, Hara responded, "So far, we have acted on the basis of collaboration with the United States. Let us wait and see what the United States does." Since Shidehara had obtained a free hand from the United States, it was only natural for the Japanese government to incline toward sending reinforcements to Siberia.

Hara Takashi's Conviction

Where did Hara Takashi's consistently pro-American conviction come from? It is obvious from Hara's background as a politician that he succeeded Mutsu Munemitsu's realistic diplomacy and was influenced by Saionji Kinmochi's liberal thinking. Saionji himself was of the opinion that the dispatch of Japanese troops to Siberia should not exceed the scale proposed by the United States. Another source of Hara's conviction was his wariness of the Imperial Army and its patron Yamagata Aritomo. As much as opportunity allowed, Hara wished to restrict the activities of the Imperial Army.

In the Hara cabinet, finance minister Takahashi Korekiyo was a constant opposing the dispatch of the Japanese troops and advocating their withdrawal, mainly from the financial viewpoint. As such, Takahashi was constantly in confrontation with War Minister Tanaka Giichi. But it is believed that Tanaka himself was aware of the inevitability of withdrawing the troops but felt he had to be seen as an advocate of a continued presence lest he provoke "restive sentiments within the Army."

When Uehara Yūsaku, Chief of the Imperial Japanese Army General Staff, tendered his resignation in protest of the government's decision to withdraw the troops, Tanaka said, "We must carry out the withdrawal even if it causes Uehara to resign." Hara also commented, "We should not let the military clique have its way. Public opinion will not support the military clique, either." War Minister Tanaka himself tendered his resignation repeatedly, but it is believed that his true intention was to make Yamagata dissuade him from resigning. Tanaka accepted the dissuasion on the condition that Yamagata rein in the Imperial Japanese Army General Staff Office. Hara's comments clearly reflected the atmosphere at the time:

> The Imperial Japanese Army General Staff Office has remained unaware of the current of history due to Yamagata's patronage. Since the situation today is totally different from that under Emperor Meiji, it is dangerous to abuse the prerogative of supreme command. It is the essence of constitutional politics for the government to take full responsibility for keeping any trouble from reaching the imperial family. And it is good for the imperial family if possible abuses of supreme command authority are controlled.

Hara was saying that the emperor's "prerogative of supreme command" was, in actuality, a façade to cover up the arbitrary conduct of the Imperial Japanese Army General Staff Office, and that abuses would undermine the prestige of the imperial family.

Finance Minister Takahashi proposed that the Imperial Japanese Army General Staff Office be abolished. On this, Hara told Tanaka:

> The other day, Nagaoka Gaishi came to me and said, "I was told that there was not enough financial leeway to improve our air force, but we would have enough funds if we abolished the Imperial Japanese Army General Staff Office. It is destined to be abolished anyway when Yamagata passes away." The presence of such a large-scale building as the General Staff Office which eclipses other ministries must provoke antipathy among the people.

Although Tanaka expressed agreement with what Hara had told him, he nevertheless suggested that they not publicize Takahashi's proposal lest it prove counter-productive. Hara concurred.

In mid-1921, the government finally decided to remove Uehara Yūsaku. At this point, Tanaka said to Hara, "I suggest we appoint some mediocre person Chief of General Staff Office in order to prevent future abuses of authority by the General Staff Office." Hara agreed with this, saying, "We should eliminate the main driver of the militarism." The term "militarism" was not born in the historical review of World War II. It had been in use in Britain, France, and the United States to justify the need to resist German militarism and join World War I. And this concept also had a profound influence on the Taishō Democracy. It was decided that Aki-yama Furuyoshi would succeed Uehara. In his diary, Hara wrote:

> For quite some time, the Imperial Japanese Army General Staff Office has been at odds with the war ministry, persisting with its militarist position, influencing the cabinet meetings, and putting Tanaka and other cabinet members in a difficult position. This personnel change is a scheme to eliminate the problem. . . . If executed as planned, I believe it will help our country take one step forward.

Nevertheless, Yamagata forced the postponement of Uehara's removal, citing Emperor Taishō's illness as the reason. Although this excuse was nonsensical, there was nothing Hara could do about it. Hara was assassinated that November, and Yamagata passed away the following February. It is indeed a matter of bitter regret that Hara did not outlive Yamagata.

CHAPTER

7

Paris Peace Conference

—Alliance Partner's Skilled Diplomacy Saves Japan—

Japan's First Big Moment as a First-Rank Country

The Paris Peace Conference marked Japan's debut on the world stage as a first-rank nation. Led by Saionji Kinmochi and Makino Nobuaki, chief delegates plenipotentiary, the Japanese delegation included future foreign ministers Matsuoka Yōsuke, Arita Hachirō, and Shigemitsu Mamoru as well as future prime ministers Konoe Fumimaro and Yoshida Shigeru (who also served as foreign minister). Despite having somehow staved off Western imperialism after opening its doors and having managed to win the Sino-Japanese and Russo-Japanese Wars, Japan was still a newcomer in world politics and was not prepared to play a major diplomatic role in the international arena. Japan's Foreign Ministry today sends new hires overseas for two years primarily for language training. This program is thought to stem from the poor language proficiency shown by members of the Japanese delegation at the Paris Peace Conference. In fact, Japan had to rely on the skilled diplomacy of Britain, its alliance partner, to escape catastrophe during the most important negotiation at the Paris Peace Conference.

After the delegation returned to Japan, Saionji reported to the emperor on the exchanges during the Peace Conference. Saionji enumerated three major agenda objectives that the delegation had failed to achieve despite

The Japanese delegation to the Paris Peace Conference (photo courtesy of the Ministry of Foreign Affairs Diplomatic Archives)

its best efforts. First, the Micronesian islands that Japan had wished to territorialize ended up being put under mandate of the League of Nations, owing to the powerful argument made by the United States. Second, Japan's proposal for the abolishment of racial discrimination was not endorsed due to adamant resistance from the British colonies. Third, though the allied powers supported Japan's position, China refused to sign the treaty on the Shandong Peninsula, garnering sympathy from some members of the US delegation.

The US Official Position and Actual Intentions

On the Micronesian islands, Japan almost got what it had wanted, since Japan was entrusted by the League of Nations with the administration of the islands. In those days, an underdeveloped region was considered incapable of self-rule, owing to its low level of civilization, and was put under a mandate of the League of Nations. The League was supposed to care for the region until it could stand on its own. In reality, however, the League entrusted an advanced country with administering mandatory rule. Until their independence after World War II, those mandated territories were substantially colonies.

In January 1918, President Woodrow Wilson gave a speech on his Fourteen Points at the joint session of Congress. This speech marked the end of American imperialism, pursued since the late nineteenth century, and the beginning of the American idealistic diplomacy known even today as Wilsonianism. The fifth point of the speech proposed, "A free, open-minded, and absolutely impartial adjustment of all colonial claims, based upon a strict observance of the principle that in determining all such questions of sovereignty the interests of the populations concerned must have equal weight with the equitable claims of the government whose title is to be determined."

At a joint session of Congress in February, President Wilson stated that, "peoples and provinces are not to be bartered about from sovereignty to sovereignty as if they were mere chattels and pawns in a game." He followed this with an Independence Day speech in which he insisted on "the settlement of every question . . . upon the basis of the free acceptance of that settlement by the people immediately concerned, and not upon the basis of the material interest or advantage of any other nation or people . . ." In this speech, Wilson also stressed that the United States would not tolerate any country or people's interfering in another country's affairs in order to expand its influence and gain material benefit. It was through this process that the US principle of self-determination was consolidated. This stance was certainly a gallant pose in the eyes of the American citizens. But it should be noted that, prior to the United States joining World War I, secret agreements had been reached between Japan and Britain over the postwar handling of territories in Asia and the Pacific and among European powers over the division of the former Turkish territories. These secret deals were realized under the guise of the mandate system.

This is a peculiarity of American politics. Whenever the US government finds it politically unfeasible to accomplish its ideals, it makes lofty speeches and adopts surface programs to avoid criticism from Congress and the media. But there was a reason the United States could not do this with Yap Island. Because the island was a relay station for the underwater cable connecting Guam and Celebes, the US government adamantly opposed Japanese control of the island and denounced the secret Anglo-Japanese agreement as unacceptable. Given American principles and the actual US interests involved, Japan worried that this issue would not be settled to its satisfaction. It was the persistent efforts and diplomatic ingenuity of Shidehara Kijūrō, who subsequently became Japanese ambassador to the United States, that solved the problem. Shidehara succeeded in bringing the negotiations with the United States to a happy end by giving the Americans the freedom to visit the island and manage the cable. This was a satisfactory settlement for the US side and Shidehara's efforts kept Yap Island from becoming an issue between the two countries until World War II.

Proposal on the Abolition of Racial Discrimination

During the Paris Peace Conference, the Japanese delegation took the initiative in the deliberations on the issue of the abolition of racial discrimination, largely because of Japan's bitter experience with the tenacious "yellow peril" argument in the West, including the Japanese immigration issue in the United States during and after the Russo-Japanese War. During World War I, it was feared in Japan that, once this war between white nations ended, those white nations would unite to confront the yellow races. In December 1918 in Yokohama, one day before the departure of the Japanese delegation to the Paris Conference, delegates received an official directive from the government that included the following instructions on the issue of the League of Nations.

> Because racial discrimination among nations has yet to be eliminated, the League of Nations could be seriously disadvantageous for Japan. If the League is going to be established, however, Japan cannot remain an outsider, which would isolate Japan. Thus, in order to eliminate disadvantages that could derive from racial discrimination, the delegation is instructed to argue as much as possible for an appropriate guarantee against disadvantages rising from racial discrimination.

This shows that the Japanese government was truly worried that the white nations, which were the overwhelming majority at the League of Nations, would act in a high-handed way and adopt all manner of pro-white rules. As it happened, however, Japan was appointed a member of the League's Council and it never suffered any racial discrimination in League operations. In retrospect, Japan was a bit paranoid and over-anxious about future racial problems. It was the principle of abolishing racial discrimination within each country that Japan took up as a specific issue during the Paris Peace Conference. Because of Britain's global hegemony since the seventeenth century, the majority of the underdeveloped fertile land in the world at that time was monopolized by the Anglo-Saxon countries. While it was the racial discrimination against the Japanese immigrants in the United States that agonized Japan the most in those days, Japanese immigrants were de facto shut out from such fertile lands as Australia, New Zealand, Canada, and South Africa. The Japanese delegation intended to raise this issue. What the Japanese side proposed was that, because League of Nations member countries would be treated equally, racial discrimination against the people of a member country should be abolished. Chief delegate Makino Nobuaki repeatedly stressed that it was only natural for the people of a member nation to demand equal treatment since each member country was determined to collaborate with other members for the sake of world peace and security, even at the expense of the life of its own people. Makino also argued that, if equal treatment was not granted for any specific member nation, members' confidence in justice and equality, the very standards that governed relations among member countries of the League, would be shaken. It should be noted here that what Japan was insisting on was racial equality among peoples of those first-rank countries responsible enough to be members of the League of Nations. It was not arguing for racial equality among all the peoples of the world.

The initial reaction of the heads of the British colonies who opposed Japan's proposal was, "Although Japan's demand is understandable, it causes problems if we have to treat not only the Japanese but also the Chinese and the Indians as equals." This would certainly have been a real problem if and when the day had come for China to join the League.

Indignant Public in Japan

Public opinion in Japan strongly supported the government position at the Paris Peace Conference. An alliance to promote the abolition of racial discrimination was organized in Tokyo, which resolved at its February and March 1918 conventions that the Japanese people would oppose the

League of Nations if it was not based on the principle of the abolition of racial discrimination. Encouraged by this public backing, the Japanese government sent strong directives to its delegation in Paris to pursue its original demand.

The Japanese proposal was a righteous argument. When the Japanese diplomatic mission in Washington, DC, attempted to lay the groundwork for its position with the US government, the latter found it impossible to oppose the Japanese argument due to its own principles. President Wilson went so far as to suggest that the proposal could be his own if Japan would soften its demand by adding such modifications as "as promptly and as much as possible." Britain also found it impossible to oppose the proposal initially and asked for time to consider it. As the objections by members of the British Empire became known, however, Britain itself became increasingly unsupportive. Australia, Canada, and New Zealand were adamantly against the Japanese argument. Australian Prime Minister William Hughes, in particular, went so far as to leave the negotiating table, claiming the proposal was utterly unacceptable to the Australian public. Hughes' attitude was so eccentric that Prime Minister Louis Botha of South Africa confided to Makino, "Strictly between you and me, I cannot help but call him a madman." Hughes consistently remained a man of unshakable views and, in the later debate on whether the Anglo-Japanese Alliance should be continued or not, he strongly argued for its continuation against all others, including Canada, who argued for its abolition.

Meanwhile, Japan tried to forge compromises in Paris, and, in the end, it signaled it was willing to drop the principle of the abolition of racial discrimination from the main text of the Covenant of the League of Nations and insert it in the preamble instead. This made the principle a non-binding proclamation of the Covenant. Nevertheless, Japan failed to obtain agreement from participating countries before going into a vote. As it turned out, eleven out of sixteen participating countries voted for the Japanese proposal, while five rejected it, including Britain and the United States. Britain found it had no choice but to represent the will of the members of the British Empire. Although the US government had been sympathetic to the Japanese proposal, it had to vote against it to prevent Australia from leaving the League, which would make the US government a target of harsh criticism and attacks from its Western states. Thus the vote left a bitter aftertaste for many of the participants. US President Wilson, who presided over the conference, declared that the proposal was rejected because it failed to win unanimous support. Makino protested—to no avail—that there were other cases of proposals being adopted by majority vote. On April 11, Makino delivered a speech in order to put Japan's position in the official record.

The Japanese public was naturally indignant. French newspapers were generally sympathetic to Japan. *La Victoire*, for instance, editorialized, "It was improper that Japan's proposal was rejected when the United States had succeeded in inserting its Monroe Doctrine in the League of Nations Covenant." *Le Temps* argued, "While we wish to express our deepest sympathy for Japan's proposal, we would also like to say that it is beyond doubt that the day will come when Japan's well-justified demand will be respected." It was widely recognized, both within Japan and internationally, that Japan occupied the higher moral ground in this dispute. Nevertheless, Japan's proposal was rejected by the countries of the British Empire and by the United States. This historical fact became one of the justifications for subsequent anti-Caucasian Asianism and anti-British/ Americanism in Japan.

Interestingly, even during World War II, despite the anti-Semitic policy of Germany, Japan's ally, the Japanese government instructed its foreign missions to treat the Jewish people equally according to the Japanese traditional race equality policy since the time of the League of Nations. Sugihara Chiune, the Japanese consul in Lithuania, saved the lives of thousands of Jewish people by issuing transit visas to third countries via Japan in line with this basic directive. Some post-World War II revisionist histories are telling this as a kind of heroic story as if Sugihara acted against the pro-Nazi instructions of the home government, but the official position of the Japanese government is clear as stated in published official records. In fact, the Japanese Manchurian Army accommodated Jewish refugees, took care of them, and helped them settle in Harbin or Shanghai about the same time.

China in Turmoil

The issue of the Shandong Peninsula became a controversial one. Since this was the issue that gave rise to the large-scale anti-Japanese movement in China, marking a turning point in pre–World War II Sino-Japanese relations, it is worth briefly revisiting the situation in China as well as Japan's foreign policy from the day of the so-called Twenty-One Demands in May 1915 through the May Fourth Movement in 1919.

When Yuan Shikai proclaimed his reign as emperor of the Chinese Empire on January 1, 1916, influential leaders and groups in various locations around China rose in revolt. This was the Third Revolution (Constitutional Protection Movement), which forced Yuan to abandon monarchism on March 22. Yuan died, disheartened, on June 5, 1916. Although Li Yuanhong succeeded Yuan as president, the real power of the regime was soon taken over by Premier Duan Qirui. Being a competent man, Duan managed to ride out numerous civil wars and power struggles and to remain an influential figure in the Beiyang Government until the Northern Expedition by Chiang Kai-shek in 1926. Meanwhile, Sun Yat-sen established a military government in Guangdong in 1917, followed by Zhang Zuolin's seizure of Manchuria in 1918, both of which posed threats to the Beiyang Government. In 1921, the Communist Party of China was organized in Shanghai.

Nishihara Loans

Japan's policies also underwent changes. Although the government of Prime Minister Ōkuma Shigenobu had announced its support for Yuan Shikai's monarchism around the time of the Twenty-One Demands, it changed its attitude as Yuan's Chinese Empire became unpopular both inside and outside of China. In the end, the Ōkuma government joined the Western powers in recommending the abolition of monarchism. As China began to show signs of disintegration during the turmoil following the Third Revolution, the Ōkuma government decided to secretly support the non-governmental anti-Yuan movements promoted by so-called *tairiku-rōnin* (Japanese adventurers in China). Because Li adopted a policy of north-south reconciliation after Yuan's death, the Japanese effort to take advantage of China's disintegration became untenable, forcing Japan to change its policy to support Li and Duan. More specifically, the Japanese government tried to control the Duan regime with economic assistance. What were called the Nishihara Loans played the central role in this. Although Nishihara Kamezō was a private citizen who had been closely associated with Terauchi Masatake since Terauchi was Governor-General of Korea, he was instructed by Terauchi and Finance Minister Shōda Kazue to enter into negotiations with the Duan government on a financial loan. The historical verdict on the Nishihara Loans remains extremely negative. It took less time for the loans to lose public support than it did for the dispatch of Japanese troops during the Siberian Intervention. As soon as the Terauchi government stepped down, the loans became a target of harsh criticism and were quickly terminated. Because the Nishihara Loans were conducted by a private citizen based on a policy decided by the provisional advisory council on foreign policy, completely ignoring the foreign ministry and going outside the normal diplomatic channels, it was only natural that Foreign Ministry officials did not think well of the program. Aside from ministry criticism based on turf issues, there was the matter of how loans were granted. The Nishihara Loans granted China loans of over 145 million yen (700 to 800 billion yen in 2003 money, assuming the current price of gold is about 5,000 times what it was then) without demanding solid collateral. This loan total exceeded the total for all of the loans extended China until then (120 million yen). As it turned out, the Japanese government failed to recover either principal or interest on these loans, except for a small amount, forcing the government, and thus the Japanese people, to bear the burden.

The Nishihara Loans were not used for economic construction as originally designed. Instead, they were diverted to war spending for the Duan government to confront the revolutionaries in the south and to private spending for government dignitaries. Worse yet, Japan was severely criticized by Sun Yat-sen's military government for interfering in the civil war. This was only natural. Internationally, the Western powers questioned Japan's intentions, whether Japan was trying to upset the Western powers' coordination in granting loans to China. Any historical incident is driven by its own historical inevitability. The Nishihara Loans were a rare exception to this rule, with faulty implementation and disastrous results.

Among the factors accounting for this failure is the East Asian economic alliance proposal advocated by Gotō Shimpei, home minister in the Terauchi government and later foreign minister. Gotō had long argued for the formation of an economic alliance in East Asia in order to counter the US Monroe Doctrine, and he insisted it was high time to invest Japan's surplus capital in China, seeing as Japan at that time had accumulated a huge amount of foreign reserves due to the war boom. It was the combination of Gotō's big talk, Terauchi's soldier-like simple-mindedness, and a general distrust of the Foreign Ministry since its mishandling of Japan's joining World War I and issuing the Twenty-One Demands that led to the decision to entrust the loan negotiations with China to a private citizen. The decision became easy prey for leading figures in the Duan government with a quick eye for gain. If there is anything positive to be said of the Nishihara Loans, it would at best be that the Duan government remained very cooperative during the period and agreed to sign the Sino-Japanese Military Treaty at the time of the Siberian Intervention.

To say a word in defense of Duan, he did not accept the Japanese offer purely for monetary gain. When asked on a TV program in later years about the Chinese dignitaries he had associated with, Yoshida Shigeru singled out Duan and praised him, saying, "He was a magnificent man who talked about nothing but his country." Yoshida added that Duan's true ambition was for China to recover eastern Siberia in collaboration with Japan. It so happened that, at that time, the United States was devoid of any legal argument for denouncing Japan's loans to China. At a time when no European countries could afford to pay attention to the Far East due to the war in Europe, it was only the United States that had both suspicions concerning Japan's advances in the Far East and the power to stop them. As described above, the United States attempted in vain to form a four-country consortium with Britain, France, and Germany, excluding Japan and Russia, to provide loans to Qing China. Given the realities in the Far East, Japanese and Russian participation was found essential, at which point the United States withdrew from the consortium on the grounds that the conditions for the loans infringed upon Qing sovereignty. Although the consortium survived the US withdrawal and subsequent German withdrawal, all the members—Britain, France, and now Japan and Russia—were involved in World War I and could not afford to oppose Japan's unilateral action. On the implementation of the Nishihara Loans, the Terauchi cabinet took the official position that the loans were intended to promote economic development with no political implications and were not to be administered by the four-country consortium. Although the United States proposed a new four-country consortium with Japan, Britain, and France, it was only in 1920 that this became a reality. Around the time of the Nishihara Loans, the United States did not carry weight on this issue.

Signing the Lansing-Ishii Agreement

There was one more reason Japan believed the United States recognized its special position in China: the Lansing-Ishii Agreement. The United States declared war on Germany in April 1917. Consequently, Japan and the United States were fighting a war on the same side. The Japanese government dispatched Ishii Kikujirō as special envoy in order to coordinate bilateral relations so as to prevent any conflict of interest between the two countries. Britain, an ally of both, naturally hoped for the bilateral coordination. On September 3, 1917, prior to the beginning of official consultations

Ishii Kikujirō (photo courtesy of the Ministry of Foreign Affairs Diplomatic Archives)

between Ambassador Ishii and US Secretary of State Robert Lansing, the British ambassador to the United States paid a visit to Ishii. The British ambassador told Ishii that, because a satisfactory agreement between the United States and Japan was vital to Britain, he had explained to the US government that Japan's desire concerning the China issue and the Micronesian islands was quite legitimate. He also gave Ishii the following advice and asked Ishii to be patient.

> Although the United States does not have any critical interest in China, it has remained very sympathetic toward China because the current secretary of state is the son-in-law of former secretary of state John W. Foster, who became an advisor to the Chinese government after retirement. It would be a great misunderstanding, however, to conclude that the United States will forever be uncompromising vis-à-vis the China issue. In short, you should consider the current US attitude toward China as deriving from the personal sentiments of the incumbent secretary of state and not take it too seriously.

It was a blessing to have an ally, particularly when it was such an influential ally as Britain. The Lansing-Ishii Agreement was an exceptional document in the history of US-Japan relations in the sense that it had the United

States endorse Japan's special position in China. Japan would never have obtained this outcome had this been negotiated solely bilaterally between the two parties. This was only possible because, first, Japan was fighting on the same side as the United States and, second, Britain lent its influence and diplomatic skills to assist the negotiations. It is no exaggeration to say that the greatest loss for Japan from the later abrogation of the Anglo-Japanese Alliance was the loss of Britain's diplomatic influence, particularly with the United States.

When Ishii visited the British ambassador on September 5, the ambassador told him:

> Although the United States unofficially recognizes Japan's special position in China, it seems hesitant to acknowledge it publicly. Because the US government has never asked foreign governments to acknowledge its Monroe Doctrine, it will not issue an endorsement even if Japan asks for one concerning China. Just as the United States appears to be content with the Monroe Doctrine without asking for foreign governments' endorsement, perhaps it may be unnecessary for Japan to ask for a US endorsement in writing concerning its position in China.

Thus the British ambassador even gave Ishii a hint about how Japan could backstep in order to prevent the failure to reach an agreement from developing into friction with the United States. Additionally, the British ambassador had been instructed by his home government to hand the US secretary of state a document outlining how Japan had contributed to the allied powers since the beginning of World War I.

The British ambassador's advice notwithstanding, Japan succeeded in getting the US government to recognize Japan's special position in China. For one thing, the Japanese government had earlier obtained a US government pledge concerning Japan's special interest in Manchuria. When US Ambassador to the Republic of China Paul Reinsch tried various ploys to make inroads into Japan's concession in Manchuria, Japanese ambassador to the United States Satō Aimaro asked Secretary Lansing for clarification in January 1917. Lansing assured Satō that the US government had never instructed Reinsch to do this because it recognized Japan's special interest in Manchuria. Although Washington had never made a formal announcement on this issue, he said, it had de facto recognized Japan's interest and did not intend to infringe on it. In addition, the British ambassador to the United States acted as a skillful intermediary, leaving both Japan and the United States wide room for compromise. This benefited Japan during the bilateral negotiations. The Lansing-Ishii Agreement was concluded on November 2, 1917, through an exchange of notes. The deal was struck by Lansing first sending a formal letter to Ishii. In his reply, Ishii directly quoted Lansing's letter, thus signaling his agreement.

Background of the Agreement

Scrutinized closely, the Lansing-Ishii Agreement was an enumeration of mutually contradictory principles, which later became controversial. First, the agreement stated that, in recognition of the general principle that special relations emerge between adjacent countries, the United States recognized Japan's special interest in China, particularly where the territories of the two countries were adjacent. Yet the agreement also declared that China was perfectly entitled to territorial sovereignty and that neither the United States nor Japan had any intention of obstructing China's independence or its territorial integrity. Pointing to the open-door principle and the principle of equal opportunity vis-à-vis China, the agreement stated that it trusted the Japanese government's guarantee that Japan would not take any action that would be disadvantageous to other countries' trade with China, even in the region where Japan had special interests.

Although there was no significant gap in interpretation between the two countries at the time the agreement was concluded, differences emerged as time went on. At the Senate Foreign Relations Committee in August 1919, Lansing announced that the "special interests" referred to in the agreement did not include political special interests. In contrast, Ishii in his memoir *Gaikō Yoroku* (Diplomatic commentaries) wrote:

> I must say it was a truly astonishing announcement. . . . Japan's special interests in China that the United States had recognized were mainly of a political nature and those with an economic or commercial nature were only indirectly involved. Otherwise, the joint declaration between our two countries would have been meaningless.

On this comment, Ishii added that it should be noted that Lansing, under pressure from the Republican members of Senate, had been pressured to play down the "special interests" as much as possible.

On this particular point, perhaps Ishii's interpretation was accurate. After all, it was obvious to any reader of the agreement that the only "special interests" that would not affect either sovereignty or territory, or China's economic interest, would be Japan's political influence in China. Furthermore, anyone knowledgeable about US domestic politics knows that the US government often does the same sort of thing Lansing did in his announcement to appease Congressional critics.

In terms of the region to which the Lansing-Ishii Agreement was applied, the United States took a very limited interpretation. At a meeting with Japanese Ambassador Satō in 1917, Lansing specifically called Satō's attention to the distinction between "Manchuria, where Japan's special interest is recognized" and "Shandong, where Japan's special interest is not recognized." It was a clear message that the United States had no intention of recognizing Japan's special interests in China but had made an exception for Manchuria. Different sources give different interpretations of the background to the agreement's conclusion. In his memoir, Ishii referred to President Wilson's damping down Lansing's resistance. In contrast, Kurobane Shigeru, author of *Nichibei gaikō no keifu* (Genealogy of US-Japan relations), states that Lansing was willing to compromise but was restricted by Wilson. Instead of speculating on what took place inside the US government or accusing it of betrayal, we should understand what this tells us about what kind of a country the United States is. Once Lansing had made a compromise going beyond what principle allowed the US government to do, it was inevitable that the US government would backtrack on this issue in Congressional committee hearings.

Saved by Britain Again

Thus Japan set out to face the discussion on the China issue at the Paris Peace Conference armed with a secret pact with Britain and the Lansing-Ishii Agreement with the United States. But the Chinese delegation announced that, because China had declared war on Germany, all of its treaties and arrangements with Germany had already been abrogated under international law. On the basis of this, the Chinese delegation demanded the direct return of the German concessions on the Shandong Peninsula. The Japanese delegation pointed out that Japan had conquered the Shandong Peninsula and declared war on Germany in 1914 before China did in 1917, and that the situation had been recognized by China itself at the time of the Twenty-One Demands in 1916. The Chinese delegation insisted that the 1915 agreement with Japan was a provisional one signed during the turmoil and had to be reconfirmed at the Paris Conference. The Chinese delegation would not give even an inch, apparently expecting backup from the United States.

In the end, it was again alliance partner Britain that saved Japan as British foreign secretary Arthur Balfour provided the Japanese delegation with classified information before the start of the consultation among members of the allied powers, saying, "The United States will initially take the stance of accepting the Chinese argument. France also takes the position that Japan might have to return Qingdao to China, depending on conditions." As the conference faced rough going, as expected, Balfour got together with Japanese chief delegates Makino Nobuaki and Chinda Sutemi for a consultation that lasted for an hour. The British Foreign Office director for Far Eastern affairs also joined the discussion.

The Japanese government was prepared to return territories to China, but it wished to retain such economic interests as the railroad and mines, as well as some settlements in China. In order to clear other countries' suspicions that Japan was greedily seeking something more, Balfour asked for clarification from the Japanese side on each and every specific issue that had been raised concerning Japan's intentions. Some of the points were mere propaganda from the Chinese side, but even the British Foreign Office had been taken in. After the consultation, Balfour instructed the British Foreign Office director for Far Eastern affairs to summarize the hour-long discussion in a memorandum, which, after modifications and corrections by the Japanese side, Balfour handed to the British, French, and US governments at a debriefing on the meeting. Although Wilson continued to oppose some parts of the memorandum, Balfour again attempted to mediate by submitting a compromise proposal. In this way, agreement was finally reached among Japan, Britain, and the United States.

Around the same time, the Italian delegation walked out of the Peace Conference over the issue of a claim to Fiume and returned home. The

United States, fearing the League of Nations would be stillborn if Japan also withdrew from the conference, compromised over Japan's arguments. The Japanese delegation, as a matter of fact, had been instructed by the home office in Tokyo not to sign the Covenant of the League of Nations if Japan's request regarding the Shandong Peninsula was rejected. In other words, the United States sacrificed its principle in order to salvage the League of Nations.

A similar process was repeated toward the end of World War II. It is believed that the Soviet Union had been prepared to be accommodating in terms of the demarcation of occupied territory in Eastern Europe, assuming Britain and the United States would find it uncomfortable for the Soviet Union to advance beyond the pre-war German-Soviet border. As soon as the Soviet Union learned about the "Four Policemen" arrangement—that is, the Soviet Union's participation in the United Nations—that the United States had really been after, the Soviet Union stopped referring to taking an accommodating stance and, instead, concentrated on the territories it occupied. Franklin D. Roosevelt, too, sacrificed actual American interests in international politics in order to realize an idealistic institution—the United Nations. This was a manifestation of American idealism. In contrast to Franklin Roosevelt, who persisted in dealing with the aftermath of World War II through the United Nations, ignoring Winston Churchill and his reliance on power politics, Woodrow Wilson salvaged the League of Nations by accepting British mediation during the Paris Peace Conference. Wilson's decision might have reflected the reality that Britain was still too powerful to ignore. It was truly thanks to Britain's support that Japan was able to pursue its dual-track diplomacy of implementing imperialistic policies and participating in the League of Nations.

It was indeed heaven-sent for a country like Japan, which was unfamiliar with international diplomacy due to its geographical and historical isolation, to have a friend like Britain. When it is recalled that Japan later had to deal with the Manchurian Incident without the benefit of the Anglo-Japanese Alliance and that Japan still had a chance to settle the issue with a mutual compromise had it accepted the Lytton Report, drafted by a British diplomat, it is easy to see how important Britain was to Japan. The Chinese delegation announced that it would sign the peace treaty with Germany except for the clause on the Shandong Peninsula. But for a country to sign this kind of treaty and not be bound by one or more of its clauses ran counter to international law practice and was unacceptable to the Paris Conference participants, including chairperson Georges Clemenceau. The Chinese delegation consequently abstained from the treaty signing ceremony on June 28, 1919. In fact, a storm of protest was blowing in China that would not allow its delegation to participate in the ceremony.

On May 4, hearing that an agreement had been reached among Japan, Britain, and the United States on April 30, some 3,000 Chinese students got together in a protest meeting at Tiananmen Square and rushed to the Japanese legation. Their rally was blocked, and students raided the residences of pro-Japanese dignitaries instead. The protest movement spread all over the country in no time and a nationwide strike was launched in June. Although the Beijing government had initially attempted to restrict the students, it instead released the students it had detained and purged pro-Japanese dignitaries as the protest movement became widespread. This was the May Fourth Movement that marked the beginning of a new era of anti-Japanese sentiment among the Chinese.

Two New Trends in the Twentieth Century

Concisely summarizing the history of that time in his *China's Destiny*, Chiang Kai-shek wrote (to paraphrase):

> The Japanese imperialists first imposed their Twenty-One Demands on China, taking advantage of Yuan Shikai's monarchical ambitions. They next provided political loans to accommodate the militarist policies of the Beiyang Army regime. That done, they concluded the Sino-Japan Military Treaty allowing Japan to advance its troops to Manchuria, conquered Qingdao, and demanded the railroad and mining concessions that Germany had held on the Shandong Peninsula. Shattering our hopes and insulting our dignity, this national humiliation fueled a strong desire for revolution among the Chinese people. The May Fourth Movement was but the most vivid expression of this desire.

Reviewing those five years of Sino-Japanese relations from the perspective of a nationalistic Chinese revolutionary, Chiang Kai-shek described it exactly as it occurred. In contrast to the historical views of Yuan Shikai and Duan Qirui, who actually engaged in dealing with Japan, Chiang represented the southern revolutionaries whose interests did not coincide with the Beiyang regime's. As the Chinese Nationalist Party became the mainstream of the Chinese revolution, Chiang's historical views thus became the orthodox historical views in China through the establishment of the Communist regime in 1949.

In the relatively short period of the first half of the twentieth century, the world was changing so fast that Japan could hardly keep up. The United States, which had been so imperialist in its annexation of the Philippines, drastically changed its attitude to embrace Wilsonianism and promised to grant the Philippines independence. The nationalism that rose like a flood tide in China, with the support of the United States, the most powerful country in the twentieth century, set a precedent for the liberation of colonies and the end of imperialism in the second half of the twentieth century. Japan had to confront these two new trends squarely, trends which it had not needed to heed in the nineteenth century.

8

End of the Anglo-Japanese Alliance

—Choice at the Crossroads of Old and New Diplomacy—

US Self-Seclusion

The United States did not join the League of Nations, despite having proposed it. The course of events that led to this situation illustrates the intricacy of relations between domestic politics and foreign policy in the United States. The League of Nations Covenant was adopted in February 1919 at the Paris Peace Conference. Even though President Wilson temporarily left Paris in an attempt to personally persuade Congress, the Senate, where the Republicans held a majority, remained strongly against US participation in the League. Of course, the Senate's opposition was partly attributable to the Republican's partisan logic of opposing any and all Democratic policies, but the main underlying factor for the Senate was American isolationism: Americans were adverse to being involved in conflicts in the old world and being responsible for the maintenance of world order. In order to appease the Senate, Wilson sought an amendment to the already-adopted Covenant, which was granted. It was this revised Covenant that he brought back to the Senate. The Senate, nevertheless, remained adamantly against the proposition and, in the end, rejected it in the spring of 1920. This rejection did not discourage Wilson, who then made US participation in the League of Nations one of his campaign issues during the 1920 presidential election. When the Republican candidate, Warren Harding, won the election, however, the probability the US would be part of the League of Nations fell to zero.

From this time on until World War II, the United States went into self-imposed seclusion within the boundaries of the American continent. Even though the United States decided not to join the League of Nations, it had to have an alternative vision of world peace lest there be no American foreign policy. Around the same time, an issue emerged that the United States actually had to solve—the issue of reducing and limiting naval armaments. The United States had continued to build naval vessels steadily since the presidency of Theodore Roosevelt, expanding its naval budget yearly. Congress, naturally, found this problematic when the war in Europe came to an end.

The Anglo-Japanese Alliance and the United States

Entangled with this was the US attitude toward the Anglo-Japanese Alliance. In the Senate in January 1921, long-serving Navy Secretary Josephus Daniels announced that there was no hope that arms reduction could be pursued internationally so long as Japan and Britain remained allied. His message was that the United States would not stop building naval vessels until it could rival the combined naval power of Japan and Britain. While this announcement alone was more of a simple arithmetic yardstick to defend the naval budget than a statement of international strategy, it was nevertheless a sensational statement.

In response, the Japanese and British governments immediately announced that the stipulations of the Anglo-Japanese Alliance would not apply to the United States. When the alliance was revised in 1911, a clause was added stating that "Should either high contracting party conclude a treaty of general arbitration with a third power, it is agreed that nothing in this agreement shall entail upon such contracting party an obligation to go to war with the power with whom such treaty of arbitration is in force," in effect exempting the United States from the application of the alliance. Because the Senate failed to ratify such treaty, however, this clause was theoretically moot. In any event, neither Japan nor Britain had ever imagined that their alliance would apply to the United States.

Setting aside whether these two countries would actually go to war with the United States, an alliance was an alliance. If the United States and Britain, two major naval powers, confronted each other due to a conflict of interests, it would be only natural for Japan to side with Britain, its alliance partner. This fact alone forced the United States to take the combined power of Britain and Japan into consideration. It was Canada that was the most worried about this. In Canada's view, the interests of Japan and the United States in the Far East continued to be in conflict, as did the shipbuilding race among the major powers. It was predicted that Japan's power would peak in 1923, after which the United States was expected to gain the advantage. This prediction then led to speculation that there would be a crisis in US-Japan relations in 1923. If that actually happened, Canada would be in trouble, sandwiched between its friendly southern neighbor and Britain, the leader of the British Commonwealth.

At the outset of the British Imperial Conference, which convened in London in June 1921, British Prime Minister Lloyd George announced that friendly relations with the United States would remain central to the British Empire's foreign policy. At the same time, however, he also praised Japan, which had faithfully abided by the Anglo-Japanese Alliance during World War I, and expressed his wish that "this well-tested friendship be long maintained." George in effect presented Britain with the major challenge of coordinating these two bilateral relations, and that issue took center stage during the conference. Once established, an alliance can be quite resilient. Although Britain had been dissatisfied with Japan's non-cooperation during World War I, it paid tribute to the Anglo-Japanese Alliance once the war was over. One can find a present day echo of this in official characterizations by the United States of the US-Japan alliance as the "cornerstone of the Pacific" no matter how frustrated it is with Japan's defense efforts or the base situation in Okinawa.

To Continue the Alliance or Not

At the British Imperial Conference, Canada and South Africa opposed the continuation of the Anglo-Japanese Alliance while Australia and New Zealand advocated continuation. Australian Prime Minister William Hughes commented:

From all accounts, I believe that the treaty with Japan should be renewed. Will we not be in the position to exercise great influence in Far Eastern politics when we are an ally of Japan, a major power in the Far East, instead of an enemy of Japan? If Japan becomes excluded from the group of West European powers, it will be internationally isolated, and the national pride of its people will be hurt where it is most painful. Britain must be aware that if it turns its back on the Anglo-Japanese Alliance, it is isolating Japan. Renewing the alliance, however, will have an effect of imposing on Japan a certain restriction that is inalienable from a treaty with such a civilized nation as Britain. Continuation of the Anglo-Japanese Alliance would therefore be beneficial for world peace, for China, and for the sphere of British civilization as a whole.

Based on this argument, Hughes suggested that the Anglo-Japanese Alliance be continued with an explicit announcement that its stipulations are not to apply to the United States.

Being relatively close to Japan geographically, Australia was a keen observer of the country. Had Japan maintained relations with Britain throughout the prewar period that allowed it to constantly consult Britain on foreign policy issues, the balance of power within Japan between nationalist expansionists and advocates of cooperation with Britain and the United States might have been different. Particularly given Emperor Shōwa's pro-Britain/United States inclination as well as the Japanese trait of remaining loyal to an ally, the arbitrary conduct of the military might well have been reined in.

Prime Minister William Massey of New Zealand gave a detailed account of how his country could not have dispatched troops to Britain had it not been for the cooperation of the Imperial Japanese Navy and said:

> Personally, I do not think there will be a second world war in the next thirty years. Because wars erupt unexpectedly, however, it is unwise to delay the necessary preparations until the last minute. . . . Imagine if Japan were on the enemy's side.

While stressing the importance of maintaining good relations with the United States, Massey concluded his remarks by saying, "I am obliged to speak on what comes to mind and what my experience tells me. I do not think I need an excuse to do so."

Prime Minister Jan Smuts of South Africa followed:

> We are at a crossroads. We will have to choose either effective consultations in the spirit of a genuine international community or a world of mutually conflicting groups and exclusive alliances, which could bring us much more critical disasters than in the past.

His comment followed the Wilsonian argument for the abolition of the already antiquated bilateral alliance and, in its place, argued for the adoption of multilateral collective security. Smuts insisted that the Anglo-Japanese Alliance should be scrapped.

Although Canadian Prime Minister Arthur Meighen did not express an opinion in formal sessions during the conference, it is obvious from subsequent developments that he led the discussions at secret meetings following formal sessions with his hard-line opposition to the continuation of the Anglo-Japanese Alliance. As a matter of fact, Britain subsequently proposed a quadruple consultation among Japan, Britain, the United States, and China, which was believed to originally have been a Canadian proposal. The proposal to include China in the consultation was de facto opposition to the Anglo-Japanese Alliance.

In the May 1920 official announcement on its attitude toward the Anglo-Japanese Alliance, the Chinese government had denounced the reference to "integrity of the Chinese territory" in the main text of the revised Anglo-Japanese Alliance as an insult to the honor and dignity of a sovereign country. Although the announcement did not oppose the Anglo-Japanese Alliance per se, it was made in response to popular opposition to the alliance within China and its intent was to signal Chinese opposition to the Anglo-Japanese Alliance. In a June 1, 1920, newspaper interview, Sun Yat-sen went so far as to say:

> I am adamantly against the renewal of the Anglo-Japanese Alliance. This is because the alliance is harmful to China. Why does Britain support Japan when Japan continues to take invasive actions? All of China is opposed to Japan's conduct. Should the Anglo-Japanese Alliance be renewed, the Chinese people will oppose Britain as

much as they do Japan.

Sun's comment was followed by expressions of opposition from various organizations in China. Most of the British Chambers of Commerce and Industry in various cities in China followed suit in expressing opposition to the renewal of the Anglo-Japanese Alliance. China was already firmly determined to oppose the continuation of the Anglo-Japanese Alliance. The only thing left for China to decide was what diplomatic tactics it could use to persuade the Western powers, including Britain and the United States, during the conference.

Balfour's Draft Proposal

At this point, the British government found itself in a quandary, since a majority of the British government supported continuing the Anglo-Japanese Alliance. This included such individuals and departments responsible for foreign policy as Foreign Secretary George Curzon, Secretary of State for the Colonies Winston Churchill, Lord President of the Privy Council Arthur Balfour, Lord Keeper of the Great Seal of England Joseph Chamberlain, the secretaries of war and navy, and the British General Staff.

There has been considerable conjecture regarding Britain's true intention vis-à-vis the Washington Conference. Some, for instance, have argued that Britain's wish to consult more closely with the United States instead of with its alliance partner Japan and its invitation to China, which adamantly opposed the renewal of the Anglo-Japanese Alliance, were evidence enough to conclude that Britain had determined to terminate the alliance from the start. Britain, however, was a democratic country just like the United States today, where nothing was decided by a single person behind the scenes. As a matter of fact, everyone who was directly engaged in diplomacy and defense preferred to continue the alliance. The question, therefore, was how to incorporate the American and Canadian wishes into Britain's policy. Nobody knew beforehand where this compromise would take Britain. And that was British-style realistic diplomacy.

That being the case, the only clue to Britain's true intention was not conjecture based upon what someone might have said but the propositions that Britain officially submitted. One such proposition was Balfour's draft proposal, which had been handed to the Japanese and US sides immediately before the Washington Conference. Aiming to protect the Japanese, British, and US territorial rights in the Pacific region, the British government proposed first that the three countries consult among themselves sufficiently and without reserve on how to protect their territorial rights should they be threatened by a third country and second that, should the territorial rights of two of the trio be threatened by the third member of the trio, the two threatened countries are free to form a military alliance, provided that it be a strictly defensive alliance and that its formation be conveyed to the threatening third country. This was a proposal for a Japan-UK-US triumvirate on Pacific affairs. What Britain wanted was the conclusion and control of a kind of re-insurance treaty with the United States, which Britain should never antagonize, and Japan, an Asian power and Britain's long-time ally. The prototype Re-insurance Treaty, of course, was the attempt by German Chancellor Bismarck to maintain peace in central Europe by forming alliances with both Russia and Austria. Considering that it would have been difficult for the United States to go into a military alliance due to its national principle as well as its domestic politics, it would be only Japan and Britain that could form a military alliance should the necessity arise. This proposal for a re-insurance treaty was, de facto, Britain's attempt to explore the possibility of prolonging the Anglo-Japanese Alliance. Although its scope was limited to the protection of territorial rights, it was nevertheless a proposal for an alliance and, as such, was a proposal for maintaining the friendship and mutual trust between Japan and Britain.

Start of Shidehara Diplomacy

Britain's need to somehow coordinate its relations with Japan and those with the United States coincided with the US need to launch an arms control conference. This enabled the convening of a nine-country conference in Washington, DC, with Japan, Britain, the United States, France, and Italy—five countries subject to naval reductions—Belgium, the Netherlands, and Portugal—three countries that had strong interests in Asia—and China taking part. The Japanese ambassador to the United States, Shidehara Kijūrō, was appointed one of the plenipotentiaries for the Japanese delegation to this Washington Conference. Because this was the start of the decade of what was called Shidehara Diplomacy, it is worth revisiting the process, based mainly on Shidehara's memoir, that culminated in the Washington Conference. Shidehara's summary of the British Empire Conference was concise and to the point:

> Believing that Japan would never betray alliance partners as long as the Anglo-Japanese Alliance is maintained, Australia recognized the continuation of the alliance as a means to guarantee its peace and security. Canada, on the other hand, insisted that relations with the United States could not be managed smoothly if the alliance between Britain and Japan remained in force. This was particularly so in that the United States would have to bear in mind the combined forces of Britain and Japan, making it difficult for the United States to boldly reduce its force levels, which in turn would make it impossible for Britain to accomplish its goal of scaling back the world powers' military force levels. Thus Canada opposed the continuation of the Anglo-Japanese Alliance.

The British government submitted the draft treaty to the Japanese government prior to the Washington Conference. According to Shidehara:

> In a nutshell, the British draft treaty concerned the Japan-UK-US military alliance. The domestic situation in the United States is very different from what it was at the time of the Washington Conference, but it has long been the national principle of the United States since the nation's founding by George Washington to avoid any entangling alliances that could put it in a difficult position vis-à-vis other countries. That was why US Secretary of State Charles Hughes filed the British draft treaty away and completely ignored it.
>
> Among the general directives we were given was an instruction on the Anglo-Japanese Alliance. When problems arose in the Anglo-Japanese Alliance and amendments or revisions were proposed by the British side, we were instructed to accept them. If the British side proposed terminating the treaty, that would be fine, too. We were directed to determine our response in light of the Western reactions.
>
> After pondering this issue on my sick bed [Shidehara was suf-

fering from gallstones], I decided to propose something like a four-country consultative pact as a counter-proposal to Britain's draft treaty on the Japan-UK-US military alliance. Under my proposal, the three countries plus France could come together and consult when a serious problem arose. Since it was a consultative mechanism and not an alliance that would bind the participating countries, I thought even the United States would find it agreeable.

After the draft was completed, I had Deputy Chief of Mission Saburi Sadao take it to Balfour. A very open-hearted Balfour immediately agreed that mine was a better idea, making one or two edits to my poor English with his fountain pen. He told Saburi, "Because this is far better than my proposal, let me withdraw mine. Please hand this to Secretary Hughes as Shidehara's proposal approved by Balfour." Because it was almost time for Saburi to visit Hughes, he took my proposal with Balfour's handwritten corrections to Hughes.

Receiving this Shidehara draft, Hughes organized a four-country conference inviting the French government. On the reason for the inclusion of France, Shidehara writes:

Since the recent visit to the United States by Ferdinand Foch, supreme commander of the Allied armies, and his enthusiastic reception, France has become increasingly popular among the American people. Since it remained questionable whether the US Senate would ratify the entente among Japan, Britain, and the United States alone, Secretary Hughes suggested it be made a four-country treaty, adding the participation of the popular France.

Hidden Danger in Trust and Self-Confidence

I have recounted the above episode at length because it brings many thoughts to mind. First, it shows how greatly Shidehara was trusted by the Japanese government, and at the same time, how confident Shidehara was about his home government's trust. Even though he was a plenipotentiary delegate, he was, after all, a mere ambassador and was not even a cabinet member. Yet he drafted a proposal that could determine the nation's fate on his own, without consulting the home government, and submitted it to the British and American governments.

One can also discern how deeply Shidehara was trusted by elder statesmen, including Yamagata, and cabinet leaders. According to *Hara Takashi nikki* (Diary of Hara Takashi), there was a consensus among these men that diplomacy should be left to Shidehara. However, I must point out that there was a hidden danger in this trust and self-confidence. In retrospect, it must be said that Shidehara's conduct was imprudent. Even allowing for some inaccuracy in Shidehara's memoir, which was written on the basis of his memories of events that had taken place some thirty years earlier, his interpretation of the Japanese government's directive to its delegation at the Washington Conference was not exactly accurate. The third of the general policies instructed the Japanese delegates to make the utmost effort to create a suitable environment for the Japan-Britain-US triple entente with the chief mission of consolidating perpetual peace in the Pacific and the Far East. The Japanese delegation succeeded in accomplishing the spirit of this directive. The fourth directive, however, read:

> When the issue of the continuation of the Anglo-Japanese Alliance is discussed in conjunction with the Japan-Britain-United States entente, the Japanese government has no opposition to its continuation. . . . If all the other participating countries in the conference argue for scrapping the alliance as a premise for the arms reduction conference, delegates are allowed to declare that clauses in the Anglo-Japanese Alliance that could be obstructive to the Japan-Britain-United States entente shall not be applied to the member countries.

In other words, the true intention of the Japanese government was, as Australian Prime Minister William Hughes rightly pointed out, to maintain the Anglo-Japanese Alliance by explicitly announcing that its stipulations would not apply to the United States.

Considering that the directive used the softer expression "[having] no opposition to its continuation" instead of "steadfastly maintain the Anglo-Japanese Alliance," however, the Japanese government's wish to maintain the alliance might not have been that strong. Also, seeing as Shidehara was not reprimanded after the Washington Conference for his conduct, it might be said that he understood the spirit of this directive accurately. Nevertheless, the directive did not say, "If the British side proposes terminating the treaty, that too is acceptable," as suggested in Shidehara's memoir. As history subsequently proved, the proposal for a four-country alliance was tantamount to proposing the abrogation of the Anglo-Japanese Alliance, which was, to say the least, a grave decision on the part of the Japanese government. What Shidehara did, therefore, was to discard the twenty-year legacy of the Anglo-Japanese Alliance on his own without due consultation with the home government or even notifying it of the significance of the consequences. Moreover, Shidehara's motivation was based on a technical reason—that Balfour's draft proposal might not be acceptable to the United States.

While Shidehara described Balfour's proposal as a "military alliance" that would be unacceptable to the United States, the proposal was actually for what Shidehara would call a "consultative pact" and left room for the continuation of the Anglo-Japanese Alliance. The proposal was, indeed, a laborious work by Balfour, who had no wish to damage the twenty years of mutual trust between Britain and Japan. It would have been at least worth trying and seeing if the United States would accept this proposal. There was no need for Shidehara to tamper with Balfour's masterpiece. All he had to do was to agree with the proposal and encourage Britain to persuade the US government to accept it as a joint Britain-Japan proposal. Even if Britain succeeded in persuading the US government, it was still possible the US Senate might not ratify the proposal, in which case the proposed alliance could have been launched with Japan and Britain alone, leaving US participation an open option. In any event, all that Britain and Japan had to do vis-à-vis the United States was to explicitly state that the United States would be exempted from the application of clauses in the Anglo-Japanese Alliance.

When the United States refused the proposal, Britain had to decide what to do next. As a country of gentlemen, it would be difficult for Britain to raise the issue of abandoning a twenty-year-old alliance. In his memoir, *Broken Thread: An Autobiography*, Major General Francis Piggott, a pro-Japanese former military attaché at the British Embassy in Tokyo, wrote that Balfour once said he felt as if he were killing his own child, obviously referring to the Anglo-Japanese Alliance. When Balfour asked his opinion, Piggott first said he should refrain from criticizing the British approach to political and economic issues vis-à-vis Japan because such things were entrusted to people with far better judgment than himself. Admitting, however, that he could at least dwell on the Japanese psychological reactions, Piggott said,

> Japan regards the Alliance as the cornerstone of her foreign policy and a permanent marriage bond, and its dissolution so soon after the war—divorce, in fact, with no unfaithfulness to justify it—might give mortal offense, More than that such action would be interpreted as ingratitude, which is a crime that ranks high in their calendar.

When German Emperor Wilhelm II announced in 1890 the discontinuation of the Re-insurance Treaty, which later historians called one of Chancellor Otto von Bismarck's masterpieces, Tsar Alexander III of Russia said he was satisfied that at least it was not Russia that had severed the alliance. It was while Britain was racking its brains over what to do that Shidehara offered his counter-proposal, which Britain gladly took on. Balfour's mind-set was, therefore, far from the "very open-hearted Balfour" Shidehara had described. As a matter of fact, instructions from the home government said, "If the British government proposes that the Anglo-Japanese Alliance be replaced by some other agreement, you are allowed to agree." Since Shidehara himself proposed the de facto abolishment of the alliance without a British proposal, strictly speaking, he was in violation of his instructions.

I personally think it would have been best for Japan to ride on the British proposal, letting Britain persuade the United States. Even if the end result would have been the same, it could at least have made Britain responsible for the judgment. Shidehara was confident that he excelled in the Japanese government in terms of his English proficiency and diplomatic ability, and he had the full trust of Japanese government leaders who believed it best to leave foreign policy to Shidehara. Given this situation, the suspicion that Shidehara might have been over-confident of his diplomatic skill seems well grounded.

Shidehara's Wilsonian Convictions

It should be noted here, however, that Shidehara's conduct was based not on petty bureaucratic wisdom but on his conviction and philosophy. Japan was then at the crossroads of major policy options—the crossroads of "old diplomacy" and "new diplomacy," —the crossroads of power politics/ realpolitik and Wilsonianism. By country, it was the pro-British policy vs. the pro-American policy. The difference between the two schools was, according to Asada Sadao's *Ryō-Taisen-kan no Nichibei kankei* (US-Japan relations between the two World Wars), the difference between collaboration with the United States as advocated by Hara Takashi and cooperation with Britain as promoted by Foreign Minister Uchida Kōsai. Immediately after World War I, Hara predicted that the equilibrium among world powers would be disrupted by the war and he was convinced that Japan-US cooperation would be essential for the settlement of the China issue. He did not think even the Anglo-Japanese Alliance would suffice and insisted the top priority should be on improving relations with the United States "even if it calls for some sacrifices." Even today, his prediction of the international situation and the measures he proposed would be praised for their big-picture accuracy. Hara was consistently convinced that cooperation with the United States was "the great principle and framework for Imperial Japan's diplomacy." By contrast, Foreign Minister Uchida claimed that it would be a matter of course for relations with Japan's British ally to take precedence over those with the United States. Maintaining the Anglo-Japanese Alliance despite the deep loathing China had for it meant protecting the two countries' respective imperialist interests by cooperating with one another. The "some sacrifices" that Hara referred to is interpreted to include Japanese interests in China that might have to be relinquished in order to promote cooperation with the United States.

Shidehara, Hara's closest confidant, made the following remark immediately prior to the closure of the Washington Conference:

Japan has made the maximum possible concessions to China without compromising reason, justice, or honor. Japan does not resent this. On the contrary, Japan is pleased to think that these sacrifices will not be wasted in terms of promoting the grand cause of international friendship and goodwill.

In the conference itself, Shidehara made three concessions. First was to offer priority rights for loans in Manchuria and Mongolia to the joint operations of the newly formed four-country consortium. Second was to give up the priority rights of the Japanese advisors in South Manchuria. And third was to officially withdraw the Group 5 demands that had been reserved for the future. As for Japan's special interests in Manchuria and Mongolia, Foreign Minister Uchida wanted the expression used in the Lansing-Ishii Agreement which had acknowledged Japan's special interests explicitly retained. This was different from Shidehara's position. But Shidehara stressed that the substance of the agreement was retained and succeeded in persuading the foreign ministry to de facto cancel the agreement, saying, "Japan is not driven by any intention to secure preferential or exclusive rights in China. Why should Japan need such rights? Japan's traders and businessmen are geographically advantaged and they are quite knowledgeable about the practical realities in China." Japan did not need any special rights in China, Shidehara argued, because it could win a free and fair competition. Seeing how deep Shidehara's conviction was, it seems quite possible that his discarding the Anglo-Japanese Alliance to promote the four-country treaty was not a simple consequence of over-confidence in his diplomatic skills. He might well have been convinced that it was time for Japan to change course. Judging from how consistent his subsequent conduct was, it seems quite plausible that Shidehara really was driven by conviction.

Is the New Diplomacy Effective for International Peace?

Yet even if Shidehara was driven by personal conviction, the question remains: Was Shidehara's foreign policy the appropriate national strategy for Japan? This question is twofold. One part asks whether what was called "the new diplomacy" was really effective in promoting world peace and Japan's security. The other part asks if it was practical for Japan to pursue this new diplomacy, given the domestic situation at that time, without the Anglo-Japanese Alliance. Unfortunately, history has already given its answer to the second question.

Certainly, Shidehara worked hard to deploy the new diplomacy, and certainly he achieved some success. However, the new diplomacy lasted for only ten years, until the Manchurian Incident. Whether the failure of this new diplomacy was truly inevitable or not calls for a deeper look at history. The Manchurian Incident itself would not have occurred in the first place had it not been for the rise of Chinese nationalism in the form of campaigns to disparage and belittle Japan. Even if the rise of Chinese nationalism had been inevitable, there are several historical "what ifs" that could have made the situation quite different, including "What if there had been no Great Depression?" and "What if Hara Takashi had not been assassinated?" Nevertheless, it is a historical fact that the domestic foundations for the new diplomacy were not strong enough to withstand the pressure stemming from the series of difficulties that arose. Even when Japan faced difficulties, it might have been able to handle them successfully if Britain had been there to help it maintain cooperative relations with the United States. Internationally isolated, however, Japan was at the mercy of its domestic forces. In other words, from the viewpoint of domestic politics, it would have been easier to maintain Shidehara's cooperative foreign policy if the Anglo-Japanese Alliance had been upheld. Frederick Moore, who was a consultant to the Japanese Embassy in Washington, DC, for fourteen years believed that, "if the Anglo-Japanese Alliance had been maintained, civil officials and the Imperial Navy could have been able to suppress the Imperial Army," and therefore lamented, "it was an error on the part of American foreign policy to have forced Britain to abolish the alliance." Moore's observation that the alliance with Britain could affect Japan's domestic politics is on the mark.

This brings us to the fundamental question of whether Japan was right to put its trust in the new diplomacy as something that could make the country more secure. It should be pointed out here that the flip side of international cooperation under the Nine-Power Treaty was Japan's international isolation, a paradox that derived from the essence of the Wilsonianism of the United States. Since no one excels Henry Kissinger in the analysis and assessment of Wilsonianism, I will discuss this along the lines of the description in his *Diplomacy*, quoting that book as appropriate. The most orthodox means to maintain peace in the old world was to maintain the balance of power by forming alliances among nations. But, according to Kissinger, "America disdained the concept of the balance of power and considered the practice of Realpolitik immoral. America's criteria for international order were democracy, collective security, and self-determination. . . ."

Alliances and Collective Security

The term "collective security" has evolved since its inception. It began as an anti-alliance concept, but it has developed into a concept supporting international treaties and alliances. This is shown in the sophistry on the North Atlantic Treaty Organization (NATO) that the US administration used in 1949 to get the Senate to ratify the treaty. Even though NATO, the first alliance treaty that the United States concluded in peacetime, was clearly an alliance to counter the Soviet Union, the US government tried to justify it by stressing, "This is a new, collective security system and, unlike conventional alliances, it is not directed at any specific country." Because it is not diplomatic to have a hypothetical enemy even in an ordinary alliance, the inclusion of the standard "this is not directed at any specific country" made the statement all the more confusing. But again according to Kissinger, the concepts of "collective security" and "an alliance" were originally diametrically opposed. "Alliances always presume a specific potential adversary; collective security defends international law in the abstract, which it seeks to sustain in much the same way that a judicial system upholds a domestic criminal code." And this type of system "contributes to security if all nations . . . share nearly identical views about the nature of the challenge, . . . regardless of the specific national interest they may have in the issue at hand"—a situation that is not realistically feasible.

Citing the Manchurian Incident, Italy's invasion of Ethiopia, Germany's control of Austria and Czechoslovakia, the Soviet invasions of Finland under the League of Nations, and the Soviet invasion of Hungary, Czechoslovakia, and Afghanistan under the United Nations. Kissinger claims, "Experience has shown these assumptions to be false," He goes on to point out, "In the Gulf War, collective security was invoked as a justification of American leadership, not as a substitute for it." Simply put, an alliance maintains peace by, according to Kissinger, creating a balance of power between antagonistic groups. In contrast, under collective security, rules are instituted for both friends and foes, and compliance by all the parties concerned ensures peace. But there is no guarantee of peace if and when a party breaks ranks.

Japan was provided with the Japan-Britain-France-US four-country treaty and the nine-power treaty on China in place of the Anglo-Japanese

Alliance that had fully protected Japan as a maritime nation. But these two new treaties provided Japan no security at all. When a country decides to defend itself isolated without any alliances, it takes an extraordinary level of security for the country to feel secure. The traditional Russian policy of keeping the border as far away as possible is a typical manifestation of this psychology. "Japan's lifeline" also went farther away from Japan—from the Korean Peninsula to Manchuria. Similar developments were also seen in Europe. Although France wanted an alliance with the US and, particularly, with Britain to prepare in case Germany sought to regain the status it had lost in World War I, what it got instead was a five-country Britain-France-Germany-Italy-Belgium treaty including various security arrangements with the East European countries. In actuality, this was the European version of the four-country treaty and the Nine-Power Treaty in the Far East. This five-country treaty was called the Locarno Treaties. As history shows, the Locarno Treaties proved useless for the security of the countries concerned.

Prior to this period, the Western powers had maintained their security with balances of power through alliances. This security was lost when the United States pointed out how antiquated their approach to security was, at which point all of the Western powers were deprived of alliances and became isolated. This was how the world looked between the two world wars. It was only the United States, which claimed north, south, and central America as its own through the Monroe Doctrine, and Britain, the ruler of the British Empire, that could enjoy a level of security no other country could emulate.

What If the Anglo-Japanese Alliance Had Been Maintained?

What would have happened if British-Japanese cooperative relations had been preserved based on Balfour's draft proposal? Seeing as both Japan and Britain shared a common interest in the maintenance of their respective interests in China, they would probably have tried to protect their respective interests as imperialist nations. Simply put, the error of Shidehara diplomacy was, at its core, Shidehara's attempt to apply a patina of American idealism to essentially imperialist Japanese diplomacy. Japanese diplomacy at that time was more in tune with British diplomacy. As discussed in more detail in later chapters, when the British government requested Japan's military cooperation to protect Japanese, British, and American residents endangered by the Nanjing Incident of 1927, Shidehara's cooperative diplomacy took the position of adamantly opposing military intervention. Major General Piggott lamented that this deprived Japan of the opportunity to regain its position as an ally of Britain. It was reported that the Japanese military attaché in London was crying when he visited the British War Office to inform them that Japan would not dispatch even a single soldier.

Had Balfour's draft proposal survived, the Anglo-Japanese Alliance would have been resurrected de facto in 1927. This would have presented China with a more challenging situation. And because of the moral obligation imposed by the Anglo-Japanese Alliance, Japan would not have been able to assist India's independence movement, either. All in all, it is quite possible that the liberation of Asia would have been delayed. On the other hand, when Japan's imperialist advance became excessive, Britain would have reined in further Japanese conduct for fear of confrontation with the United States, which would have significantly affected the balance between the hard-liners and the moderates in Japan. It might have been able to prevent the Manchurian Incident altogether or, even if the incident had taken place, it could have been settled along the lines proposed by the Lytton Report.

It remains unknown whether the British Empire had made it easier for Japan to enter its market, given the Great Depression that had erupted earlier. In any event, however, the alliance would have been able to keep the domestic Japanese situation resulting from the depression from impacting Japanese foreign policy. It also seems to be beyond doubt that Japan would not have entered such an unrealistic and quixotic arrangement as the Tripartite Pact with Nazi Germany and Fascist Italy. What would have happened consequently? While international situations change drastically when there is a major war, changes will be more gradual in war's absence, at least in the Far East. Nevertheless, the trend to decolonization and anti-imperialism would have arrived, even if it might have been delayed by half a century. Japan's privileged position in China would have been lost, and there is a good possibility that the Korean Peninsula would have obtained independence either through guerilla warfare like that in Algeria, with China as the hinterland, or by some peaceful method that was more in tune with the times around the liberation of the Portuguese colonies in the mid-1970s. Considering that former members of the Soviet Union obtained their independence only in 1991 and, for that matter, China still retains the territory of the Qing Empire, however, Japan might have retained its colony on the Korean Peninsula a little longer than Portugal did its colonies. In any event, the leases on Lüshun and Dalian would have expired sooner or later and these territories would have been returned to China around 1997 when Britain returned Hong Kong.

In the end, the resulting situations would have been more or less the same. Meanwhile, the liberation of the Asian peoples and the resolution of China's semi-colonial status would have been delayed, forcing zealous nationalists there to endure another half century of setback and humiliation. On the other hand, East Asian peoples might have been spared the miseries and enormous human sacrifices of World War II. For Asia simply to have maintained peace throughout the twentieth century, the "century of war," would have been a great accomplishment. Since ancient times, there has been nothing else that causes as much pain and anguish as war. As demonstrated by the process by which sovereignty over Hong Kong was reverted, British realistic diplomacy has proved capable of maintaining peace. Given the course of events that did take place, it is perhaps meaningless to discuss which course would have been better for Japan and the world. Nevertheless, the debate will continue over whether Wilsonian idealism or traditional realism is the better approach to maintaining world peace in the years ahead.

CHAPTER

9

Peace and the Military

*—The Insight and Skillful Diplomacy
that Made the Washington Conference a Success—*

What Made Arms Reduction Possible?

Shidehara Kijūrō took a two-year sick leave after the Washington Conference, returning to the government in 1924 as foreign minister. The subsequent eight years until the Manchurian Incident in 1931 are referred to as the era of Shidehara Diplomacy. If Shidehara's cooperative diplomacy can be characterized as the light of the era, the Japanese military was the dark. While the fifty years after World War II undoubtedly mark a time in Japan's modern history when the authority of the military was enervated, it was earlier equally weak in the ten years after Hara Takashi formed his first cabinet in 1918. This period coincided with the era of arms reductions resulting from the Washington Naval Treaty. The Washington Conference was such a complete success and an epic development for world arms reduction that neither the leftist historical view of post–World War II Japan nor the militarist historical view before and during World War II dares dispute what was accomplished at the conference.

Simply put, the signatories to the treaty agreed to the 5:5:3 ratio for the number of capital ships Britain, the United States, and Japan would hold. They also agreed to maintain the status quo with regard to fortifications and naval bases in their Pacific island territories. The treaty imposed a ten-year moratorium on competition in naval construction among the major naval powers. As far as Japan was concerned, the treaty enabled it to cut its naval budget, which had shot up to 500 million yen, or one-third of the total government budget, in 1921 to 280 million yen in 1923 and 230 million yen in 1925. Thus the treaty greatly contributed to reducing Japan's financial burden.

Behind the success of the Washington Conference was the fact that the financial situations in all of the participating countries were similar. Since the introduction of the HMS *Dreadnought*, every naval power had been forced to procure expensive state-of-the-art dreadnought-class and later super-dreadnought-class vessels, putting tremendous pressure on government finances. All the participants in the naval construction race secretly hoped that their competitors would stop building any more ships so that they themselves could ease back. A somewhat similar situation emerged toward the end of the 1980s during the arms control negotiations between the United States and the Soviet Union. Since the humiliation it had suffered at the United States's hands in the Cuban Missile Crisis of 1962, the Soviet Union had steadily built up its military for nearly twenty years. Its military preparations had caught up with and even surpassed those of the United States by the early 1980s. Threatened by Soviet military expansion, the United States started its own military buildup in cooperation with its allies at the time of the Soviet invasion of Afghanistan in late 1979. It was around this time that the United States mobilized Japan's financial resources, which had until then been kept, so to speak, in strategic reserve. This led to the so-called Reagan-Nakasone era in US-Japan relations. When the United States launched the Strategic Defense Initiative (SDI or the "star wars" initiative), the Soviet Union could no longer compete with it financially or technologically. At this point, the Soviet Union had no choice but to ask the United States not to pursue its space defense program.

In terms of the military budget burden, the United States was also very close to its limit at the time. It was in 1987 that Paul Kennedy wrote *The Rise and Fall of the Great Powers* to warn the United States that it would eventually fall, just as other empires had fallen, unless it got its bloated military budget under control. As is the case with all competitions, however, no matter how hard the race, the point is to ensure it is even harder for your opponent. As a matter of fact, the Soviet economy was already de facto defunct. When Mikhail Gorbachev was appointed General

Secretary of the Communist Party of the Soviet Union in 1985, he initiated *perestroika* in an attempt to completely reorganize Soviet politics and the economy. In a few years, this policy led to the demise of the Soviet empire.

Another similarity between Japan in the post–Washington Conference period and the Soviet Union during the Cold War could be the ill-timed end of the economic boom. When the Soviet Union was competing with the United States, a race it had no hope of winning in the first place, it unexpectedly benefitted from two oil crises in the 1970s that brought windfall earnings to the Soviet Union, at that time the world's largest oil producer. Although this revenue gave the Soviet Union substantial financial leeway in its competition with the United States, that leeway ended abruptly in 1986 when oil prices collapsed. In the case of Japan too, it appeared for a time that the increased tax revenue from the World War I–driven economic boom could finance the grand naval construction program. Military spending had been increasing remarkably starting in 1917, and by 1920, when the postwar depression set in, it accounted for nearly 50 percent of the Japanese government's general expenditures. With the depression, it became impossible to sustain the naval construction program, let alone accomplish the whole range of ambitious goals. In retrospect, had Japan been forced to stay in the naval construction race with the United States without benefit of the Washington Naval Treaty, it might have met the same fate as the Soviet Union in the 1980s around the time of the Great Depression or even earlier—certainly long before its defeat in World War II. Japan was no match for the United States from the start. Ironically, it may have been the Washington Naval Treaty that allowed Japan to retain a naval capability somehow competitive with the United States, and this could have been a contributing factor behind World War II. For men and states alike, good can come out of a misfortune, and vice versa.

Katō Tomosaburō, Shidehara's Good Partner

The Washington Conference owed its success to the United States, which exercised leadership throughout the conference by proposing significant reductions in its own naval armament. But it would have been difficult to accomplish what it did if it had not been for Japan's cooperation, which was made possible by the wisdom of Navy Minister Katō Tomosaburō and Shidehara Kijūrō, and the mutual trust between them. Katō succeeded Yamamoto Gonbei, who had ruled the Japanese navy during and after the Russo-Japanese War. After serving five consecutive cabinets as navy minister, starting with the Ōkuma Shigenobu cabinet of 1916, Katō eventually became prime minister himself. He remained a central figure in the Imperial Navy until his death in 1923. Never abusive or pretentious, he was a man of few words

Katō Tomosaburō (photo courtesy of Kyodo News)

whose judgment was always moderate and correct. Detesting flowery language, he always deleted unnecessary ornamentation and self-serving expressions from the draft speeches and remarks his secretaries prepared. He was the embodiment of the silent navy man who did not believe in verbal arguments. Katō was always unpretentious, never posing as a hero or a patriot. Had he survived ten years more, the controversy over whether the government was or was not encroaching on the emperor's sovereign right to command the military would not have been an issue at the time of the London Naval Conference in 1930.

During the First Sino-Japanese War, Katō served as the chief gunner aboard the state-of-the-art cruiser *Yoshino*. He fired the first salvo at Qing's *Tsiyuen*, which marked the beginning of the war. Although Japan's official military history claims it was the Qing side that fired first, I have proven in my *Mutsu Munemitsu and His Time* that it was unthinkable, given the strategies of the two sides, that the Qing would initiate hostilities. It seems beyond doubt that Captain Kawahara Yōichi of the *Yoshino* and its chief gunner Katō thoroughly understood the strategic intention of Foreign Minister Mutsu and Navy Minister Saigō Tsugumichi and fired first. Alarmed by the seriousness of the "fire" command he received from Katō, the gunner immediately sent a sailor to Katō for confirmation. To this, Katō replied, "Fool! Would I lie at such a critical moment? Hurry up!" This statement very well summarized Katō's style—sharp and to the point. At the time of the Battle of Tsushima during the Russo-Japanese

War, it was Commander-in-Chief of the Combined Fleet Tōgō Heihachirō and his chief of staff Katō who decided on operations. Before the start of the battle, Katō, recalling how Admiral Horatio Nelson was killed during the Battle of Trafalgar, asked his commander-in-chief to retreat to the enclosed bridge of the battleship *Mikasa* for safety. Tōgō would not heed Katō's advice, saying, "I do not need any protection. I am an old man. Younger people should retreat instead so that they can serve the country in the future." Thus Katō divided staff officers into several groups but remained on the bridge with Tōgō throughout the battle.

The below brief review of the Washington Conference, where Navy Minister Katō and Ambassador Shidehara acted as plenipotentiaries is basically in line with Shidehara's memoir. Shidehara writes:

> It appears that Minister Katō had already decided to accept the 5:5:3 formula from the beginning, even though he never told anyone. Thus I thought we could reach an agreement during the conference. Minister Katō was more concerned about the maintenance of the status quo in the military facilities in the Pacific than the number of naval ships.

If the United States constructed an impregnable fortress on Guam, for example, it would be impossible for Japan to fight a war with the United States even if it were allowed to maintain a force of up to 70 percent of the strength of the US naval force. Shidehara thus thought, "Minister Katō must have judged that a war is possible even with the 5:5:3 formula as long as the status quo in the military facilities in the Pacific is maintained." The negotiations ran into such difficulties that, at one point, Katō was mentally steeling himself for the conference to break up. Shidehara stepped in and demonstrated his diplomatic skills. Admitting he was a complete layman in military affairs, Shidehara showed Katō a draft proposal for how to conclude the negotiations. While Katō said, "We can live with this proposal, but I do not think it will be acceptable to the United States," Shidehara nevertheless encouraged Katō to give the proposal a chance on the assumption that it could not do any harm to try. When Katō handed the proposal to US Secretary of State Charles Hughes, Hughes looked it over, put it in his pocket, and said, "Let me think about it." While Katō was disappointed by Hughes' cold reception, Shidehara said, "Hughes is a smart man and he would immediately challenge something he did not like. His silence is a good sign." Although Katō teased Shidehara, saying, "You are soft-hearted and swell-headed. That's your problem," Hughes did shortly contact Katō for an appointment. When the two met, Hughes told Katō that he had no objections to the Japanese draft proposal. Unconvinced, Katō asked Shidehara to confirm the State Department's position, to which Shidehara replied, "It was the US Secretary of State himself who agreed with your proposal. How can I go to the State Department for confirmation?" The draft treaty was thus accepted.

Shidehara's ability as a diplomat was impeccable. Working at the same level as first-class Anglo-Saxon diplomats, he could understand them perfectly and talk with them persuasively. He was a rare breed among post-Restoration Japanese. Although Shidehara's diplomacy based on cooperation with Britain and the United States was later overwhelmed by domestic political events and the military, his abilities were fully utilized during the decade following the Washington Conference. In this, he was aided by his good partner, Navy Minister Katō. A time when competent officials with abundant common sense were able to serve the country well, this could very well be Japan's "good old days."

Yamagata Aritomo's Death

The Washington Conference also provided Hara Takashi an opportunity to restrain the military. Prime Minister Hara proposed that he serve as acting navy minister while Katō was away in Washington, DC. Although Katō himself had already agreed with this arrangement when he was appointed plenipotentiary, the Imperial Army adamantly opposed it. This had been anticipated. Even though it was a temporary measure, the Imperial Army objected on the grounds that it would set precedence for a civilian war/navy minister. Needless to say, Yamagata Aritomo fiercely opposed the proposal, as did War Minister Yamanashi Hanzō. But Hara would not give in. Having obtained Imperial Navy agreement, he decided to test his prerogative as a prime minister whose party held an absolute majority in the House of Representatives. At the same time, though, Hara approached Yamagata behind the scenes through Tanaka Giichi in an attempt to win him over. Subsequently, Hara succeeded in persuading War Minister Yamanashi to drop his objection on the condition that the Imperial Army would not be asked to accept appointment of a civilian as its acting minister. Because this was a mere tacit understanding, however, Hara had no intention of being constrained by it once Yamagata passed away. Unfortunately, Hara was assassinated three months before Yamagata died of illness, and it was Prime Minister Takahashi Korekiyo who succeeded to the post of acting navy minister until Katō returned from Washington, DC.

The winds of time were blowing strongly against the military. Until Yamagata's death, all of the party politicians refrained from saying or doing anything that would displease him. Prime Minister Hara no exception, he remained highly cautious where Yamagata was concerned. Yamagata passed away on February 1, 1922. Immediately after his death, the entire Imperial Diet erupted with anti-military arguments as if the lid had been taken off a boiling cauldron. The Proposal to Amend the Official Rule on Appointing War/Navy Ministers submitted in the wake of Yamagata's demise used such vehement expressions as "the current rule violates the principle of constitutional government and . . . allows arbitrary conduct by the military. It behooves the government to promote the sound development of constitutional politics by promptly amending the current rule." This proposal was adopted by unanimous decision in the House of Representatives. This was a quick flowering of the seeds Hara had sown before his own demise. Had he survived a little longer, even half a year longer, he would have used his muscle to turn this success into some form of concrete accomplishment. However, Takahashi Korekiyo, who succeeded Hara as prime minister, was not capable of actually appointing civilians to military ministerial posts despite the Diet resolution. And Katō, who succeeded Takahashi, went only as far as to "study its implementation," even though he agreed with its philosophy.

Hara Takashi's Realism

Hara's assassination was a great loss for Taishō Japan. According to the Meiji-Shōwa journalist Maeda Renzan, the Japanese people enthusiastically welcomed the formation of the Hara cabinet. Citizens loved to call Hara a *heimin* (commoner) premier and his cabinet a *heimin* cabinet to the extent that the word *heimin* became a buzzword. People used it extensively as in "a *heimin* restaurant" and "a *heimin* tavern." It was the first full-fledged party cabinet since the formation of the Jiyū-tō party in 1881. It had been twenty-one years since Mutsu Munemitsu died in 1897, regreting his failure to achieve parliamentary politics in his lifetime. His dream was finally realized by Hara, who had inherited Mutsu's hopes. Undeniably, it took too long. Hara was already sixty-three years old when his cabinet took office. The day of his first cabinet meeting, Prime Minister Hara told Maeda, "I am afraid you will all be disappointed with me. Had I formed my cabinet ten years earlier, I would have accomplished a lot. As I grew older, however, things around me became so complicated that I now realize that I cannot do everything I wish." Anyone who hopes for parliamentary democracy in Japan must wish that the Hara cabinet had been formed ten years earlier and that Hara had survived ten years more. Despite his remark to Maeda, Hara turned his energies to the tasks he had set for himself as soon as he became prime minister. First, though, he had to consolidate his power base. He extended suffrage, lowered the minimum tax for a voter from ten yen to three yen, and introduced the single-seat constituency system. Reading the draft proposal for this reform, Inukai Tsuyoshi of the opposition Kokumin-tō party lamented, "If this proposal is passed, we must be prepared to have Hara as our prime minister for at least ten years." As Inukai feared, when the general election was held in 1920, Hara's Seiyūkai succeeded in picking up an additional 115 seats (bringing the total to 278) to hold an absolute majority in the House of Representatives.

Hara also expanded his influence in the House of Peers, which had long been a political stronghold for the Yamagata forces. Among its members was a powerful gathering called a "study group" formed mainly of viscount members. While this group had before opposed party politics, it recognized the changing times and decided to increase its political power by becoming closer to the ruling Seiyūkai. In response, Hara appointed Ōki Enkichi, a leader of the study group, to his cabinet. At this point, the 150-member "study group," the largest faction within the House of Peers, became the de facto government party of the Hara cabinet, followed by the Association of Count Members of the House of Peers, completing Hara's control of the House. For the next three years or so, Hara succeeded in overcoming the resistance of indecisive and bigoted conservatives and in making realistic and sensible decisions on such important matters as higher education and the withdrawal of Japanese troops from Siberia, This pragmatism was the very essence of Hara Takashi.

Some post–World War II critics expressed disappointment with Hara who, they say, was not as progressive as popularly believed. As evidence, these critics cited Hara's slowness to implement universal suffrage as well as his cautious attitude toward the democracy and socialism movements. But it was only natural for Japanese political leaders at the time to be wary of popular movements. Hara's attitude should not be interpreted as mere subservience to Yamagata. Ordinary people in pre–World War II times felt a chill down their spines at the words "the reds." This reaction is considered reactionary and right-wing in some corners of society today influenced by Communist propaganda during the Cold War. Yet now that the Soviet state has collapsed and Russians themselves have stopped denying the appalling tragedies during the Communist dictatorship, this reaction has been proven to be neither unreasonable nor excessive. Democracy needs moderation and compromise in order to be sustained. In this sense, Hara Takashi was a genuine democratic leader who compares well with democratic leaders in the Anglo-Saxon world. Nevertheless, it is questionable whether Hara can be judged solely by what he accomplished as prime minister before he was assassinated. The slightly over three years of the Hara cabinet would have been just the first half, or even less, of the Hara era had his government lasted for the decade Inukai predicted. In these "first years of the Hara era," during which Hara repeatedly demonstrated his realistic judgment and dauntless actions on important issues, Hara's actual concern was to reward his followers. They had long suffered from the decades of *hanbatsu* domination, and consolidating the foundation of party politics was to be Hara's way of rewarding them. Hara's pursuit of this goal led to uninhibited drives to expand his party's influence as well as a shameless quest for concessions. These actions drew scathing criticism from the public, but Hara paid them no heed. Hara once told the journalist Baba Tsunego, "If you continue to hit the nail that sticks out, as you have attacked my cabinet, there will be no outstanding statesman in Japan." And Hara continued to pursue what he believed in.

It would have been well worth watching what Hara would have done to establish parliamentary democracy in Japan after consolidating his base, particularly after the death of Yamagata, had Hara survived even a few more years. It was regrettable that Takahashi Korekiyo, who succeeded Hara, did not have the political clout to cash in on the absolute majority in the Imperial Diet which he inherited and reflect those aims in policy. Because the transformation of the Seiyūkai after Hara's demise was an important turning point for politics in Taishō-Shōwa Japan, I will return to it later.

Imperial Defense Policy

At this point, it is well to look back at the post-Russo-Japanese War trends in the Japanese military. As soon as the Russo-Japanese War was over, the outlook for national defense became a major issue in Japan. It was only natural to debate what to do with the war preparedness machinery, which had grown during the war as Japan had poured every possible resource into it. The natural course of action would have been arms reduction, but the Imperial Army thought differently. Judging from Russia's previous conduct in the Balkans, it was obvious that Russia would not give up its ambitions because of a setback or two. Rather, it was assumed Russia would return, better prepared this time and having learned from its previous attempt. This was by no means an unreasonable or irrational judgment call on Japan's part. This thinking was later endorsed by Joseph Stalin's reference to "retaliation for defeat" when the Soviets violated the neutrality pact and attacked Japanese troops toward the end of World War II. Although Japan won the Russo-Japanese War, it had had to fight the enemy with inferior forces throughout the course of the war, resulting in a legacy of anxiety over the inadequacy of its military. There was also a more bureaucratic problem. Officers and soldiers who survived the fierce battles during the Russo-Japanese War had to be rewarded with promotions. Given that, it was utterly unthinkable Japan would opt for arms reductions and deprive those officers and soldiers of the posts to which they were entitled.

It was against this background that the Imperial Defense Policy was formulated promptly after the Russo-Japanese War. Tanaka Giichi of the Imperial Japanese Army General Staff Office drafted the policy, and Yamagata edited it. Based on the lessons Japan had learned in the Russo-Japanese War, this draft policy argued the need for convergence and coordination between the Imperial Army and Imperial Navy strategies. In addition, Tanaka also argued that strategy should be coordinated with political maneuvers, but, interestingly, Yamagata dropped that particular portion of the policy draft. Here, one can see the genesis of the

later contrast in political philosophy between Tanaka and Yamagata—
while Tanaka came to the forefront of Japanese politics during the Taishō
Democracy years fully utilizing his flexibility of ideas, Yamagata clung
to the autonomy of military command and continued to resist the development of parliamentary politics. In terms of actual forces, the Imperial
Army sought to maintain 25 regular divisions. This means it wanted to
maintain the same level of preparedness in peacetime as it had during the
Battle of Mukden in the Russo-Japanese War: 16 regular divisions and
nine first and second-line reserves. Because there were 17 divisions including the Imperial Guard Division at the time the policy was drafted, the
army planned to add eight more regular divisions. The Imperial Navy was
much more complex. Seeing that the Russian fleet had been annihilated
during the Battle of Tsushima and that Britain—ruler of the seven seas—
was Japan's ally, these two navies posed no threat to Japan's security. But
since it had been the Imperial Navy that had finally decided the outcome of
the Russo-Japanese War by winning a historically unprecedented victory,
the Imperial Navy had tremendous influence and immense public popularity. It was unthinkable that its contribution should go unrewarded.

At the time, it was Yamamoto Gonbei who decided Imperial Navy policy. Although Saigō Tsugumichi had been the navy minister for five and
a half years after the First Sino-Japanese War, he was such a modest and
broad-minded person that he left all naval affairs to Yamamoto. Yamamoto was thus the real power center for the navy in those days. Yamamoto
had succeeded Saigō as navy minister and remained in the post for some
seven years, including during the Russo-Japanese War. After he resigned,
he had his disciple, Saitō Makoto, succeed him and retained his leadership
and influence in the Imperial Navy.

Even before the conclusion of the Anglo-Japanese Alliance, Yamamoto had been determined to learn from Britain, a fellow "island empire."
Yamamoto sent Lieutenant Commander Satō Tetsutarō to Britain for this.
Satō himself had read Alfred Mahan enthusiastically even before he was
sent to Britain; after his study in Britain, he stayed in the United States
for a while to study personally under Mahan. When the Anglo-Japanese
Alliance was signed in 1902, Yamamoto ordered Satō home. Back in
Tokyo, Yamamoto directed Satō to report on his studies in Britain and
the United States in the *Teikoku kokubō-ron* (Study on Imperial defense),
which Yamamoto circulated among the public after submitting it for view-

ing by the emperor. Also influenced by Mahan, Yamamoto was himself convinced that the defense priority should be placed on the navy and not on the army because Japan would be able to maintain its security and prosperity as long as it controlled the seas. When the Imperial Japanese Army General Staff Office proposed an army-navy joint memorandum for resolving Korean affairs on the eve of the Russo-Japanese War, Yamamoto refused the proposal, saying, "Losing Korea is not a problem. It is enough if we can defend the home territory of the Japanese Empire."

It should be recalled that Mahan's theory was originally a general argument that possessing powerful sea power would guarantee a country's security and prosperity rather than a strategy against a specific hypothetical enemy. The motto "He who commands the sea has command of everything" was regarded as an immortal principle when the British Empire was at its peak. Japan fought the Russo-Japanese War with what was called a 6+6 fleet (six old-type battleships and six cruisers). Satō's ambitious proposal called for Japan to possess eight battleships and eight cruisers, all of the dreadnought design introduced after the Russo-Japanese War. While the hypothetical enemy for the Imperial Army was Russia, the Imperial Navy's hypothetical enemy was the United States. The navy's strategy appeared reasonable, given the bilateral friction over the issue of Japanese immigration as well as President Theodore Roosevelt's grand naval construction plan, but the navy's true intention was to achieve Mahan's ideal of becoming a great naval power with no hypothetical enemy. Thus started the great naval construction race between the United States and Japan, driven more by theory and each country's wish to enhance its own prestige than by realistic necessity. Germany's Kaiser Wilhelm II also admired Mahan. Although Mahan himself must have never intended it, his thesis ignited the naval construction race in Europe which became one of the causes of World War I, as well as a similar race between Japan and the United States in the Pacific.

Two Additional Army Divisions vs. the 8 + 8 Fleet

Although Prime Minister Saionji added a note saying that the new policy was contingent upon future national resources, he reported to the emperor that the defense policy drafted by the Imperial Army and Navy was "extremely appropriate." Political historian Tsunota Jun criticizes Saionji's attitude as "a harbinger of national policy as a phatic construct, a trend that critically harmed Taishō and Shōwa Japan." It was certainly a bad practice common to many policy decisions throughout the Taishō and Shōwa eras. Instead of clarifying policy essence and arguing vehemently as Itō Hirobumi, Mutsu Munemitsu, and Komura Jutarō had done, the government leaders in the Taishō and Shōwa eras did not dare resist forceful demands. Instead, they let those voices have their way and simply added some rhetorical disclaimers. The Twenty-One Demands incident with Qing, in which the controversial Group 5 was adopted as a mere "wish," illustrates how harmful this attitude was for Japan. In any event, Japan's long-term goal was set, even though it was unreasonable on the face of it to pursue such a financially taxing defense plan during peacetime. Sadly, this same attitude has persisted to equally pernicious effect in the post–World War II setting as well. Although defense experts pointed out the absurdity of limiting the defense budget to 1 percent of GNP, the proposal was adopted with only a slight change of wording—to "aim to limit the defense budget to within 1 percent of GNP." Once the 1 percent limitation was put into words, however, it became a sacrosanct rule that required strict adherence.

When the Imperial Army demanded an additional four divisions in 1907, the Saionji government provisionally allowed the addition of two divisions, the remaining two divisions to be considered later, the government said, in light of the financial strain. As noted above, this question of two more army divisions haunted all subsequent governments until the Ōkuma Shigenobu cabinet finally granted the Imperial Army's wish. With its naval construction plans having been approved by the Imperial Diet twice, in 1907 and again in 1911, the Imperial Navy had a firm footing for building its 8+8 Fleet. And because public trust was so strong in the wake of the grand victory in the Battle of Tsushima, the Imperial Navy's political position was much better than the Imperial Army's was, the army having no immediate enemy.

Yet just as the Yamamoto Gonbei government submitted a supplemental budget to the Diet in 1913 to further finance the 8+8 Fleet, the Siemens scandal broke, jeopardizing not only the supplemental budget but the Yamamoto government itself. This Siemens scandal involved Vice Admiral Matsumoto Yawara, a future navy minister-hopeful who took a bribe of some hundreds of thousand yen from the shipbuilder as a commission. Although Matsumoto had kept the money in the bank untouched for future use as political funds if and when he became navy minister, it was undeniable that he had committed a crime. Matsumoto publicly apologized for his wrongdoing and pleaded guilty. As a result of this scandal, the trust that the people had had in the Imperial Navy and naval leaders since the Battle of Tsushima was eroded precipitously. Although the 8+8 Fleet plan survived as a long-term goal and was pursued by Yamamoto's successor, Navy Minister Katō Tomosaburō, it was obvious to all concerned that the financial situation once the World War I boom ended precluded the 8+8 navy. This was the situation in Japan when the Washington Conference was convened.

Theoretically Correct Ugaki Proposal

The Washington Naval Treaty was a historical accomplishment. Although arms reduction had been talked about earlier, nobody believed it possible. But the Washington Conference succeeded in getting all the major powers to reduce their naval forces. It was only natural Japan should hope for a similar arrangement for the Imperial Army. After all, Tsarist Russia, the Imperial Army's number-one hypothetical enemy, had fallen and Russia had lost the ability to threaten Japan militarily, sporadic guerilla warfare by partisans in Siberia notwithstanding. Not even the Imperial Army could resist the current of history. Thus when opposition parties proposed reductions to the army's war preparedness budget in the Imperial Diet in the wake of Yamagata's demise, the ruling Seiyūkai was cornered into submitting its own army reduction plan as a counter-proposal. Minister of war in the Katō Tomosaburō cabinet Yamanashi Hanzō had to downsize the Imperial Army twice during his tenure for a total of 60,000 officers and soldiers—the equivalent of five army divisions.

War Minister Ugaki Kazushige in the Katō Takaaki cabinet which was formed in 1924 had an even greater impact on the army. While War Minister Yamanashi contributed to government finances by cutting the Imperial Army budget by 15 percent, Ugaki made no such budgetary contribution because he used any savings for the army's modernization program. Ugaki's reduction, nevertheless, had more of an impact than previous attempts because he dared to cut four army divisions in one stroke. As far as soldiers and bureaucrats are concerned, the most demoralizing change is a reduction in posts. Outstanding young officers who dreamed of becoming regimental commanders, divisional commanders, or eventually army generals some day, had to retire due to a dearth of posts. The loss of four army divisions meant the loss of sixteen infantry regiments. Each regiment was the pride of the town where it was stationed, and the regimental colors were bestowed personally by the emperor. Commanders of the abolished regiments were seen weeping bitterly as they returned their colors. The deep-seated grudge thus generated against Ugaki is considered a major factor that later blocked his appointment as prime minister, even though, on the eve of World War II, he was considered one of the few who could stop the military from running amok. Yet as policy, Ugaki's force reduction was correct and necessary. Reforming the Imperial Army was an urgent imperative at that time.

World War I provided incentive for the development of various weapons and military technologies, including aircraft, armored tanks, toxic gas, radio transmitters and receivers, and anti-aircraft guns. Armies in Europe and the United States were revolutionized. Japan's army alone was left behind in this. Journalist and military commentator Itō Masanori writes in his *Gunbatsu kōbō-shi* (Rise and fall of military cliques) that, "Without exception, all the Japanese officers I met in Europe in those days lamented that the Imperial Army would degenerate into a third- or fourth-rate army if it were not modernized with the funds that would be freed up by terminating troop dispatches to Siberia." Itō himself lamented the inflexibility of the Imperial Japanese Army General Staff Office, saying,

> The military capability of the twenty-one divisions in the Imperial Army had already declined to a level lower than seven or even five divisions of the leading European armies. However, the plan the Imperial Japanese Army General Staff Office submitted in 1921 embodied a hope to expand the number of divisions to 25 during peacetime and 40 in wartime, revealing its continued preoccupation with the number of divisions instead of qualitative modernization.

In terms of government finances, once the World War I boom ended, a period of administrative and financial reorganization began. On top of that, the government had to deal with the huge financial burden of relief and reconstruction efforts related to the Great Kantō Earthquake of 1923. Given this financial situation, the only way to finance Imperial Army modernization was to dramatically reallocate the army budget. In this sense, Ugaki's troop reductions were a well-grounded measure and their execution demonstrated great leadership.

The Era of Anti-Militarism

The mood and the times were fiercely anti-militarism and enthusiastically pro-democracy. This era is described as similar to the post–World War II era. It is hard to imagine that the period was to be immediately followed by the early-Shōwa ultra-nationalism. Internationally, the anti-militarism argument started during World War I. According to Henry Kissinger, once World War I erupted, the escalation of the scale of war was so rapid that the correlation between diplomacy and military strategy was lost. Although the causes of the war were known to be the power struggle in the Balkans and the naval construction race between Britain and Germany, no one thought to stop the war by eliminating these causes. The sacrifices of war had simply become too great by that time for such remedies to be considered. Thinking their suffering derived from the enemy's essential depravity, says Kissinger, the participants in World War I became convinced that no true peace would ever be achieved until the enemy was completely defeated.

In seeking to mobilize an entire nation to fight a war, it is imperative to make people believe friends are absolutely righteous and foes absolutely evil. Modern war propaganda was born for this purpose. The winning side's propaganda remains as history, while the losers' is destined to be eliminated from history. Japan's propaganda was more effective in Asia during World War II because it included the element of Asia's liberation from Western colonial rule. Having no other negative information, the Allies in their war propaganda had to stress the cruelty of the Japanese forces. The propaganda tended to be filled with such exaggerated adjectives as "horrific" and "hair-raising" because the Allies did not have enough facts to back up their allegations. The history textbook issue and the apology issue that have lingered in Japan more than half a century after the end of the war are after-effects of that wartime propaganda.

During World War I, Britain and the United States labeled the war democracy's fight against militarism. Theoretically, this embodied as much contradiction as the characterization of World War II as democracy's fight against fascism—the contradiction obvious to all when Russia was counted as a democracy in either case. However, the purpose of propaganda is, after all, to win the war, and people could not care less about such trifles. Because Japan joined the British-American side in World War I, it was regarded as on democracy's side, making anti-militarism and pro-democracy the order of the day in Japan. The country entered an era when *minshu-shugi* (democracy) was openly celebrated. This made the time when Yoshino Sakuzō had translated "democracy" as "*min-pon shugi*" in 1916 because he was afraid to use the word "*min-shu shugi*" seem to be in the remote past. Itō Masanori writes, "Those were the days when soldiers and officers were reluctant even to board a train in uniform and preferred to go out in plain clothes if at all possible. Graduates of prestigious women's schools declared they would never marry a military officer." A daily newspaper carried a letter to the editor in August 1922 that reads:

> When a military officer tries to hire a *jinrikisha* at a train station, the rickshaw puller arrogantly scolds the officer, jeering, "You must be joking. Why don't you walk?" While even the most foolhardy gangster would not meddle with a soldier before, today it is the gangsters that pick quarrels with soldiers, abuse them verbally, and even raid barracks. How truly bizarre!

Francis Piggott, former military attaché to the British Embassy in Tokyo, described the tendency among the Japanese people to show strong aversion to anything military during this brief period:

> It was an interesting historical fact that respect for the Imperial Army among the Japanese people deteriorated from 1922 through 1923. Japanese people in those days were apparently ignorant of the meaning of militarism. They seemed to think that anything military, ranging from officers on a train to senior military officers attending a public ceremony, was a manifestation of militarism . . .

It has been pointed out that it was this tendency that gave rise to deep-seated resentment among young officers and that this was one remote cause of the later rise of militarism in Japan. It appears, however, that Japan's anti-militarism did not last very long. To quote Piggott again, "this unpleasant but not dangerous misunderstanding vanished into thin air in a few months." On the Ugaki reduction three years later, Piggott writes,

> It was conducted in a totally different atmosphere. You can imagine how different it was if I say the popularity of the Imperial Army had reached its apex. Therefore, abolishing four army divisions provoked petitions and protests from various corners of the private sector. It was only after the army explained that, even though the number of divisions was reduced, the Imperial Army's combat readiness would be reinforced, not weakened, and the Japanese people could continue to be proud of and trustful of their army that people approved the army reduction.

It should be noted that the Great Kantō Earthquake hit Tokyo and vicinity between the Yamanashi and the Ugaki decisions. The Imperial Army under War Minister Tanaka Giichi dedicated itself to disaster relief operations, regaining the people's trust.

A Starting Point for Modern Japan

All of the above brings back to mind how things were during the Taishō Democracy. Given the long-held resentment of the arrogant military and *hanbatsu* that had obstructed parliamentary democracy in Japan, it is quite understandable that the death of Yamagata triggered an outpouring of resentments during the Taishō Democracy when anti-militarism was the global norm. At the same time, given the fresh memory of the military's dedication during the First Sino-Japanese and Russo-Japanese Wars as well as the trust the military earned with its post-earthquake disaster relief operations, it is also understandable that the Japanese people started questioning whether treating the military so harshly was justified. There was a fundamental freedom in the Japanese people's reactions during the Taishō Democracy. Both the aversion to and sympathy for the military were indigenous and spontaneous sentiments, not something imposed from outside. And because both of these sentiments were expressed free of restrictions, a natural check and balance emerged between them.

In seeking the source of modern Japan's identity, I would say Taishō Democracy is definitely one of modern Japan's starting points. Even now, more than half a century since the end of World War II, the Japanese people are still looking for their own identity and no one in Japan is confident about Japanese society today. This is, perhaps, attributable to the fact that postwar Japanese society was not constructed by the Japanese people themselves. The postwar constitutional regime was formulated by the Allies' early occupation policy with the purpose of depriving Japan of military potential. Although the United States later reversed course to allow and encourage the country's rearmament, stringent provisions that make amending the constitution practically impossible have preserved the constitution until today. In the half century during the Cold War, it was the anti-US-Japan Security Pact—anti-militarist thinking that originated in Moscow and Beijing—that most vocally defended the constitution bequeathed Japan by the Occupation Forces. Frankly speaking, this movement to keep the constitution unchanged has been nothing more than an anti-US-Japan Security Pact, anti-national defense campaign to facilitate direct and/or indirect invasion of Japan by the Communist forces. Since the movement had such political undertones, its logic failed to convince the Japanese people. It has simply corrupted the thinking of the post–World War II Japanese and failed to contribute to the construction of a new identity. In contrast, the political regime during the period of Taishō Democracy was accomplished by the Japanese people by their own hands. Study of the writings of such Meiji greats as Itō Hirobumi, Mutsu Munemitsu, and Itagaki Taisuke reveals how genuine and sincere these Meiji leaders were in seeking to establish their own political system in Japan. It should also be remembered that it was the Japanese people themselves who fought through the bitter battles with *hanbatsu* and military cliques to achieve their ideal political system. This is distinctively different from the post–World War II regime that has hardly any roots in the Japanese intellectual tradition.

The late psychologist Kawai Hayao introduced the term "*jinen*" (自然), meaning the state of a thing that it is destined to be. The concept of "constellation" is also used to stress that that which is indigenously created combining the celestial dispensation and mystery of nature is viable, while that which is artificially and exogenously created is not. Golfers know that once you destroy the existing constellation in an attempt to improve your swing, your score is miserable for quite some time before it gets better. A person's mental state, Kawai's specialty, is so difficult to reorganize it might not be possible in a single lifetime. It seems the same thing can be said about a state and its people. Post–World War II Japan has not yet achieved the constellation or state of *jinen* in which people can feel spiritually comfortable. It was definitely in this state though, during the Taishō Democracy. Those were the days in which, for better or worse, the Japanese people were responsible for their society and the state they built themselves. Those were the days when the Japanese people were confident in themselves and this confidence gave them spiritual stability.

CHAPTER

10

The Blossoming of Shidehara Diplomacy

—A New Departure for Japan's Diplomacy—

Hara and Takahashi Cabinets

It was after Shidehara Kijūrō became foreign minister in the Katō Takaaki cabinet (the Three-faction Pro-Constitution Cabinet) in 1924 that he began to implement his long-cherished aspirations and policies. The eight-year period between the formation of this cabinet and the assassination of Inukai Tsuyoshi in 1932 became the golden age for democracy in Japan. During these eight years, all the prime ministers also headed political parties, and the military complied with the policies of the party governments. In the latter half of this period, two major parties, the Seiyūkai and the Minsei-tō, won enough seats to govern. This was the realization of the British-style parliamentary democracy—and a two-party system—which Itagaki Taisuke and Ōkuma Shigenobu had dreamed of since the Freedom and People's Rights movement in the Meiji period and which Mutsu Munemitsu had secretly cherished as a future goal for Japan. What follows is a brief recounting of the process that culminated in the blossoming of party politics in Japan.

When Hara Takashi was assassinated, both the Seiyūkai and the elder statesmen requested Saionji Kinmochi form a new cabinet. Saionji declined the nomination and suggested Finance Minister Takahashi Korekiyo succeed Hara instead. Upon this recommendation, the Seiyūkai elected Takahashi its president, giving birth to the Takahashi cabinet in 1921. Takahashi was a totally unselfish man with a sophisticated sense of humor. Adored as a doyen in Japan's finance and monetary policies, he was such a first-rate person that no one spoke ill of him even after his assassination during the February 26 Incident of 1936. Takahashi was instrumental in floating a foreign loan at the time of the Russo-Japanese War and served the Japanese government as Governor of the Bank of Japan before he was appointed finance minister in the first Yamamoto Gonbei cabinet (1913–14). Although he had retained his membership in the Seiyūkai since that time, he had no political ambitions. Unlike Hara Takashi, who assiduously memorized the personal histories and factional affiliations of all the party members, Takahashi was decidedly uninterested in such things. In fact, he could hardly identify party members by name or appearance. Although he grudgingly agreed to become prime minister to help the government prepare for the imminent Washington Naval Conference, he steadfastly refused to become Seiyūkai president. In the end, he was persuaded to assume that position on the condition that he would not have to be involved in party affairs. Once he became Seiyūkai president, however, he found himself so bothered by trivial party business day in and day out that, he reminisced, he wished he could find a suitable successor and quit at the earliest opportunity.

In retrospect, Takahashi cannot evade the accusation that he lacked the sense of responsibility needed to be the leader of a major political party and succeed Hara Takashi when Hara was assassinated. Even though it was not Takahashi's intention, it nevertheless remains a historical fact that, with the weakening of the Seiyūkai under Takahashi's leadership (or lack thereof), politics in Japan deviated from ideals and national policies and pursued party interests instead. Each party became obsessed with its political ascendancy, devoting its energies to obstructing the other parties. Takahashi bears no small responsibility for this. Eventually Takahashi realized his responsibility and devoted himself to politics, but it was already too late. To be sure, it would have been no easy task for anyone to succeed Hara Takashi. Using his Diet majority to the fullest, Hara worked shamelessly to make the Seiyūkai even stronger, even to the point of defending protégés who had unsavory reputations. While this drew some criticism, Hara successfully overcame his difficulties by arrogantly cashing in on his party's absolute majority in the House of Representatives and with careful political maneuvering in the House of Peers. Political scientist Oka Yoshitake has commented that any one of the many difficulties Hara faced "would have toppled an ordinary cabinet." After Hara's assassination, the Takahashi cabinet managed to control the House of Representatives with its absolute majority. The cabinet quickly got into trouble in the House of Peers, however. Takahashi attempted to fend off attacks by reshuffling his cabinet. In the reshuffle, he moved to replace Education Minister Nakahashi Tokugorō and Railway Minister Motoda Hajime, two frequent targets of criticism because of scandals. Nakahashi and Motoda, however, refused to resign, igniting an uncontrollable intraparty feud between the pro-reshuffle faction and the anti-reshuffle faction. This eventually led the whole cabinet to resign.

Disillusionment with Party Politics

In selecting Takahashi's successor, elder statesman and former Prime Minister Saionji Kinmochi declined to be involved, citing illness. The selection was left instead to another former Prime Minister, Matsukata Masayoshi, who recommended Katō Tomosaburō. Because Katō died of illness a little over a year after he formed his cabinet, Yamamoto Gonbei had to form his second cabinet in the midst of turmoil in the aftermath of the Great Kantō Earthquake of 1923. It was the second consecutive supra-party government, but the formation of supra-party governments was supported by the public at the time. According to an August 1923 issue of the weekly *Tōyō Keizai Shimpō*, although the Japanese people had ardently desired democracy since the beginning of the Taishō era, they became so disenchanted with the factional feuds which were the reality of party politics during the Hara and Takahashi administrations that they ended up "cursing party politics." Referring to the next cabinet toward the end of Takahashi's tenure, the Meiji-Shōwa scholar on government Yoshino Sakuzō said, "The idea of leaving politics to the regular constitutional government practice [of government by the majority party] makes even less sense than giving a dying patient health tips meant for a healthy person." He said, "Not even such a shameless person as myself would feel comfortable" recommending the regular constitutional way today.

This disillusionment with party politics was attributable to the uglier side of democracy as demonstrated during the thirty-seven months of the Hara administration. The public saw politicians putting party interests before the national interest, rewarding party hacks with government offices, looking for special favors, indulging in blatant corruption, and spending more time tearing each other down than building the state up. Admittedly, such things are everyday newspaper headlines today. In fact, they are so routine that democracy cannot be sustained if voters become disenchanted every time such incidents take place. Nevertheless, the people's despair was all the more profound because of their high expectations of Japan's first attempt at democratic government. For better or worse, we have to admit that democracy in today's Japan resembles politics during the Taishō Democracy. Considering the advice from Edwin Reischauer and his associates that was adopted by the General Headquarters of the Occupation forces, it is only natural that we would see the political system during the Taishō Democracy resurrected in post–World War II Japan. In fact, the conduct of the Liberal Democratic Party politicians who have governed Japan for half a century in the post–World War II era resembles that of the Seiyūkai and Rikken Minsei-tō party members—who were among our grandfathers' and great-grandfathers' generations—so much that the two are almost undistinguishable.

One major reason a stable parliamentary democracy has been sustained in post–World War II Japan is the fact that it has its roots in the political system of the Taishō Democracy. The Japanese people accomplished Taishō Democracy with their own hands through bitter struggles dating back to the the Freedom and People's Rights Movement. Yet some people claim the Occupation Forces granted democracy to a Japan where there had been no hint of democracy before.

Conditions for Mature Democracy

One factor that was absent during the Taishō Democracy but has been instrumental in sustaining a stable democracy for over half a century in post–World War II Japan is the Japanese experience with autocratic rule by the military clique in the years between the Taishō Democracy and postwar democracy. The damage inflicted on Japan by the military clique's autocratic rule was so deep and so widespread that people assume today's democracy is, for all its faults, a better system than what they experienced in the past. As far as democracy is concerned, Japan has undergone an experience that seems to validate the famous saying attributed to Winston Churchill: Democracy is the worst form of government, except for all those other forms that have been tried from time to time.

In order to sustain democracy, people need to be tolerant, almost to the extent of resignation, with respect to its shortcomings. To attain this mindset, people seem to have to go through certain political experiences. In retrospect, British parliamentary government also matured only after a series of trials and errors, starting with the Magna Carta (1215) and going through Oliver Cromwell's Puritan Revolution (1642), the Restoration of 1660, and the Glorious Revolution of 1688. In Taishō Japan, people became so weary of corruption under this "worst form of government" that they decided to entrust the government to the clean and efficient military. The military was indeed free of corruption. No one suspects Generals Tōjō Hideki or Itagaki Seishirō made a personal fortune. It is said that the first target of the Occupation Forces was Itagaki's house. Because Itagaki was called an "emperor of Manchuria," they looked for a hoard of Chinese treasures. What they found was a simple commoner's house devoid of almost anything of value. And yet these people led Japan to total destruction. It is no doubt at least partly due to this experience that democracy in today's Japan has been resilient.

But it was difficult for democratic politics to take hold in a Japan where people still believed in the possibility of an ideal form of government to which they could entrust their dreams and expectations. This was all the more difficult when the same people—who had not yet reached Churchill's resigned frame of mind—believed there were viable alternatives to democracy. One alternative that is often suggested is that of rule by a philosopher-king—rule by people who are genuinely concerned about the general wellbeing and the national interest instead of people whose major concern is their own and their party's interests. Past attempts at philosopher-king rule have mostly ended up as autocratic rule, which was more harmful to the governed. Nevertheless, ever since Plato's characterization of it as the ideal form of government, rule by a philosopher-king has remained an impossible dream for mankind. For pre–World War II Japanese, who had not yet experienced autocratic rule by the military clique, there were always alternatives to democracy. Immediately before the Taishō Democracy, for instance, a quick and easy alternative was to return to the supra-party governments that had ruled Japan since the Meiji Restoration. This was an option that was not without merit, particularly during the national modernization process, such that its revival did not meet strong resistance from the people, who, by that time, had become weary of the problems inherent in party politics. That was why the Japanese people did not at first oppose the revival of a supra-party government which came after the Hara and Takahashi cabinets.

Kiyoura Cabinet Resigns and Three Pro-Constitution Factions Form a Cabinet

It was, however, only until the Yamamoto Gonbei cabinet that people tolerated supra-party governments. The political parties' disappointment at the formation of the Yamamoto cabinet was immense, because they had been confident that the Katō Tomosaburō cabinet would be succeeded by democracy. They chose not to make a political issue out of it, however, because the Yamamoto government declared it would tackle the national crisis caused by the Great Kantō Earthquake. But when Kiyoura Keigo, President of the Privy Council, was appointed to form a cabinet after the Yamamoto cabinet resigned in only three months as a way of taking responsibility for the Toranomon Incident (an assassination attempt on then Prince Regent Hirohito) in 1923, the political parties could take it no longer. Further annoying advocates of party politics, Kiyoura formed a cabinet entirely of House of Peers members, except for ministers of war, navy, and foreign affairs. This was an anachronistic arrangement by anyone's reckoning. After witnessing how Kiyoura formed the cabinet, even Saionji Kinmochi himself, who had recommended Kiyoura to the emperor, confided to people around him that "it was a mistake to have recommended Kiyoura."

It was at this time that the Seiyūkai broke apart. Takahashi became seriously worried that such irresponsible conduct on the part of political parties would further disillusion the people to the point that they could even turn to socialism. When reactionary trends in politics become excessive, they run the risk of triggering a groundswell of sentiment in favor of a revolution. Given the strong impact the Russian Revolution had had on Japanese society at that time, it was only natural that Takahashi and others were concerned about the possibility of a revolution. Determined to devote the rest of his life to defending the constitution against such a scenario, Takahashi resigned his peerage and decided to run for the House of Representatives. One can only wish Takahashi had come to this determination earlier and concentrated on leading the Seiyūkai to defend parliamentary democracy right after Hara's death.

Although Takahashi's resolution was genuine, he was unfortunately without the political clout needed to influence the general current of the Seiyūkai. The anti-Takahashi faction within the party, which had resisted his earlier attempt to reshuffle the cabinet, insisted that the party continue to cooperate with the Kiyoura government from outside the cabinet. Their real purpose was to stay as close to the locus of political power as possible, and they might even have feared that the opposition Kenseikai might get closer to the government. It is easy to stigmatize the anti-Takahashi faction as power-mongers, but a more dispassionate view would characterize their conduct as a party-politics inevitability. Eventually, the anti-Takahashi faction left the Seiyūkai to form a new Seiyū-Hon-tō. Having more seats in the Diet than the Seiyūkai, the Seiyū-Hon-tō became the dominant political party and endorsed the Kiyoura cabinet.

At this point, the remaining members of the Seiyūkai got together with Katō Takaaki's Kenseikai and Inukai Tsuyoshi's Kakushin Kurabu to form a three-faction, anti-Kiyoura, pro-constitution alliance. Subject to a barrage of criticism from the three-party alliance in the Diet, the Kiyoura cabinet counter-attacked by dissolving the House of Representatives. The three-party alliance, however, achieved a landslide victory in the subsequent general election in May 1924. In past elections, the incumbent side had always had the advantage. After all, it could utilize the powers associated with the home ministry to influence prefectural governors and the police and could also use its political might to raise funds and put pressure on people sympathetic to the opposition parties. The result of the 1924 election, however, showed that incumbency could no longer determine the outcome of an election. As a result of the election, Saionji Kinmochi recommended one person to the emperor as the next prime minister: Katō Takaaki, president of the Kenseikai, the largest part of the three-party alliance.

The Era of Regular Constitutional Government Practices

Saionji had become the most powerful figure in Japanese politics after the death of Yamagata Aritomo. What, one may wonder, was his political philosophy? Saionji was exposed to liberalism while he was studying in France. For Saionji, however, liberalism mainly took the form of Western individualism, and he saw it as the antithesis of the traditional feudal thinking in Japan. In terms of political thinking, Saionji opposed and suppressed advocates of anti-party conservatism, who, like Yamagata, believed that a party government would infringe upon Imperial sovereignty. As soon as Saionji got involved in the freedom and people's rights movement, however, his attention shifted more toward keeping the movement from going too far left. This distinguished him from other, more usual Freedom and People's Rights Movement advocates. In a speech Saionji delivered when he succeeded Itō Hirobumi as president of the Seiyūkai, he declared that he completely shared Itō's political convictions and there was therefore no need to amend the party's platform and manifesto. The Seiyūkai's platform was the product of a compromise Hoshi Tōru and Hara Takashi made to invite Itō to the party. Among other points, it even declared, "Appointment and dismissal of cabinet members is the emperor's prerogative, and it can be either a member or a non-member of the Seiyūkai."

On this point, Itō and Saionji differed from Mutsu and Hara, for whom the realization of a party government was a long-cherished dream. For Saionji, a party government was just one realistic option, a supra-party government being the other, in the context of the times. Particularly when the public was fed up with the undesirable, albeit inevitable, features of party politics that it had experienced for the first time, he thought it perfectly reasonable to entrust Katō Tomosaburō, Yamamoto Gonbei, and Kiyoura Keigo with the government. That said, Saionji was distrustful of Katō Takaaki after witnessing his arbitrary behavior in deciding Japan's participation in World War I, his mishandling of the Twenty-One Demands, and his subsequent non-cooperation with the provisional council on foreign policy research.

The trend of the times, however, again turned favorable to constitutional government. Having once become tired of the undesirable features of democracy, the public was now fed up with a succession of supra-party cabinets. This was a sign Japan's democracy was maturing through bitter experience. Reading the trend of the times, Saionji was insightful enough to follow the regular procedure of a constitutional government now that Katō's Kenseikai was elected the dominant party. Saionji was also magnanimous enough to overlook Katō's past behavior. It was at this point that the rule of parliamentary democracy or, as a popular phrase of the time put it, "regular constitutional government practice" was firmly established in Japan. The Japanese people had finally succeeded in establishing parliamentary democracy with their own hands after many twists and turns starting with the Freedom and People's Rights Movement. Although the people who had experienced it had for the most part already died, the next eight years were "the good old days" of democracy in Japan. This overlapped the seven years of Shidehara Diplomacy.

Shidehara Kijūrō, Minister for Foreign Affairs

On June 9, 1924, when Katō was ordered by the emperor to form a cabinet, he invited Shidehara to his house and asked him to become his foreign minister. Shidehara thus became the first career diplomat who had formally passed the foreign service examination to become foreign minister. His appointment was highly appropriate in everyone's eyes. Since both he and Katō were married to Iwasaki Yatarō daughters, one might expect criticism about nepotism or special relations with the Mitsubishi zaibatsu and opposition to Shidehara's appointment. Shidehara's rise, however, was so natural and reasonable that, amazingly, no such criticism was heard. To this point, Shidehara had been a model bureaucrat: he was never intrusive, aggressive, or offensive. Once he attained the position of responsibility, however, he started to fiercely pursue what he had long believed in, opening a new page in Japanese diplomacy. He demonstrated that he knew how best to behave as a bureaucrat and, subsequently, as a statesman. In a press conference immediately after he assumed the post, Shidehara said, "The age of Machiavellian maneuvers and imperialistic strategy is completely of the past now and diplomacy must pursue the great cause of justice and peace." In line with this, he declared, "In short, Japan must comply with and further advance the noble spirit of the Treaty of Versailles and various treaties signed at the Washington Conference."

In the Imperial Diet session that convened on July 1, 1924, Shidehara made a historic speech on foreign policy. Foreign Minister Shidehara's diplomacy remained highly consistent throughout his tenure, and its fundamental elements were all compacted in this speech. Shidehara himself laboriously drafted this lengthy speech. I wonder when the custom of writing one's own thoughts went out of style among the Japanese. Itō Hirobumi, Mutsu Munemitsu, and Komura Jutarō had all written coherent and flawless treatises whenever they faced a matter of grave national concern, yet today's Japanese politicians no longer do this. It is not just that the custom has gone out of fashion; they are probably incapable of writing a treatise even if they wanted to. For one thing, Mutsu, Komura, and Shidehara were brighter than the brightest; they were people whose superiority had been widely recognized by their contemporaries since childhood. They were endowed with unrivaled insight, philosophy, and writing ability. What really happened was the extinction of a system in which the best and the brightest automatically rose to the top of the policy-making ranks. Instead, politics has become the playing field for ex-bureaucrats who have given up on their careers in officialdom and seek life-support in politics. With this, a system emerged in which those who win the battles became cabinet members with the help of their faction's support and the seniority system.

Historic Foreign Policy Speech

In his July 1924 foreign policy speech, Shidehara set out by declaring, "The essence of the diplomacy of the Empire of Japan is to advocate the legitimate rights and interests of the Empire while respecting the legitimate rights and interests of other powers," in order to maintain peace in Asia and, eventually, the world. Instead of one-sidedly asserting Japan's rights, Shidehara declared Japan would also respect those of its global partners. This mutual respect of rights and interests was the very essence of Shidehara Diplomacy. The Nine-Power Agreement signed at the Washington Conference affirmed China's sovereignty and territorial integrity. Nevertheless, given the chaotic conditions in China at the time, Japan still could have expanded its rights and interests in China either by threat of force or by bribery. Yet Shidehara's position was that Japan would protect its own rights and interests but refrain from pursuing an expansionistic policy that would violate the rights and interests of others, a position that he maintained consistently throughout his tenure.

Shidehara also said in his speech, "Commitments a country has officially made to other countries . . . must not be altered . . . even if the government or cabinet changes." The commitments that Shidehara referred to included the Twenty-One Demands. These were demands, but he amended them at the Washington Conference to such an extent that, realistically, China should have felt content with them. The amendments made considerable concessions from what Japan had gained from the Demands, with the exception of its special interests in Manchuria and Mongolia. When Wang Ch'ung-hui, Chinese chief delegate to the Conference, was about to depart Washington, DC, for home, he took the trouble of approaching Shidehara through the crowd of participants to say, "To tell you the truth, I have misunderstood Japan terribly. It was a great personal gain for me to be able to understand Japan during this conference." Now that Shidehara had so magnanimously made the maximum concessions, he expected both Japan and China would comply with their international commitments and exercise restraint to maintain peace in Asia. Given conditions at the time, this was perhaps the best anyone could hope for.

In his Diet speech, Shidehara also stressed, "Japan will not interfere in China's domestic politics. Japan will not take any action that ignores the legitimate positions of China. At the same time, we in Japan trust China will not take any action that ignores our legitimate positions." To be sure, Shidehara had the necessary sincerity and persuasiveness to convince the Chinese delegates he personally contacted. Yet when China itself was in total disarray owing to internal conflict with any and all contending forces competing for legitimacy bearing the banner of nationalism, Chinese self-restraint was easier said than done. From the Chinese viewpoint, the post–Washington Conference regime consolidated not the foundations for stable peace as Shidehara hoped but the very unequal relations of the past that had to be broken down. And the subsequent inclination of the United States to become more sympathetic to China's nationalistic demands triggered a tragic setback for Shidehara Diplomacy. But that was to be much later. Meanwhile, Shidehara Diplomacy did everything it could to promote mutual trust between China and Japan, greatly contributing to the enhancement of Japan's international credibility.

Persistent Non-Interference in Domestic Chinese Politics

Soon after Shidehara was appointed foreign minister, the civil war in China intensified. In time the tensions led to the Second Zhili-Fengtian War, the armed struggle between Zhang Zuolin of the Fengtian clique, who had ruled Manchuria, and Wu Peifu of the Zhili clique, which was in possession of Beijing. Until then, Japan had both overtly and covertly sided with Zhang Zuolin, who had, for his part, protected Japan's special interests in Manchuria and Mongolia to the extent that Japan's special interests there were guaranteed as long as Zhang controlled Manchuria. But the opposing Zhili clique became dominant and, at one point, it appeared it would cross through the Shanhai Pass and invade Mongolia. Fearing the consequences for the interests that Japan had built up in Manchuria, some in Japan staged demonstrations at the Ministry of Foreign Affairs demanding more assistance to Zhang and railing against Shidehara's indecisive foreign policy.

Nevertheless, Shidehara did not flinch. On the contrary, on October 13 Shidehara officially requested the two warring parties "to respect and protect the interests of Japan and its citizens in China because Japan will strictly maintain its non-interference position," thus making the non-intervention policy an international commitment. Shidehara consistently and firmly believed that, if Japan tried not to hurt China's feelings and maintained a policy of strict non-interference, the Chinese would respect Japan's interests in Manchuria. Needless to say, the Chinese side welcomed this Japanese government attitude. China's Foreign Minister Ku Wei-chün officially replied, "In the spirit of Sino-Japanese friendship, the Chinese government will do its best to protect Japan's interests."

When Zhang's Fengtian clique seemed certain to be defeated, however, Minister of Agriculture and Commerce Takahashi Korekiyo insisted at a cabinet meeting, "At this point, our only option is to aid Zhang Zuolin," and even Prime Minister Katō said, "What Shidehara insists on is nothing but an empty theory," tipping the balance in the cabinet meeting predominantly in favor of intervention. Shidehara, nevertheless, refused to give even an inch, citing three reasons:

1. Japan would lose its international credibility if it deviated from the internationally announced policy of non-intervention.
2. Even if Wu Peifu conquered all of Manchuria, Japan could still make

Wu respect Japan's vested interests there.

3. Feng Yuxiang, currently of the Zhili clique, had originally been an archrival to Wu Peifu and would never let Wu conquer Manchuria unchallenged. There was a good possibility, Shidehara said, that Feng's army would attack Wu's lines from behind.

The fact of the matter is that the local agency of the Imperial Japanese Army had schemed to use Feng to aid Zhang Zuolin. Both War Minister Ugaki Kazushige and Minister Yoshizawa Kenkichi, who was stationed in Beijing, knew this. Shidehara probably had information on Feng's possible moves from these two. But there was no knowing whether Feng would actually betray Wu and, moreover, because Shidehara would not change his conviction on non-interference regardless of what Feng did, this third reason was just an accessory. The cabinet meeting became entangled and no agreement could be reached. At this point, Katō proposed a break and invited Shidehara to an anteroom to ask if there was any room for compromise on his part. But Shidehara declared, "No, I cannot bend my principles. As far as this case is concerned, there is no room for compromise." He even pulled out a letter of resignation, which he had prepared beforehand. Seeing this, Katō said, "Now that I know you are so firmly determined, let me tell you I honestly do not have any objection to the policy of non-intervention myself," refusing to accept the letter of resignation. Subsequently, when the cabinet meeting was resumed, it was agreed that no conclusion could be reached, and the meeting was adjourned.

It was during dinner that day that participants were informed that Feng Yuxiang had indeed staged a coup and seized Beijing, forcing Wu Peifu to turn around and confront Feng. Upon hearing this, Shidehara requested an emergency cabinet meeting after dinner, at which he briefly explained what had happened in China. Hearing Shidehara's debriefing, Agriculture and Commerce Minister Takahashi took the trouble of coming over to Shidehara from the other side of the table, shaking his hand, and saying, "Great! Thank goodness! Japan was saved by your tenacity." Takahashi was pleased that Japan had not lost its international credibility as a result of a hasty decision. Recalling this episode with Takahashi, Shidehara later reminisced:

Takahashi was this kind of person. Although he had been arguing fiercely with me only moments ago driven by intense patriotism, he was overjoyed at the turn of events which proved that Japan was better off for not having done what he had advocated. His words and deeds were truly gracious, reminding me of a fresh breeze and the clear moon. I felt tears well up uncontrollably in my eyes.

Those were the good old people in the good old days. Prime Minister Katō was also generous with his compliments for Shidehara's conduct in this incident. In December of the same year, Katō said:

> Japan adopted the policy of non-intervention in cooperation with Britain and the United States. When the two Chinese warring parties confronted each other across the Shanhai Pass, however, some in the Japanese government wanted to abandon the policy of non-intervention, and the debate within the government grew heated and complex. Nevertheless, Foreign Minister Shidehara remained steadfast. . . . That our conduct was impartial was recognized by the Western powers as well as by the leaders of the Fengtian and Zhili cliques. Former British Prime Minister Ramsay McDonald openly declared, "As far as the China issue is concerned, Britain shall follow Japan's initiative," while the new Foreign Secretary Austen Chamberlain told our Ambassador Hayashi that Britain would be sure to coordinate its China policy with Japan.

If only Japan had maintained this kind of mutual trust with Britain, it would never have joined World War II. Had the Anglo-Japanese Alliance been sustained, this bilateral relationship of trust would have been much more stable. Although it was Shidehara who severed the Anglo-Japanese Alliance tie, he nevertheless remained convinced of the crucial importance of cooperative relations among Japan, Britain, and the United States. History shows that things did not quite turn out as Shidehara had intended, but if it had been at all possible to maintain mutual trust with Britain, Japan would have been able to pass on what it had gained during the First Sino-Japanese War, the Russo-Japanese War, and World War I to subsequent generations.

Persistence with Principles, No Room for Compromise

Before the Shidehara Diplomacy was interrupted in 1927 by the Tanaka Giichi cabinet, the idea of sending Japanese troops to China became an issue twice: once on the occasion of Guo Songling's mutiny against Zhang Zuolin in mid-1925 and again on the occasion of the 1927 riot in Hankou that threatened the security of foreign settlers. In the first incident, the majority of the cabinet was inclined to favor troop deployment; in the second incident, Britain proposed a joint force. In both cases, Japanese troops would have been sent to China had it not been for staunch opposition from Shidehara, who never budged even an inch from his position of non-interference. Foreign Minister Shidehara consistently and persistently upheld the principle he had clarified when he took office. He did not compromise even once throughout his tenure. This uncompromising attitude aroused antipathy toward Shidehara Diplomacy in some corners of Japan, which we shall come back to later, but I would like here to briefly review Shidehara's other accomplishments in the first half of his tenure.

In his foreign policy speech immediately after assuming the post of foreign minister, he touched upon relations with the Soviet Union to say, "I believe that the Soviet Union and Japan should eventually become friendly neighbors. We are destined to come closer together." Based on this conviction, he came to grips with the Russo-Japanese negotiations that had started one year earlier. As with all subsequent negotiations with the Soviet Union, these negotiations required a tremendous amount of time and patience and were not concluded until January 1925, eight years after the severance of diplomatic relations in 1917. With this agreement, both countries fully recognized the Portsmouth Treaty and normalized diplomatic relations based on this understanding. In the course of discussions, the Japanese side demanded reparations for the massacre of Japanese residents in Nikolayevsk-on-Amur and repayment of Russia's military debts during World War I. Consequently, over and above what it had acquired through the Treaty, Japan obtained coal and oil concessions in northern Sakhalin in exchange for the withdrawal of Japanese troops from the region.

As soon as this Soviet-Japanese Basic Convention was concluded, the Soviet side claimed that the new era in Soviet-Japan relations would affect the whole of world politics. Shidehara, who did not believe in realpolitik or power politics, immediately dismissed the Soviet claim. In a Diet session, Shidehara stressed that Japan and the Soviet Union were neighbors that had to maintain friendly relations and that "the Soviet-Japanese Basic Convention is merely an attempt to restore diplomatic relations and coordinate relations between two countries which share many interests." The foundation of Soviet-Japanese relations thus stabilized and remained unshaken until World War II.

Supporting China's Restoration of Tariff Autonomy

Shidehara actively pursued "economic diplomacy" in order to advance his peace diplomacy as well as to salvage the Japanese economy, which had been in the depths of the post–World War I recession. To this end, he appointed his confidant Saburi Sadao director-general of the foreign ministry's trade bureau, expanded and upgraded trade-related offices and agencies within the ministry and overseas diplomatic missions, and actively concluded and revised trade agreements with a number of countries.

Shidehara was particularly keen to develop Chinese markets for Japanese products. In August 1925, the Chinese government proposed to Washington Conference participants that an international conference be convened to discuss the restoration of China's tariff autonomy. Foreign Minister Shidehara took the initiative in supporting China's proposal, which succeeded in drawing support from the other powers. Ever since the Opium Wars, China's tariff rate had been set at 5 percent. Due to the decline in the price of silver and other developments, however, actual tariff revenues for the Chinese government were less than what 5 percent would have brought in. At the Washington Conference, the participating countries agreed on a real tariff rate, instead of the nominal rate of 5 percent, for China. As a matter of fact, Britain and the United States proposed an across-the-board increase in China's tariff rate to 12.5 percent, but Japan opposed the proposal on the grounds that it would hurt Japan's low-range exports much more than it would British and US high-range exports. Instead, Japan proposed differential tariff rates of 50 percent for high-range products, 20 percent for middle-range products, and 5 percent for low-range products.

While it might really have been Shidehara's conviction regarding cooperative diplomacy and economic diplomacy that drove his support for the convening of the Special Conference on the Chinese Customs Tariff and China's demand for tariff autonomy, he also had an ulterior motive in seeking to secure China's friendship and trust. Shidehara knew that having China's trust would be an advantage in accomplishing Japan's claims. Things unfolded exactly as Shidehara had calculated. At the Special Conference on the Chinese Customs Tariff, an agreement was reached first on the principle in November, followed by negotiations on details including the differential tariff rates before working out a definite plan. Meanwhile, the Japanese delegation was instrumental in salvaging the conference when several crises threatened to bring negotiations to a halt. But because the instability of Chinese politics de facto invalidated the Chinese delegation, the participating countries not including China adopted and signed the final agreement as an informal plan.

This conference had the effect of drastically changing China's attitude toward Japan. Horiuchi Tateki, Japanese chief delegate to the conference, reminisced:

> The Japanese attitude during the Special Conference on the Chinese Customs Tariff was very favorably received by the Chinese people, particularly the "young China" that had been on the rise in those days, as a volte-face from the former imperialistic and high-handed attitude.

Because the Japanese delegation took the initiative in all of the issues discussed during the conference:

> Even the British chief delegate, Kenneth Stewart, began to say the Japanese delegation should take the lead whenever a need arose to negotiate with the Chinese side on important issues because it was most deeply trusted by the Chinese side. It was perhaps due to this development that we saw various occasions on which Beijing citizens showed whole-hearted friendliness toward the Japanese delegation. Moreover, anti-Japanese movements gradually waned in Shanghai and other cities, edged out by a pro-Japanese air, which was extremely delightful.

Japan's reputation was so improved that some in Britain and the United States even accused Shidehara of having violated the agreement among the world powers for coordinating their actions vis-à-vis China. On those accusing voices, Shidehara reminisced:

The Japanese government had intended to support China's request for tariff autonomy from the beginning. . . . I remember that we had told the British and American representatives of this stance of ours. In those days, Western diplomats stationed in China normally went to Beijing via Tokyo. It was therefore in Tokyo that I met with the British and American representatives on their way to Beijing and shared with them my prediction that the Chinese side would probably stress the issue of tariff autonomy in the coming conference.

Toward the end of the previous year, in what became his last visit to Japan, Sun Yat-sen called for the abolition of the unequal treaties that had been imposed on China. On his deathbed in March 1925, he left his last will that China should accomplish freedom and equality. Shidehara must have known of these episodes when he tried to persuade the British and American representatives to the conference, saying:

While China might abuse its tariff autonomy, causing problems for the Western powers, it would not be fair, on the other hand, to deny China that authority. Japan went through a similar ordeal, and it was through the revision of our treaties of commerce and navigation with the Western powers that we were eventuallyable to regain our tariff autonomy, which had been denied us since the one-sided imposition of a fixed tariff rate by the Ansei Treaties of 1858. Tariff autonomy is an inalienable right of a sovereign nation. Even if China were to temporarily abuse its tariff autonomy and impose an unjustifiable tariff on its trading partners, disturbing the Western powers' trade, China itself would realize the long-run disadvantages of its conduct and properly revise the tariffs, including abolishing them where necessary. Since I had said this to the British and American representatives beforehand, I do not deserve to be accused of making an attempt to out-flank them.

Sympathetic but Unsentimental Observation

It was only natural that the attempt to accomplish equality, a long-cherished desire for China, included efforts to restore China's jurisdiction. Shidehara also took the initiative on this issue, proposing to the US government that it convene a conference on this matter. That proposal came to fruition in the form of a committee meeting in Beijing in January 1926. The entire country in turmoil and foreign residents in China under constant threat, however, prospects were dim for an early settlement of this issue. In the end, the committee concluded, "the most urgent issue for China at this point is the modernization of its legal and jurisdictional provisions, and it would be premature to restore legal autonomy."

On this particular point, Shidehara made a sympathetic and yet unsentimental observation that can be summarized as follows. Japan has long been understanding of China's wish to liberate itself from the bondage of unequal treaties with the Western powers. I must point out, however, that what China wishes to accomplish at this time is significantly different, in terms of methodology and procedure from the path Japan took. As we went through the hardships imposed by unequal treaties and set out to revise the treaties, we first blamed not the Western powers but ourselves for our inadequacies. Instead of loudly denouncing imperialism, we calmly devoted our attention and energy to improving domestic governance. The Western powers willingly agreed with the revision of their treaties with Japan when they saw the domestic modernizations that we had accomplished. Even while foreign residents in Japan were enjoying their extraterritorial rights, we did not curse the Western powers' imperialism. Instead, we concentrated on developing and modernizing our country. Even during the period of the unilaterally imposed tariffs, we never violated the treaties to impose higher tariffs on imports. Instead, we tried to manage our finances. Unequal treaties are the result of the inadequacies of domestic politics, not the cause of turmoil in domestic politics as China claims. We are not necessarily suggesting that China should fully emulate what Japan did, but we feel obliged to request self-restraint by the Chinese officials and citizens because we sincerely hope that China will become an equal partner as soon as possible.

Shidehara's remarks were logically consistent and eminently sound from the common-sense perspective of the nineteenth century through which Japan had struggled to survive. The tide of the twentieth century, when freedom and equality were the indisputable grand principles, was about to reach Asia. Convinced that existing treaties, even unequal ones, had to be complied with, Shidehara held the view that the revision of treaties was possible only when the world powers recognized the improvements in the domestic conditions in the countries concerned. Shidehara thus believed that Japan would be prepared to recognize China ahead of the Western powers when China showed commendable progress. But Shidehara's philosophy was already being overtaken by the the anti-imperialist trend of the times, which continued to advance aggressively. This was the beginning of the tragedy of Shidehara Diplomacy.

CHAPTER

11

The Tide Turns

—Public Resentment of Shidehara's Cooperative Diplomacy—

Changing Tide Undercuts Shidehara Diplomacy

The Japanese public had strongly resisted Shidehara's cooperative diplomacy from the beginning. It seems universally true that hard-line diplomacy is more popular than cooperative diplomacy, but this has been particularly true in Japan with few, if any, exceptions since Commodore Matthew Perry's arrival at Uraga in 1853. Nevertheless, Shidehara dauntlessly persisted in promoting this policy he believed in, paying no heed to criticism of what was called his weak-kneed diplomacy. It was fortunate for Shidehara that the domestic situation in Japan allowed this. This was at the peak of the Taishō Democracy and, internationally, coincided with the era of international cooperation centered around the League of Nations and the post–Washington Conference international regime. Those were the days when not even Japan's military would dream of defying the authority of the central government.

Politics has a life of its own. Even under the Meiji Constitution which, theoretically, established the independence of military command, politics, military, and bureaucracy in Japan were under the control of cabinets that were responsible to the Diet, a system befitting parliamentary democracy. It was the international situation, rather than the domestic political situation, that eroded the foundations for Shidehara's cooperative diplomacy. Had the post–Washington Conference regime survived a little longer, so would have Shidehara's cooperative diplomacy and, by extension, parliamentary democracy in Japan. The changing international situation, however, did not allow this. In January 1923, most of what is now Guandong province came under the control of the Kuomintang (Chinese Nationalist Party) led by Sun Yat-sen. More accurately, it was the warlord who supported the Kuomintang who secured control of Guandong in a power struggle among local warlords. When this happened, China watchers outside the country saw it as just one of numerous alignments and realignments among warlords. Yet this turned out to be a critical turning point in modern Chinese history, one that decisively influenced subsequent Sino-Japanese relations. It was also a setback for Shidehara Diplomacy.

China in Turmoil

The Soviet Union's China policy also played a role here. In 1919, with the fervor of the proletariat revolution still at a high point, the Karakhan Manifesto announced that the Soviet government was prepared to renounce all special privileges and unequal treaties that the Tsar's government had acquired from China. This decision was greeted with great joy by Chinese nationalists, and it provided the foundation for the future development of Soviet-China relations.

Subsequent Soviet Communist Party policy emphasized the development and strengthening of the Communist forces within China and the establishment of a people's republic in Mongolia. The Soviet government assisted Mongolia's quest for independence from China both overtly and covertly, and it dispatched the Red Army in July 1921 to help Mongolia achieve independence from the Republic of China. Soviet recognition of Mongolia's independence followed. This did not meet with the same strong resistance in China that greeted Japan-backed Manchukuo's later declaration of independence. For one thing, the Manchu people by that time had become a minority in Manchuria due to massive migration of Han Chinese who fled their war-torn homeland. Although the Han Chinese migration had been forbidden under the Qing Dynasty, the Qing's fall triggered their exodus to Japan-controlled Manchuria, where relative peace prevailed. While the Mongols in Inner Mongolia had already been half sinicized, those in Outer Mongolia still retained a strong ethnic identity. It also helped that Soviet socialism was seen as the star of hope for oppressed peoples. A further factor was that China was in a state of total confusion, torn by struggles among warlords, and the warlord who happened to control Mongolia at that time was too weak to resist the Soviet interference. China nevertheless continued to stubbornly reject Mongolian independence. It was only after World War II, when the Soviet Union was a victorious superpower and the international order became a fait accompli, that China finally recognized the Mongolian People's Republic. Had this not occurred, Mongolia would still be in the same status as Tibet and Xinjiang—targets of the Chinese government's sinicization policy.

Also in July 1921, representatives of Communist groups from all over China, including Mao Zedong, gathered in Shanghai to convene the first national convention of the Communist Party of China. Although the Soviet government attempted to improve its relations with the Beiyang government in Beijing, it found this difficult given the close relations between the Beiyang government and the Western powers. Instead, it started to pay more attention to the activities of Sun Yat-sen's revolutionary forces in the south.

From Sun's perspective, it was only natural he should accept Soviet approaches when diplomatic relations with the Western powers were being monopolized by the Beiyang government. After all, the Soviet Union had succeeded in carrying out the Russian Revolution, and this must have been a dazzling presence for Sun. Thus, in January 1924, the first convention of the Kuomintang formally adopted the party line of "cooperation with the Soviet Union and accommodation of Communism." Having been repeatedly deceived by warlords with whom he had formed partnerships in the past, Sun recognized the need to possess his own armed forces so that he did not have to rely on this or that warlord. On the advice of his Chief of Staff Chiang Kai-shek, who had been sent to the Soviet Union the previous year, Sun decided at the Kuomintang convention to establish a military academy. While Chiang Kai-shek was appointed the academy's commandant, Soviet educational advisers were assigned to the academy and the future premier of the People's Republic of China, Zhou Enlai, was designated the acting director of political education. This was the Whampoa Military Academy, which had a decisive influence on the

Chinese revolution, producing numerous generals for both the Kuomintang and the Communist Party, including He Yingqin and Lin Biao.

Because Commandant Chiang took the initiative in observing strict school rules and set a good example in disciplining the cadets, he became deeply respected and loved by the graduates. It was, indeed, thanks to the strong support of Whampoa Military Academy alumni that Chiang was subsequently able to overcome a run of political crises. Although Chiang was later criticized for corruption and nepotism, he had devoted his pure passion to the cause of revolution in his youth and this experience became a life-long asset. It was his experience as the commandant of the Whampoa Military Academy that helped Chiang amass more power and influence than Wang Jingwei, Sun's closest confidant within the Kuomintang and someone who was considered superior to Chiang in competence and insight. Although the academy was initially ready to accept 300 cadets, some 3,000 applied. In response, the academy adopted an intensive training course so that it could accept more cadets, turning out a massive corps of military officers in no time. Efficiently drawing upon the nationalistic energy of Chinese youths, the academy contributed to the formation of a powerful military force. In only two years, this military force was strong enough to launch the Kuomintang's Northern Expedition.

People in Japan do not appear to have been fully aware of these developments in China. While a number of Japanese revolutionaries and adventurers participated in the First Revolution (Xinhai Revolution), no one from Japan took part in this new venture by Chiang Kai-shek. This venture was mainly backed by the Soviet Union. One may say this was the point where Japan's pan-Asianism, which had been going on since the Meiji era, reached its limit. Even after the Northern Expedition started, people in Japan interpreted it as nothing but an intensification of personal strife among warlords and failed to realize that it was the dawn of a new era in China. This misperception was typically revealed in the analysis by Yoshida Shigeru, Consul-General at Mukden and later prime minister, who reported back, "The instability of the political situation in China is attributable to personal strife among warlords, . . . which has become even more intense since the establishment of the Republic of China in Nanjing."

It should be recalled here that Shidehara Diplomacy was based on the strict principle of non-interference in other countries' internal affairs. Japan therefore took the position that it was for China itself to decide which of the domestic forces would represent the country and that Japan would pursue courteous diplomatic relations with the legitimate representative of China thus chosen. This was the period when the urge to be part of the new forces in China was the lowest in Japan, including in the military. Japan's failure to establish a strong relationship with Chiang, who had studied at a military academy in Japan and remained pro-Japanese until the end, might be one factor behind the failure of Japan's China policy through to the end of the World War II.

Spread of Soviet Communism

The Western powers, including Japan, were more concerned about the spread of Soviet Communism in southern China, and they were naturally cautious and suspicious about the advance of the Northern Expedition by the Republic of China, which was known to tolerate Communism. Prior to the Northern Expedition, labor union movements had already become rampant in China under the influence of the Russian Revolution. These activities occasionally developed into bloody incidents. In 1925, the May Thirtieth Movement erupted in Shanghai. In the beginning, it was a strike by workers at a Japanese factory. Because of a confrontation with the management, the factory strike soon developed into a Shanghai-wide strike whose major target was the British businessmen who held the real power in the Shanghai International Settlement. The strike in no time spread to Hong Kong, at which point the Kuomintang government declared it was breaking off economic relations with Britain. The subsequent economic blockade of Hong Kong by the Kuomintang government and the general strike in the territory lasted sixteen months. During those sixteen months, Chinese residents in Hong Kong were discouraged from contacting and talking with British residents, and large numbers of Chinese employees working in British households there moved to Guandong. Under the circumstances, it was only natural Britain would be cautious about the further spread of Kuomintang influence.

This First United Front by the Kuomintang and the Communist Party of China, however, did not last long. To begin with, "united front" is a favorite strategy of the Communist Party. Simply put, with this strategy, the Communist Party seeks to form coalitions with other forces in order to establish its existence while it is still weak; then it takes the first opportunity to capture the initiative and ruthlessly purge all its former partners. There is, in fact, no knowing how many social democrats were victimized in this way in the course of the Russian Revolution. While this may strike you as a cold and heartless strategy, Communist principles hold that anything is justified as long as it serves the cause of the revolution. Communist Party theorists, however, have a habit of explaining everything theoretically, inadvertently revealing even their hidden intentions. This happened, for example, when police under the command of Zhang Zuolin raided the Russian embassy in Beijing and found a Comintern directive. Seeing that directive, Chiang decided to purge the Communist elements in Guangdong in March 1926 in order to guard his rear before launching the Northern Expedition. This marked the end of the First United Front.

In July 1926, only two years after the establishment of the Whampoa Military Academy, Chiang Kai-shek launched the Northern Expedition with eight armies, or a total of 100,000 troops. The opposing Beiyang Army forces, including Wu Peifu, far exceeded Chiang's army in terms of troop strength, and they took advantage of their numerical superiority to put up respectable resistance everywhere they met Chiang's army. Nevertheless, Chiang's army under the competent command of Whampoa Military Academy graduates continued to win fierce battle after fierce battle, gaining public support for the well-disciplined soldiers. In major cities, labor union support contributed to easy victories for Chiang's revolutionary army, which seized Shanghai and Suzhou in March 1927 and gained general control of the Yangtze River basin before finally making a triumphant entry into Nanjing.

Nanjing Incident of 1927

It was at this point that the Nanjing Incident happened. The following explanation of the background relies mainly on Shidehara's memoir. He wrote, "The Northern Expedition army entered Hankou in 1927, where large posters welcoming Borodin were found everywhere. Not a single poster welcomed Chiang Kai-shek." The Communist Party of China, which had fled Guangdong to escape Chiang's anti-Communist coup, and the left-wing faction of the Kuomintang entered Wuhan ahead of Chiang's army and established a joint Kuomintang-Communist Party government there. Mikhail Borodin, who had been a Russian advisor to Sun Yat-sen in Guangdong during the First United Front, became the representative of the Wuhan government and confronted Chiang's anti-Communist government. Shidehara continued:

> When Borodin insisted in his speech, "We must fundamentally reform China," the Chinese public in the audiences jeered, "Who's this 'we' he's talking about? He looks like a Caucasian and behaves as if he were an emperor." When the Japanese consul in Hankou reported on this episode to the foreign ministry in Tokyo, I thought it could be the beginning of Borodin's failure and downfall. I started paying closer attention to developments in China.

This was, indeed, a shrewd observation. As Shidehara predicted, Russia's role in the Chinese revolution turned out to be short-lived; instead, the Kuomintang and the Communist Party of China assumed the initiative. Shidehara refrained from referring to the threat of Soviet Communism and stuck to his non-interference principle—that is, leaving Chinese domestic politics to the Chinese people. This decision showed that, in addition to being faithful to his own principle, Shidehara understood the Chinese people's nationalism and the limits to Russian influence. Although Chiang's army was powerful enough to defeat Wuhan if it wished, Chiang headed for Nanjing instead, deliberately avoiding a showdown with his former comrades. As Shidehara wrote:

> Subsequently, Chiang Kai-shek's army went down the Yangtze River and entered Nanjing. Being a mixed bag of hastily trained soldiers and Communist elements, this army committed violent acts and looting whenever it found a foreign resident. One or two British and American residents were murdered. Fortunately, no Japanese residents were killed, although the Japanese residents too were thoroughly robbed just like all the other foreign residents.

This was what the Nanjing Incident was all about. While a certain amount of violence and looting is more or less inevitable when an army seizes a city, it appeared that there was some intentional riotous conduct planned by the Communist elements in the case of the Nanjing Incident. The head of political affairs of the 6th Army of the Kuomintang National Revolutionary Army, which entered Nanjing, was a member of the Communist Party. He had been allegedly instructed by Borodin to deliberately cause friction with the Western powers by assaulting foreign residents there, because this would create problems for Chiang. Chiang's personal memoir also recorded the incident as a conspiracy by the Communist Party. Having conjectured the Communist Party's intention from what had happened in Hankou and Nanjing, Chiang immediately ordered National Revolution Army Chief of Staff Bai Chongxi to foil the Communist Party's scheme of an all-out revolt in Shanghai, thus preventing Shanghai from falling into Communist hands. When the Nanjing Incident subsided, Chiang imposed a purge on the 6th Army and executed all of those who had been involved in assaulting foreign residents.

On the Nanjing Incident, Shidehara continued:

When the Incident occurred, there were three gunboats moored in the port on the Yangtze River. Hearing that their nationals had been killed, British and American gunboats bombarded what was judged to be a Chiang stronghold for about an hour. The Japanese gunboat alone did not join the salvo.

Some in Japan spread the rumor that it was Foreign Minister Shidehara who issued the directive prohibiting the Japanese gunboat from firing. Needless to point out, I was in no position to command a military ship. Having learnt earlier that a large number of Japanese settlers had been massacred in Nikolayevsk-on-Amur in 1920 at the time of the Japanese troop dispatch to Siberia, I feared riotous behavior by Chiang's army might escalate to threaten the lives of the Japanese residents if the Japanese gunboat fired its guns,. I thus pleaded with the captain of the gunboat to refrain from opening fire. This must have been unbearable for him, but he nevertheless willingly agreed to do as I asked. I was told later that the captain simply refrained from giving the order to fire, never confiding his decision to any of his crew. That was why younger officers misunderstood and thought I had ordered him to hold fire. As a result, I was the focus of Japanese resentment.

This is no doubt a very accurate description of what really took place. It was indeed unthinkable for such a competent ex-bureaucrat as Shidehara to inadvertently interfere with such a controversial affair as the command authority. Also, while it might have been possible to evacuate British and American residents, who were fewer in number, to a specific spot, a sole gunboat could not possibly have defended all the Japanese residents. The captain's conduct was, therefore, well justified. But there were unfortunate incidents, including a Japanese navy lieutenant who was assaulted by the mob at the Japanese consulate together with some Japanese settlers. Complying with his captain's order, this navy lieutenant did not resist the mob and endured the humiliation of the moment. But finding the humiliation unbearable as an Imperial Navy officer, this young officer disemboweled himself upon his return to the gunboat. Public opinion in Japan was outraged at this incident.

China's Multiple Hearts

To continue with Shidehara's memoir:

> Hearing of the massacre and looting in Nanjing by Chiang Kai-shek's army, foreign missions in Beijing immediately convened a conference to discuss what diplomatic actions to take. Their quick reaction notwithstanding, they could not figure out whom they should negotiate with because there was no such thing as a central government in China. The sphere of influence of Zhang Zuolin, who controlled Beijing at that time, was confined to northern China and Manchuria. His authority did not extend to central and southern China. After proposals and counterproposals, the conference decided to issue an ultimatum to Chiang Kai-shek. It even decided on the wording of the ultimatum.
>
> What the conference drafted was a severe denunciation of Chiang Kai-shek. The participating foreign missions decided that the ultimatum should be handed to Chiang Kai-shek after their home countries had endorsed it. The ultimatum would be followed immediately by military action.
>
> As soon as I received the telegraph from the Japanese minister

stationed in Beijing asking for instructions, I invited the British and American ambassadors to separate meetings at the Foreign Ministry and told them, "While we have no intention of interfering with what your government is going to do about this ultimatum, I wish to have your government's full understanding as far as the position of the Japanese government is concerned. What will Chiang Kai-shek do when he receives this ultimatum? In my judgment, he only has two options: he can either accept it or he can reject it. If he accepts the ultimatum, he will most certainly be criticized for cowardly compromising and for humiliating China. Since Chiang has not yet consolidated his position inside China, his government might well be toppled under a salvo of criticism from younger revolutionaries. This would lead to a state of further disorder in China. Given the relatively small number of settlers from your country, it would not be too difficult to evacuate all of your settlers in the event of political disorder. Japan, however, has more than one hundred thousand settlers there, and it would be simply impossible to transfer all of them to a safe haven. Even if Japan decided to dispatch troops immediately, it would still be some time before the Japanese soldiers actually reached Nanjing. Meanwhile, it is inevitable that a number of Japanese settlers would be assaulted and robbed.

If, on the other hand, Chiang Kai-shek adamantly rejects the ultimatum, Britain and the United States would probably have no choice but to jointly dispatch troops to penalize Chiang with firepower. But I must urge you to exercise caution when dispatching your troops. Every country has only one heart like a man, except China, which seems to have multiple hearts. If a country has only one heart, the entire country will be paralyzed when this heart is crushed. Since China has multiple hearts, however, its heartbeat will not be arrested even if one heart is crushed, and it is utterly impossible to crush all of its hearts all at once. There is thus no knowing how long it would take for Britain or the United States to accomplish its objective if you adopt an adventurist policy and try to conquer China militarily.

Shidehara's characterization of China as having multiple hearts was reported back to the US government by its ambassador to Japan and found its way into the State Department record.

As a matter of fact, the Japanese military during the Second Sino-Japanese War (1937–45) first thought the war would be over when Nanjing fell. When this did not happen, the Japanese then became convinced that the fall of Wuhan would end the war. History shows, however, that Japan was defeated before its troops reached Chongqing, China's third heart. It is astounding that Shidehara accurately predicted the difficulty of dealing with China already at the time of the Nanjing Incident in 1927. Moreover, his prediction was far more accurate than those by British and American China experts. In Japan, some criticized Shidehara as having only been stationed in Western countries and lacking experience in China. For the most part, this criticism was rooted in jealousy, because postings to the Western countries were then the fast track for a diplomat.

Why, then, was he able to foresee the situation in China so accurately? The only possible answer to this question seems to be Shidehara's sincere attitude toward learning—that he must have earnestly and objectively, but somewhat relaxedly, observed and studied the situation in China. On the basis of his analysis, Shidehara told the British and American ambassadors:

> Prolonged disorder in China may do little harm to Britain or the United States. Having great interests in China, however, Japan finds it unacceptable to take part in such an adventure. Japan will not sign the joint ultimatum toward China. This is my final decision, and I hope you will be good enough to convey my analysis and conclusion to your home governments.

Sanctions against China would be ineffective if Japan, China's closest neighbor and the most powerful regional military, would not participate. Thus the idea of issuing an ultimatum came to naught. Shidehara concluded this chapter of his memoir:

> At the same time, I tried to advise Chiang Kai-shek via a mutual acquaintance. I did this as an individual rather than as foreign minister of Japan. I had my acquaintance suggest Chiang consult the Western powers at the earliest opportunity and eliminate the causes of the conflict in a single stroke, making reparations for the damage his forces had caused and apologizing for the wrongdoings. It

appears that he understood my true intention because he did exactly as I had advised. It was after Chiang's negotiations with the Western powers were settled that Japan belatedly joined the effort to deal with the aftermath of the Nanjing Incident, making Chiang punish offenders and pay reparations.

Behind the subtle expression of the "belatedly joined the effort" was the delay caused by the complications in Sino-Japanese relations at the time of the Tanaka Giichi cabinet. That cabinet succeeded the Wakatsuki Reijirō cabinet in which Shidehara had served as foreign minister. The essence of Shidehara Diplomacy becomes clear when one compares his handling of the Nanjing Incident's aftermath with the Tanaka government's handling of the Jinan Incident in 1928.

Formation of the Tanaka Giichi Cabinet

It was the handling of the aftermath of the Nanjing Incident that agitated Japanese public opinion so much as to eventually bring Shidehara Diplomacy to an end. When Prime Minister Katō Takaaki died of an illness, Wakatsuki Reijirō succeeded him and kept his cabinet without any reshuffle. But the Wakatsuki cabinet fell in April 1927, one month after the Nanjing Incident, leading to the formation of the Seiyūkai cabinet headed by Tanaka Giichi. The direct cause of the Wakatsuki government's downfall was the Shōwa financial crisis of 1927. Triggered by an inadvertent reference to the failure of the Watanabe Bank by Finance Minister Kataoka Naoharu on March 14, ten days prior to Chiang Kai-shek's army's triumphant entry to Nanjing, a run began on those smaller banks that were the subject of bankruptcy rumors. By April, talk had expanded to include even Suzuki Shōten, one of the zaibatsu in those days, and the Bank of Taiwan. The situation was so critical that the Japanese government found it imperative to issue an extraordinary imperial ordinance to salvage the Bank of Taiwan. This is equivalent to bailing out a bank with taxpayer money. Under the Meiji Constitution, the issuance of an extraordinary imperial ordinance called for consultation with the Privy Council. The Council, however, rejected the plea for the extraordinary imperial ordinance, forcing the Wakatsuki cabinet to resign.

While the handling of the financial crisis appeared to be the cause of the fall of the Wakatsuki cabinet, it is reported that most of the deliberations at the Privy Council were devoted to criticism of the Wakatsuki cabinet's China policy, with a particular focus on the Nanjing Incident. Particularly vocal was Itō Miyoji, counselor to the Privy Council, who took the initiative in denouncing Shidehara Diplomacy. Itō's denunciation can be summarized as follows.

The policy of non-resistance has only damaged the prestige of the Empire of Japan, depressed the morale of the military, and endangered the life and property of Japanese nationals in China. While the Kuomintang revolutionary movement appears to expand to northern China, it should be noted that the Communist forces of the Comintern are behind this development. The Wakatsuki government badly misunderstands the situation.

In the course of the deliberations, Itō made the totally groundless accusation that the Foreign Ministry had banned newspaper articles on the Nanjing Incident lest the people know the truth. He even used the vulgar metaphor "The husband is always the last to know" in the presence of the emperor. Hearing this, Shidehara passed a memo to Wakatsuki to obtain his approval to speak up and reproached Itō, saying, "How dare you slander the Foreign Ministry with this lie in the presence of His Imperial Majesty." Unable to argue back in front of the emperor, Itō confronted Shidehara furiously after the conference as if he were about to assault him. For his part, Shidehara rolled up his sleeves preparing for a fist fight. It took the people around them to separate the two.

Because its plea for the extraordinary imperial ordinance was rejected by the Privy Council, the Wakatsuki cabinet resigned the same day. In accordance with the standard constitutional government procedure, Tanaka Giichi, president of the opposition Seiyūkai party, received an Imperial mandate to form the next cabinet. Since Shidehara was already a member of the House of Peers by that time, he continued to participate in national politics in that capacity after resigning as foreign minister.

Tanaka Giichi, a First-Rate Common Man

What kind of person, one may wonder, was Tanaka Giichi? Post–World War II leftist historians criticize him harshly. In retrospect, it must be admitted that the historical interpretation that the arbitrary conduct of the Japanese military clique that led Japan to ruin began during the Tanaka cabinet is justified. This has been the major cause of criticism of Tanaka Giichi. However, that situation should be interpreted as an unintended turn of events, not at all what Tanaka intended, rather than the intended consequence of Tanaka's policies.

Looking first at the objective facts, Tanaka was a bright and highly competent hope from the Chōshū *han*. The Meiji government sent him to study in Russia and he was invited to discuss Russia policy with none other than Itō Hirobumi when he returned home, even though he was a mere army major. It is said that Tanaka was also a favorite of Yamagata Aritomo, another Meiji giant, and the Imperial Army appointed him its liaison with Yamagata. This does not mean, however, that Tanaka was particularly good at winning Yamagata's favor. Shōwa political commentator Hosokawa Ryūgen observed:

> When advocating what he believed in, Tanaka paid no heed to the status of the person he was addressing. He would not shy away from having a heated argument even with Yamagata Aritomo in order to make his point. It was Tanaka's straightforwardness and his earnest study of any subject before taking a stance that Yamagata admired.

When he felt he had to stick to his convictions, Tanaka had sufficient discretion and self-confidence to ignore how he would be regarded.

Having observed the lack of trust between aristocratic officers and commoner soldiers in the Russian army, Tanaka feared the Imperial Japanese Army might have a similar weakness. To avoid this pitfall, he volunteered to command the Third Infantry Regiment himself and applied experimental officer/soldier education as he saw fit with the special permission of the divisional commander. Prohibiting physical punishment as doing "no good and much harm," he ordered officers to treat each and every subordinate with affection and tender care, except during military drills, which must be severe. There was one problem soldier in Tanaka's regiment: a socialist whom nobody knew how to handle. Tanaka took the trouble of training this soldier personally whenever he found time, transforming him into a model soldier in the end. While it is regrettable that Tanaka's teachings failed to take root among the Japanese officer corps, this episode nevertheless points to his original thinking. It was because Takahashi Korekiyo, who succeeded Hara Takashi as president of the Seiyūkai, had such a high regard for Tanaka's discretion that he handed the party presidency to Tanaka.

Because the Hara Takashi cabinet had inherited a massive long-term military plan from the Terauchi Masatake cabinet, Finance Minister Takahashi had a hard time drawing up a budget for the coming fiscal year. In the end, Takahashi invited both Navy Minister Katō Tomosaburō and War Minister Tanaka Giichi to his office and said,

> Both army and navy are proposing grand schemes. Do you both really need to do all of this simultaneously? Shouldn't there be priorities in terms of urgency and importance? Would you please consider what I have said not as war and navy ministers but as ministers for military affairs or ministers for state affairs?

While Katō remained silent, Tanaka readily backed off, saying, "Navy's plan should be given the priority, since it is bound to be restricted by the service life of a warship. I understand that the navy's plan is to be completed in 1927, so we can wait until then to launch our own plan." Ever since this exchange, Takahashi greatly admired Tanaka as a person. Anyone who knows even a little about the bureaucratic world cannot help but marvel at Tanaka's magnanimity. A bureaucrat or a minister who can make such a courageous remark at such a critical moment appears only once every few decades. It takes someone who has full confidence in his own judgment and knows that the respect and trust of his subordinates will not be affected no matter what he decides. Tanaka was also a heavyweight financially, raising so much money as to become a target of scandal rumors. He distributed the funds lavishly. Nevertheless, he never enriched himself personally, and when he passed away, his family was left with only his debts. On this point, Tanaka was distinct from the average postwar Japanese politician, to say nothing of the plutocrats.

It is undeniable that, among pre–World War II prime ministers starting with Hara Takashi all the way to Tōjō Hideki, Tanaka was a first-rate leader in terms of his competence, insight, breadth as a man, and leadership. When it comes to his political ideology, however, his was nothing more or less than an ordinary common-sense Japanese longing for the Empire to prosper. He was not an advocate of imperialist expansion, like Komura, nor was he an ultra-nationalist or a militarist. In the sense that he was a realist and a man of common sense in his pursuit of imperialist policies, Tanaka was, indeed, a product of Taishō Democracy. It was this lack of any particular political conviction, other than a vague patriotism, that enabled Tanaka to get along with Hara Takashi's anti-militarism. Nor did he feel particularly uncomfortable when Japanese public opinion later made a right turn as a reaction to Shidehara diplomacy. Simply put, he was just an ordinary Japanese citizen as far as his politics were concerned. Some people are uncommonly capable in dealing with day-to-day problems but show little, if any, interest in larger, historical, long-term issues. They are first-rate people, but they are never insightful statesmen. I believe Tanaka was one such person.

Mori Kaku, a Product of Imperialism

It was Mori Kaku, Parliamentary Vice Minister for Foreign Affairs in the Tanaka Giichi cabinet, who led its policies in the direction of the new Shōwa militarism. At first, Tanaka had considered appointing Honda Kumatarō, the most avid critic of Shide-hara Diplomacy among the Japanese diplomats, foreign minister. But because it appeared Honda's appointment would not have the full support of the foreign ministry, Tanaka decided to serve concurrently as foreign minister himself and appointed Mori Kaku of the Seiyūkai vice minister for foreign affairs. Tanaka did not necessarily have a high opinion of Mori's personality or insight, but Mori turned out to be quite a competent asset, and he skillfully managed the Tanaka cabinet's foreign policy as its

Mori Kaku (photo courtesy of Kyodo News)

de facto foreign minister. It thus seems worthwhile spending a few paragraphs on the person of Mori Kaku.

Simply put, he was a typical Japanese nationalist in the pre–World War II era of militarism. Mori embodied the ideal characteristics of a Japanese man as commonly cherished in the minds of Japanese boys and girls before and during World War II. This is why I believe it is meaningful to create a record of what kind of person Mori was before witnesses to this prewar history perish. It is said that, when he was in junior high school, Mori spent every spare moment looking at the world atlas. Staring at the atlas, he and his friends worked out plans to make the Pacific Ocean Japanese territorial waters. In a letter he wrote when he was seventeen, he said, "If you wish to know my intention, read the section on the great enterprise in chapter 6 of *Ukishiro monogatari*." *Ukishiro monogatari*, or tale of the floating castle, is an adventure novel written by Yano Ryūkei and published in 1890. To summarize the great enterprise section:

> Do you not know of the hero who, with the help of only 300 Cossacks, conquered Siberia and dedicated it to the Russian tsar? Do you not know, either, of the man who put the majority of the Indian subcontinent under his control with a miniscule trading company?
>
> How dare the Westerners behave so outrageously! If they are allowed to act so insolently, what prevents us from seizing masterless lands and conquering countries that are too weak to govern themselves? International law is but an argument and it is not a law.
>
> We are about to advance to all corners of the earth to conquer uninhabited lands and obtain great territories that are tens of times as large as Japan and dedicate them to His Imperial Majesty. . . If Japan is unable to maintain these territories for some reason, we are willing to become their kings ourselves.

Those were the days when such terms such as "world domination" inspired many young people.

Longing to do something in China, Mori joined Mitsui & Co., Ltd. upon graduation from university and ended up spending a total of seven years, including his time as an apprentice, in Shanghai, during which he studied rigorously, including mastering the English and Chinese languages. When his treatise based on his experiences in Changsha was published in the monthly *Chūō Kōron*, it attracted the attention of Minister of War Tera-uchi Masaki, who took the trouble of phoning the president of Mitsui & Co., Masuda Takashi, to tell him how impressed he was with the treatise. Ordered by Masuda to return to Tokyo temporarily, Mori, at the tender age of 26, was invited to dinner by the war minister. There, accompanied by Masuda, Mori freely expressed his views on Japanese China policy. While this may appear highly irregular in today's context, it seems to show that the ancient Oriental kings' traditional willingness to travel thousands of miles to seek the counsel of a wise man was still alive.

Although Mori was subsequently stationed in New York temporarily, he soon returned to Shanghai. The Xinhai Revolution erupted, and Mori worked hard to support the revolutionaries. Mori made an arbitrary deci-sion to gift the revolutionaries 150,000 yen. This was at a time when Count Inoue Kaoru, then advisor to Mitsui & Co., as well as Japan's Ministry of Foreign Affairs, were opposing the revolutionary forces. It was a Mitsui & Co. house rule that expenditures in excess of 100,000 yen from the secret budget required top management approval. When Masuda reprimanded Mori for exceeding his authority with his arbitrary conduct, Mori elo-quently expounded on the situation in China rather than being intimidated. He even declared, "it would benefit Japan eternally for Mitsui, and there-fore the Empire of Japan, to acquire concessions in the Yangtze River basin when the revolution is accomplished." Although Masuda had to reprove Mori at that time, he was later heard to say, "While the company may have lost 150,000 yen in Shanghai, I made a lucky find. That Mori is a hell of a man!" Subsequently, Masuda became a prime advocate for the acquisition of concessions in China. Rumor has it that he even plotted to acquire Man-churia. This appeared to mark the beginning of Mitsui's support for the Chinese revolution. As a Mitsui advance force, so to speak, Mori continued to establish numerous new companies in China. Needless to say, however, Mori's true aim from the beginning was to serve the country. As such, he had no intention of remaining with Mitsui & Co. Ltd. forever.

He joined the Seiyūkai in 1918 when he was 36 years old. Resigning from Mitsui & Co. in April 1920, he successfully ran for a seat in the House of Representatives in May. From that time on, Mori steadily estab-lished his presence within the party and became the parliamentary vice minister for foreign affairs, which was de facto the foreign minister, in 1927, Secretary-General of the Seiyūkai in 1929, and Chairman of the Seiyūkai General Council in 1930. When the Inukai Tsuyoshi cabinet was formed in 1931, Mori was appointed chief cabinet clerk (equivalent to today's chief cabinet secretary). Throughout his career, Mori had the full opportunity to engage in state affairs as a powerful Seiyūkai figure until his death in 1932 at the age of 50. Mori was a pioneer and the harbinger of Japanese militarism, both in name and in substance.

Comintern vs. Chinese Nationalism

When the Jinan Incident erupted in 1928, even elements within the Imperial Army hesitated at first to send troops to Shandong. Prime Minister Tanaka himself could not make up his mind. Facing this indecisiveness, Mori high-handedly forced the cabinet to decide on the troop dispatch. He threatend Tanaka, saying that if the government could not decide to send troops, the Seiyūkai would adopt doing so as a party decision and force Tanaka to resign as Seiyūkai president should he defy the party decision. Although Mori's childhood dream was to conquer the world, he was very much a realist, unlike the later militarists, when it came to actual foreign and military policies. After all, he, too, a member of the Seiyūkai party, a Hara Takashi legacy, and was in that sense a child of Taishō Democracy. Regarding the naval reduction agreed at the Washington Naval Conference, Mori said:

> There is no way Japan can compete with the United States in an arms race. To begin with, any confrontation with the United States would deprive Japan of its market for Japanese silk as well as its supply of raw cotton, the consequences of which would be simply horrifying. Japan was fortunate in having such an insightful statesman as Hara Takashi, who managed to maintain bilateral cooperation by compromising where he could but standing firm on the uncompromisable. This enabled Japan to reduce its military budget and put government finances in order.

This highly sensible assessment reveals Mori's background as a visionary businessman. As far as China policy was concerned, Mori was supportive of the territorial integrity, open-door, and equal opportunity policies at the time of the Washington Naval Conference. But he added, "In order for China to maintain its territorial integrity, China itself will have to become more prosperous, which it cannot do single-handedly. It will be imperative China draw on capital and technology from the more advanced nations." This was also an observation based on Mori's experience doing business in China. To be sure, Mori at that time shared Shidehara's view that, given an equal opportunity, Japan would be in the most advantageous position vis-à-vis China in terms of geography as well as past experience. Mori acquired this self-confidence in the course of doing business in China.

What Mori was apprehensive about and criticized Shidehara for was the erosion of Japan's advantageous position in the face of Communism's expansion in China. Mori was thus at the forefront of criticizing the Shidehara Diplomacy. In a Diet session in 1926, he demanded Prime Minister Wakatsuki clarify his position vis-à-vis Russia's influence in China, quoting a monthly *Gaikō jihō* treatise written by Kawakami Toshihiko. In essence, Kawakami's treatise argued "The spread of Russian influence in China today is no different from the situation in China on the eve of the Russo-Japanese War, even though the form of penetration is quite different." Mori stood in the Diet, asking:

> Although I requested Foreign Minister Shidehara's response to this view, he has not provided me with a clear-cut answer. Moreover, he retorted by claiming, "Russia is a nation friendly to Japan and is not an enemy. There have been some rumors about Russian conduct, but there is no concrete evidence. It would be dangerous to formulate a policy based on vague conjecture." What does the prime minister have to say about this?

In 1927, Mori visited China with Yamamoto Jōtarō and Matsuoka Yōsuke to observe the situation there. Yamamoto was Secretary-General of the Seiyūkai at that time, but he had been Mori's superior at Mitsui & Co. and was a kindred spirit for Mori. Matsuoka later became Vice President of the South Manchurian Railway Company under President Yamamoto. The visit to China was a trip by a trio of like-minded people. After returning home, Mori spoke about his trip at Kōjunsha, the first business executives club in Japan, three weeks before he was appointed parliamentary vice minister for foreign affairs in the Tanaka government. He devoted almost half of his speech to the Comintern's influence in the Chinese revolutionary movement. Pointing out that it was the Russian-backed Comintern that was behind the revolutionary movement in China, he warned that, left untouched, Chinese unification would be accomplished with the help of the Comintern, instead of Japan, within a few years.

Today, seventy years later, it is still unsettled whether it was Shidehara or Mori who made the more accurate judgment. Shidehara's judgment that Borodin's attempt would fail because Chinese nationalism was more influential than the Comintern was an accurate observation of the situation in China at that time. In fact, Chiang Kai-shek's Kuomintang took the lead in the revolution in no time and almost succeeded in unifying China. Taking a longer view, however, the Kuomintang was, in the end, defeated by the Communists' united front strategy, putting China under the control of the Communist Party and paving the way for a Sino-Soviet monolith. While this was exactly what Mori had predicted, the Chinese Communist Party was soon at odds with the Soviet Union and China became a nationalistic socialist country. Taking this, too, into consideration, one must say that Shidehara's judgment that the essence of the Chinese revolution was nationalism was an accurate one. Depending on the timeframe one prefers, both Mori and Shidehara can be judged to have been correct. While a longer-term judgment is generally believed to be more accurate, given the limited life span of a man, a more limited timeframe may be applied in assessing the accuracy of predictions. After all, it would have been no comfort for the Carthaginians to learn that the Roman Empire fell 1,600 years after their own ruin.

Mori concluded his Kōjunsha speech with the following argument.

Finally, I would like to add that the interests that the Japanese have established in the Yangtze River basin over the past twenty years have been fundamentally eroded, making it impossible for the Japanese settlers to continue their lives there. This has been caused by the economic and political revolution in China, in line with which some elements among the Chinese population intend to deliberately ruin the Japanese settlers . . . Although the Japanese government suggests that the settlers should put up with some inconveniences, it is cruel to demand that they put up with the hardship they are suffering with no end in sight.

It was Mori himself who had taken the initiative in establishing concessions in the Yangtze River basin. That these concessions were like candles flickering in the wind must have been an accurate description of the situation there. From the vantage point of an ex-businessman, the situation in China was much harsher than it appeared to Shidehara. It should be pointed out, however, that it was Chinese nationalism, not the Comintern or "some elements among the Chinese population" as Mori claimed, that was responsible for the situation. And it was the clash between this Chinese nationalism and Japan's vested interests in China that soon eroded the foundation of Shidehara Diplomacy and eventually led to the Manchurian Incident.

CHAPTER

12

Tanaka Diplomacy and Chinese Nationalism

—The Adverse Impact of Zhang Zuolin's Assassination—

The First Shandong Expedition

The Tanaka Giichi cabinet was launched in the midst of the Shōwa financial crisis of 1927. Prime Minister Tanaka appointed Takahashi Korekiyo finance minister to manage the financial crisis. Although Takahashi had been the president of the Seiyūkai prior to Tanaka and was a former prime minister, he willingly accepted the appointment so that he could deal with the crisis. Nobody in those days doubted Takahashi's knowledge of and insight into monetary and financial affairs. His appointment had a reassuring, calming effect on the Japanese public. In the end, the crisis was somehow brought under control with injections of funds from the government. The amount exceeded that suggested in the Wakatsuki cabinet's relief proposal, which had been crippled by the Privy Council's earlier rejection, which powerfully indicates that the Wakatsuki government's fall was more attributable to the climate of the times—which was critical of Shidehara Diplomacy—than to the cabinet's failure to tackle the financial crisis effectively.

Japan was still in the midst of the Taishō Democracy era, and people's general preference at that time was pacifism and international cooperation. Criticism of Shidehara Diplomacy did not necessarily derive from

Japanese imperialist and expansionist desires. Rather, it came more from the Japanese residents in China and the business sectors in both China and Japan who felt that their interests were threatened. In January 1927, the Sino-Japanese Business Association and the United Council of Osaka Spinning Companies issued a joint statement, saying, "If Japan cannot persuade the Western powers to jointly dispatch troops to suppress the irrational conduct of the Chinese, Japan should go it alone." After the Nanjing Incident of 1927, the Japan Chamber of Commerce in Shanghai made a hard-line proposal that the Imperial Japanese Army dispatch troops to China. Because this proposal was derived from the Chamber's urgent need to defend the lives and property of its members and their families, it aroused sympathy among the Japanese people. It was against this background that the Tanaka cabinet was formed. Since Tanaka had been criticizing Shidehara's weak-kneed diplomacy, his cabinet naturally departed from the principle of non-intervention Shidehara advocated and adopted a platform of protecting the Japanese residents in China.

The Nationalist Government of the Republic of China was established in Nanjing around the same time as the Tanaka cabinet was formed in April 1927. The Nationalist Government revolutionary army quickly started the Northern Expedition, hoping to put Beijing under siege. At the time, there were 1,600 Japanese residents in Beijing, 6,700 in Tianjin, 14,000 in Qingdao, and 2,000 in Jinan, these last two in Shandong on Chiang Kai-shek's Northern Expedition route. Japanese investments in these regions totaled 200 million yen. This situation made it imperative the Tanaka cabinet adopt a platform calling for protecting Japanese residents in China. Public opinion at that time, however, remained cautious. Finance Minister Takahashi was also hesitant to finance a troop deployment to China, given that the country was in the midst of trying to manage its financial crisis. Under the circumstances, the Tanaka cabinet decided to dispatch 2,000 troops to Qingdao from Lüshun (Port Arthur) instead of from Japan. When it formally notified the governments in Beijing, Nanjing, and Wuhan of the reason for the troops, the three governments strongly protested the Japanese action. Boycotts of Japanese products erupted in numerous locations in China, and some people started demanding economic ties with Japan be severed.

Chiang's Northern Expedition was effectively blocked by the Beiyang Army, and the Japanese troops soon returned to their original posts.

It became obvious at this point, however, that Chinese nationalism and the Japanese government's decision to protect Japanese residents in China were on a collision course. If the mere announcement of a troop deployment could cause such a commotion, it was patently obvious that a bloody incident—inevitable once the military started taking action—would quickly ignite Chinese nationalism.

This was only a prelude to the turmoil of the Shōwa era. If a similar situation occurred in Manchuria, however, the Japanese government would have no choice but to meet the expectations of the Japanese residents in the region by protecting them, which would inevitably put Japan on a collision course with China. Some intellectuals in China might have sympathized with Japan's policy and even have tried to protect Japan's interests if the Japanese government had stuck with the policy of non-interference and dampened down the demands for protecting Japanese residents in China. There was no knowing, however, whether the powerful surge of the campaign to restore Chinese sovereignty would have allowed such accommodative conduct. Unless both sides had been endowed with extraordinarily sensible diplomacy and the leadership needed to put it into action, they were destined to experience tragedy.

Far East Conference and the Tanaka Cabinet's China Policy

Tanaka was well aware that the situation was fraught with danger. The China policy that the Tanaka cabinet announced at the outset, both domestically and internationally, was by no means extreme. On the contrary, it was commonsense to indicate that the government was prepared to recognize the legitimate wishes of the Chinese people and to argue that there must be a way to satisfy those wishes without worsening the relations between China and the foreign powers. But it also announced that Japan could not remain unconcerned about the activities of the Communist Party of China.

In fact, all Japanese, except for a very few exceptions such as Shidehara, were worried about the Communist Party. According to Mori Kaku, Japanese interests in the Yangtze River basin had been obtained through the strenuous efforts of the Japanese residents there rather than by state or military power. Mori thought that those residents should continue what they had been doing, but he found this formula did not always work and detected the emergence of a new, unprecedented situation. It was understandable that he and the Japanese people attributed the new situation to Comintern activities. Actually, the source of the threat was Chinese nationalism, but there were enough reasons to blame the threat on the communists, and, in fact, most Japanese were convinced that the communists were to blame.

In later years, during the International Military Tribunal for the Far East (Tokyo War Crimes Tribunal) in 1946, the defense counsel argued, "Japan had good reason to fear that the spread of Communism in China would in time spread to Japan, eventually ruining the country. This was why Japan feared the advance of Communism in China." Quoting President Harry Truman's speech to Congress in which the president, at the outset of the Cold War, demanded an emergency measure to block the spread of Communism, the defense counsel argued that what Japan had done was essentially the same as the US response. In response, the prosecution demanded that this argument be stricken from the record. The defense counsel defended its position so skillfully that the odds appeared to be against the prosecution. It was at this point that William Webb, President of the International Military Tribunal for the Far East, said, "I will not tolerate an insult to any of the countries represented in the panel of eleven judges [i.e., any of the Allied Powers or, more specifically in this context, the Soviet Union]." This remark was tantamount to a blatant aversion to defying any of the victorious countries, regardless of any legal principles. Kojima Noboru has written in his *Tōkyō Saiban* (International Military Tribunal for the Far East) that President Webb's indiscretion prompted pained looks on the faces of participants throughout the courtroom.

Prime Minister Tanaka convened a conference of officials and Diet-members engaged in China affairs in order to thoroughly analyze and discuss developments in China. This conference became popularly known as the Tōhō Kaigi (Far East Conference). The Far East Conference was convened on June 27 and lasted eleven days. Prime Minister cum Foreign Minister Tanaka participated, as did Parliamentary Vice Minister for Foreign Affairs Mori, who served as co-chair of the conference. Senior officials attended from the ministries of foreign affairs, war, navy, and finance, as did Yoshizawa Kenkichi, Japanese Minister to China; consuls general stationed in various cities in China; the Governor-General of

Kwantung Leased Territory; and the commanding officer of the Kwantung Army. Ministers for finance, railways, education, home, and communications attended as observers. Mukden Consul General Yoshida Shigeru, who later became prime minister, also participated. Because the Manchurian issue was naturally a central item on the agenda, his remarks carried special weight in the discussion. Being a professional diplomat, Yoshida kept his formal remarks moderate and impartial. Taking into consideration his words and deeds around the time of the conference, however, it is not difficult to read between the lines. What Yoshida really wanted to emphasize was that Japan had to manage Manchuria using its own strengths and policies instead of relying on Zhang Zuolin for its protection. As such, Yoshida's stance was actually in line with that of the most radical faction among the conference participants. When Yoshida met with Mori Kaku prior to the conference, they instantly recognized they were kindred spirits. Yoshida wrote to Makino Nobuaki, his father-in-law, saying, "We found ourselves in complete agreement concerning Japan's China policy." During the Far East Conference, Yoshida and Mori communicated secretly between themselves. Some believe that these two were the behind-the-scenes leaders of the conference.

Nevertheless, and contrary to what Mori and his comrades had intended, the Far East Conference did not result in any fundamental change in the conventional policies toward China. On July 7, the last day of the conference, Prime Minister cum Foreign Minister Tanaka proposed the Outline of Policies on China, but the document's substance was mostly moderate and reasonable. The major difference between the Outline and Shidehara diplomacy is to be found in the unpublicized Article 7, which stated that the Japanese government would support pro-Japanese leaders in Manchuria. In Article 8, the Outline stated, "Should political upheavals reach Manchuria and Mongolia, disturbing public order and threatening Japan's special positions and interests in these regions, the Japanese government will protect them regardless of the source of the threat." It should be pointed out that Shidehara had no argument with the need to protect Japan's special interests in Manchuria and Mongolia. The only difference was his emphasis on their protection through peaceful diplomacy. If and when those interests were violated by force, not even Shidehara would have opposed taking counter-measures.

Prime Minister Tanaka's Memorandum to the Emperor

Despite its lukewarm content, the Far East Conference had a great impact for the image it projected. With Japan in deep economic recession, the Japanese people were fervently longing for social reform, and the Japanese residents in China felt uneasy about Shidehara Diplomacy. Against this background, Mori Kaku loudly announced at the Far East Conference that the time was ripe for the Seiyūkai government to develop new Asian policies. While this announcement inspired and encouraged some in Japan, it also provoked suspicion in China and among the foreign powers concerning Japan's new imperialist policy. It is said that Tanaka secretly submitted a memorandum to the emperor reporting on Japanese policy immediately after the Far East Conference. But it was a mysterious document; no original has been found anywhere in Japan, and it exists only in a Chinese translation published by a Chinese daily newspaper. Scholars today are generally agreed that the "translation" was a fabrication. Still, it depicted a plan for Japan to initially conquer Manchuria and Mongolia, then all of China, then all of Asia, and, eventually, the entire world. Anyone with any experience in intelligence could see at a glance that the document was a fake. The document was akin to the so-called Hong Kong Intelligence, a series of misinformation reports that was circulated during the Cold War when Hong Kong was the intelligence center for inside knowledge on China, including such fake stories as secret directives by Mao Tse-tung. But the purported Tanaka memorandum to the Emperor was a cleverly designed document used to warn of Japan's ambition and the Japanese threat. Forged specifically for this purpose, it was widely cited all over the world, including, not surprisingly, in China.

As a matter of fact, Tanaka's China policy was not as grandiose or megalomaniacal as the Tanaka memorandum depicted. It was much more pragmatic and realistic. On July 19, Tanaka appointed Yamamoto Jōtarō president and Matsuoka Yōsuke vice-president of the South Manchuria Railway Company. Although Yamamoto had already been a heavyweight at the cabinet level by then, having served as Seiyūkai secretary-general, Tanaka talked him into accepting the appointment. It was said that it took Tanaka's mastery of personnel matters to make Yamamoto, and earlier Finance Minister Takahashi, agree to appointments that were clearly below their levels. Takahashi was indifferent to fame and wealth, while

Yamamoto had long aspired to manage Manchuria and Mongolia, which must have contributed to his acceptance of the appointment. The appointment of Mori Kaku as parliamentary vice minister for foreign affairs later haunted Tanaka, but it was a promotion of a man of unusual ability and achieved at least some success. These appointments indicated that Tanaka was indeed a first-rate person when it came to practical business, even though he may have lacked a philosophy.

Tanaka's scheme was a realistic one given the reality of Manchuria. It was based on Japan's reliance on Zhang Zuolin, whom Japan had long backed since his bandit days, to defend Manchuria and protect Japan's interests there. Realizing that Mori Kaku and Yoshida Shigeru's words and deeds had provoked Zhang's antipathy, Yamamoto asked Tanaka to rein them in. At the same time, Yamamoto laid the elaborate groundwork for reaching an agreement with Zhang on the construction of five railroads in Manchuria and Mongolia. Yamamoto's efforts included consultations with Zhang's close aides and a well-timed visit to Beijing in October during which Yamamoto met with Zhang three times in four days. Moreover, Yamamoto confided his plan to acquire the Chinese Eastern Railway, which was under Soviet control in those days, and run it jointly with China. Yamamoto showed commendable skill, which enabled him to make remarkable progress on some of the long-standing issues for Japan. Tanaka's Manchurian policy made steady progress as well. But Yamamoto and Tanaka's efforts went up in smoke within a year when Zhang was killed in an explosion. Hearing of Zhang's death, Tanaka said, "That is the end for me," while Yamamoto was heard to say, "I may as well pack up and go home."

Chiang Kai-shek's Second Northern Expedition

Chiang Kai-shek resigned as commander-in-chief of the National Revolutionary Army after the defeat in the grand battle in the summer of 1927. Chiang had become influential among Kuomintang leaders despite his youth due to his military success during the Northern Expedition. Knowing he would be the target of harsh criticism once he lost a battle, Chiang wisely resigned on his own initiative. His resignation was followed by a trip to Kobe in September to obtain Soong Ching-ling's permission to marry her daughter, Soong May-ling. Soong Ching-ling was a younger sister of Sun Yat-sen's widow. After getting the necessary approval, Chiang met Prime Minister Tanaka on November 5.

Their discussion was recorded in detail and has been interpreted in Japan as a record of good communication between the two sides. But it is important to read between the lines here because the Japanese record tends to emphasize China's agreement with the points Japan raised. When the other party says, "Although I basically agree with what you said," as the prelude to a carefully worded rebuttal, the Japanese record tends to keep the content of "what you said" in full—which essentially can be omitted or abbreviated—giving the impression the other party has agreed with the Japanese points. In fact, the Sankei newspaper's *Shō Kaiseki hiroku* (Secret memoirs of Chiang Kai-shek) says Chiang expressed disappointment with the meeting's outcome.

When the talks took place, Yamamoto had just reached an agreement with Zhang Zuolin in Beijing on the Manchurian railroads. Thus it was only natural for Tanaka to hope the stability of Zhang's Beiyang government would not be threatened, and he suggested Chiang first devote his efforts to unifying southern China instead of rushing into the Northern Expedition. While agreeing with Tanaka on the primacy of southern China's unification, which was a matter of course, Chiang responded by saying conditions in China were so unbearable for the Chinese people that, his own views aside, they felt obliged to stand up and work to unify the country. He went on to attribute the anti-Japanese movements rampant in China to Japan's support for Zhang Zuolin and concluded that the Manchuria/Mongolia issue would be easily settled once Japan stopped supporting warlords and started contributing to the Chinese revolution. It should have been obvious from this that Tanaka and Chiang were on a collision course. It was unthinkable that Tanaka, who intended to rely on Zhang to protect Japan's interests in Manchuria and Mongolia, would abandon Zhang and assist the National Revolutionary Army. After all, Chiang himself had to flee to Japan alone, having just sustained a crushing defeat by the Beiyang Army. It was truly beyond imagining at that time that this same Chiang would redouble his efforts to drive Zhang from Beijing in only half a year and succeed in unifying China. As a matter of fact, Chiang himself, when he set out for Japan, was thinking about studying in the West for five years or so.

Prior to meeting with Tanaka, however, Chiang had already received a telegram from Wang Jingwei of the Kuomintang urging him to return home immediately and resume his former post as commander-in-chief of the National Revolutionary Army. Immediately after his talk with Tanaka, Chiang returned to China to prepare for the second Northern Expedition. Largely staffed by graduates of the Whampoa Military Academy, the National Revolutionary Army was a modern military force compared to the other warlords' armies and its advantage in a normal battle was obvious. However, it had had to begin the previous Northern Expedition only half prepared due to the power struggle within the Kuomintang. But Chiang's situation was totally different this time. When Chiang resigned, it was obvious to all that the National Revolutionary Army had to have him as its supreme commander. That was a personal victory for Chiang. As a result, Chiang was able to set out on the second Northern Expedition in February 1928 leading a grand army that was no comparison to the previous one. The National Revolutionary Army advanced north gathering momentum every step of the way and reached the Shandong border by April. Given its oft-stated policy, the Tanaka cabinet then had to dispatch Japanese troops to fulfill its commitment to protect Japanese residents and interests in China.

Jinan Incident a Turning Point in Sino-Japanese Relations

Opinion on the troop deployment was divided even within the Imperial Japanese Army. By this time, it was obvious it was only a matter of time until Chiang made his triumphant entry to Beijing. It was only natural, given this situation, that some within the Japanese Army insisted that Japan should rely on Chiang to protect the Japanese residents and that this would allow Japan to minimize its own presence in China. Those who advocated troops be deployed cited the Nanjing Incident and emphasized that relying on Chiang, no matter how trustworthy he might be, would not be enough. They insisted that the policy of protecting Japanese residents and interests in China should be pursued as announced.

In the end, the decision was made to dispatch Japanese troops to China. Once the military is dispatched overseas, however, it tends to act according to its own logic. Although Chiang's army entered Jinan peacefully, there was small-scale friction with the Japanese residents there, which was inevitable given the lax discipline of Chinese troops at the time. Once clashes occured, the Japanese Army would not agree to a truce unless the Chinese side offered "conditions that would extol the Imperial Army's prestige and eradicate the roots of the problems." The home government had to respect this stance. This, in turn, ratcheted up the Japanese government's perception of the situation as "a golden opportunity to impose decisive chastisement on the opponent." The resultant all-out confrontation between the two armies then gave the Japanese side an excuse to dispatch reinforcements to conquer Shandong.

The Jinan Incident of 1928 turned out to be a major turning point in Sino-Japanese relations. Huang Fu, the pro-Japanese and mild-mannered foreign minister of the Nanjing government, was replaced by the very competent Anglophile Wang Zheng Ting, who, instead of consulting directly with Japan, chose to criticize Japan in such forums as the League of Nations and the Western mass media in order to isolate Japan internationally. In time, the Japanese army's conduct was suspected of being a deliberate attempt to block the northward advance of the National Revolutionary Army in order to assist the Zhang Zuolin government. This perception further worsened Chinese public opinion against Japan. While the anti-foreign movement in China had previously been mainly against Britain, Japan became the central target all of a sudden in the Jinan Incident's wake, a situation that lasted until Japan's defeat in World War II.

Japanese newspapers unanimously criticized the cruelty of Chinese soldiers. While some, including the *Jiji Shimpō*, pointed out that the troop dispatch had actually made things worse for the Japanese residents and called for more self-restraint regarding future deployments, this was a minority position. On the whole, Japanese newspapers demanded Chiang Kai-shek's army redress its inexcusable lack of discipline and its soldiers's cruel conduct.

Shidehara remained silent for about a year after the formation of the Tanaka cabinet, simply watching Tanaka's foreign policy unfold. In his private letters, however, Shidehara characterized Tanaka's Manchurian/ Mongolian policy as "appalling" and said, "While I always knew Tanaka was not a man of thoughtfulness or foresight, I did not know he was so devoid of common sense." In October 1928, Shidehara made an uncharacteristically long speech at Keio University titled *Gaikō kanken* (One man's views on foreign policy). In this speech, he harshly criticized Tanaka's diplomacy:

I do not think that the Japanese government originally intended to interfere in China's domestic politics by obstructing Chiang's Northern Expedition. If it had, it should have temporarily evacuated the Japanese residents to safe havens such as Qingdao. Instead, the Tanaka government, without any deep thought, abruptly decided to dispatch the Japanese troops to protect Japanese residents and interests in China. As a result, the government's financial burden has already soared to between 60 and 70 million yen and there have been hundreds of casualties among Japanese officers and soldiers. Moreover, not a few Japanese residents there have suffered looting, carnage, and rape at the hands of Northern Expedition soldiers. Although I hear that the Tanaka government is planning to withdraw the Japanese troops when the Kuomintang government becomes a little better organized, this sounds to me like an excuse for the failure to settle this issue so far.

The next year (1929, Shidehara spoke in the House of Peers deploring the situation:

At the time of the Nanjing Incident, Japan did not send any troops to China—and there were no casualties among the Japanese residents then. It is ironical that the Jinan Incident involved a number of casualties among the Japanese residents despite the dispatch of Japanese troops. The Tanaka government's China diplomacy has become a complete failure with this dispatch of troops to Shandong resulting in the fundamental destruction of the friendship with China that Japan had nurtured over many years.

The unification of China was undoubtedly a major event in the history of Asia in the twentieth century. The fact that it was not the more principled Shidehara foreign policy but the Tanaka foreign policy of catering to the nationalistic current in Japan that was in effect at this critical juncture had a major impact on Japan's subsequent fate. In the same Diet session, Shidehara noted: "The Tanaka government's failure is attributable, after all, to the neglect of authentic diplomacy and to the penchant for changing direction freely for domestic political and party reasons."

One of the causes for the rightward tilt in Japanese diplomacy in the early Shōwa years was undeniably the Seiyūkai's pursuit of party interests—i.e., its attempts to improve its own standing versus the Minsei-tō party by denouncing and attacking Minsei-tō policy and to thus take advantage of the rising tide of ultra-nationalism in Japan. While the bipartisan system is considered the ideal form of party politics, competition between two parties in itself has the potential to destroy democracy. Seen in this light, it might be that the Seiyūkai's having an absolute majority under Prime Minister Hara Takashi was a better arrangement. It was truly regrettable that the Seiyūkai broke up after the Hara assassination. Also, this viewpoint prompts re-evaluation of the decades-long one-party domination by the Liberal Democratic Party in post–World War II Japan. Unless politics becomes mature enough to allow the functioning of bipartisan (or supra-partisan) diplomacy, this might remain democracy's eternal dilemma.

Zhang Zuolin's Death in an Explosion

After the Jinan Incident, Chiang Kai-shek's army advanced further north. Beijing was doomed. In the cabinet meeting on May 16, Minister of War Shirakawa Yoshinori reported that, because the efforts by Zhang Zuolin's army had already become half-hearted, it would be difficult for it to reverse the situation. Shirakawa also reported that other Western powers had already strengthened protection for their residents in Beijing and Tianjin, where plain-clothes spy soldiers from Chiang's army had been moving around freely. More worrisome for Japan than the safety of the Japanese residents in Beijing and Tianjin was the danger of the turmoil's spreading to Manchuria and threatening Japan's interests in that region. On May 17, Prime Minister Tanaka invited the ambassadors of Britain, the United States, and other countries to his office to explain Japan's position on the civil war in China. On May 18, he sent an official memorandum to warn both Zhang Zuolin and Chiang Kai-shek, saying, "Maintenance of public order in Manchuria is the top priority for Japan. If Manchuria is threatened by the disturbances of war advancing into Beijing and Tianjin, Japan will have no choice but to take all necessary measures to maintain public order in Manchuria." At the same time, Minister Yoshizawa in Beijing had been trying to persuade Zhang that he should withdraw to Manchuria and concentrate on its defense instead of fighting Chiang's army. Yoshizawa, however, found that Zhang was not to be persuaded.

It was at this point that a misunderstanding emerged between Prime Minister Tanaka and the Japanese Army in China. If Zhang refused to be persuaded and was defeated by Chiang, his routed soldiers would flee over the Great Wall into Manchuria. This would adversely affect public order in Manchuria. Furthermore, if Chiang's army crossed the Great Wall line to pursue Zhang's troops, the anxiety of Japanese residents and the threat to Japan's interests in the region would be far greater than during the Jinan Incident. In either case, the Imperial Japanese Army was expected to assume that it was its duty to disarm any troops that entered Manchuria over the Great Wall, no matter which side they were on. In order to do this, the Japanese Army concentrated its Kwantung Army in Mukden so that it could be deployed promptly to the region around Jinzhou near the Great Wall if that became necessary. As the Kwantung Army saw it, if that scenario actually came about, it would de facto be the responsibility of the Japanese military to maintain public order in Manchuria. That would present a golden opportunity for the Kwantung Army to carry out its plan to somehow separate Manchuria from China proper—an opportunity the Kwantung Army had been secretly looking forward to.

However, Prime Minister Tanaka's original scheme was to get Zhang to withdraw peacefully to Manchuria. Tanaka planned to have Zhang protect Japan's interests, including the Manchurian railroads, and these negotiations were already well underway. In the end, the Tanaka government's efforts paid off and Zhang was persuaded to withdraw his troops from Beijing. This actually generated a sense of frustration among the Kwantung Army officers in that their scheme to use force had misfired. Their frustration culminated in the bombing assassination of Zhang. It was Colonel Kōmoto Daisaku, senior staff officer of the Kwantung Army, who actually carried out the plot. In doing this, he was convinced that his act represented the consensus of the Kwantung Army leadership, including its commander-in-chief.

Dissatisfaction with Zhang among the Japanese residents in Manchuria and within the Kwantung Army had been mounting. Originally from the Manchurian mounted bandits called Lülin, Zhang was a warlord who had expanded his influence under the protection of the Japanese military, but he had gradually become uncontrollable. Particularly after he captured Beijing and started calling himself Grand Marshall, he became all the more pompous, and it was increasingly obvious that he wanted to free himself from the Japanese restraints. This was only natural. because Zhang was, after all, Chinese. Among the Japanese in Manchuria, however, he was harshly criticized as an ingrate.

When Zhang's train departed Beijing, it was sent off ceremoniously by the military band. At dawn on June 6, the train exploded as it approached Mukden station. Zhang was mortally injured and died shortly afterward. It is believed that the bomb was planted by the engineer corps of the Kwantung Army at the secret order of Colonel Kōmoto. Although a cover-up was trotted out to make the explosion look like the work of Chinese scoundrels, everyone suspected that it was the Japanese military that was behind the assassination.

There were moves within the Kwantung Army, including by Colonel Kōmoto, to use this incident as leverage to conquer Manchuria. Taking advantage of this mood at a cabinet meeting, War Minister Shirakawa proposed that the government authorize the Kwantung Army to deploy to the region along the Beijing-Mukden railway. Because many cabinet members, Prime Minister Tanaka included, opposed this proposal, the Kwantung Army's plot was crippled completely. In the end, the Tanaka government decided to back Zhang's son, Zhang Xueliang, and pursue the same policy as it had with his father. Although the Japanese government could have supported someone else, it deliberately chose Zhang Xueliang. But it was an unreasonable proposition from the beginning to expect to win the son's goodwill after killing his father.

Although Zhang Xueliang believed that it was the Japanese military that had killed his father, he decided to wait for a chance to avenge his father's death. He harbored his grudge deep in his heart, making the long-term success of the Japanese policy utterly unattainable. In retrospect, it was Zhang Xueliang who led the anti-Japan movement in Manchuria, eventually provoking Japan to start the Manchurian Incident in 1931. It was also Zhang Xueliang who facilitated the reconciliation between the Kuomintang and the Communist Party of China through the Xi'an Incident (1936) to form the anti-Japan united front. Zhang Xueliang's scheming was behind each and every turning point in Japan's path toward war and defeat.

As soon as the Japanese government announced its support for Zhang Xueliang in early July, he sent a telegram to Chiang Kai-shek pledging his allegiance. Toward the end of the month, he decided to fly the national flag of the Republic of China—a sun in a blue sky—throughout the entire territory of Manchuria. The Japanese side did everything it could to dissuade Zhang Xueliang from carrying out his decision. But the only thing he agreed to do was to observe the situation in China for three more months before deciding his relations with the Kuomintang government in Nanjing. And after the three-month period, toward the end of 1928, the national flag of the Republic of China flew all over Manchuria, marking the complete failure of the Japanese government's attempt to use Zhang Xueliang. The Japanese side had no choice but to console itself, saying that it was only the flag that had changed in Manchuria, nothing else.

The Kellogg-Briand Pact

A non-belligerency treaty called the Kellogg-Briand Pact was signed in the spring/summer of 1928, a period of great turmoil that saw Chiang Kai-shek's second Northern Expedition, the Jinan Incident, and the assassination of Zhang Zuolin. Japan was a signatory to the pact. A non-belligerency pact proclaims that war is unjustifiable as a means to settle international disputes and that the signatories renounce, in the names of their respective peoples, war as a tool of a state. It is the origin of Article 9 of the Constitution of Japan, which proclaims, "the Japanese people forever renounce war as a sovereign right of the nation and the threat or use of force as means of settling international disputes."

Such a pact is rooted in pacifism, which was the mainstream at the time, and the denial of power politics. According to Henry Kissinger's *Diplomacy*, France had been too weak compared to Germany in terms of national power since the beginning of the twentieth century, and not even the outcome of World War I changed that. What France really aspired to was an alliance with Britain and the United States, but it was forced to accept, instead, the so-called Locarno Treaties among Britain, France, Germany, Italy and, additionally, the East European countries.

It was somewhat analogous to Japan's experience of being deprived of the Anglo-Japanese Alliance and having it replaced by the largely useless Four-Power Treaty among Japan, the United States, Britain, and France. But because Germany's revival was a real threat in Europe, France must have been much more uneasy than Japan.

To quote Kissinger:

Driven by the desire to be perceived as doing something, [French Foreign Minister Aristide] Briand . . . submit[ted] in June 1927 a draft treaty to Washington according to which the two governments would renounce war in their relations with each other and agree to settle all their disputes by peaceful means. The American Secretary of State, Frank B. Kellogg, did not quite know how to respond to a document that renounced what no one feared and offered what everyone took for granted. The approach of the election year of 1928 helped to clear Kellogg's mind; "peace" was popular, and Briand's draft had the advantage of not involving any practical consequence.

Since Briand's argument was well in tune with the Wilsonian notion of collective security, it was easy for the United States to embrace it. In contrast to a traditional alliance, which, whether explicitly announced or not, is an attempt by countries to cooperatively defend themselves against a hypothetical enemy, collective security aims to achieve peace through a collective commitment to peace among the countries concerned and their hypothetical enemies. As has already been noted, Kissinger argues that the concepts of "collective security" and "alliance" are diametrically opposed by definition. History has shown collective security arrangements such as the Four-Power Treaty imposed on Japan or the Locarno Treaties in Europe turned out to be completely useless in settling disputes or preventing wars.

Since it was a treaty that no one could oppose, however, all the world powers found that they had to sign it. While all the signatories agreed with the treaty in principle, each country had specific points that it could not agree to because of the inconvenience the treaty would cause. Common among them was the argument to exclude the right of self-defense and conduct that they were obliged to take due to other existing treaties. Britain additionally reserved the right of self-defense in specific areas of the world where Britain had special and close interests. The secretariat of the League of Nations explained that those "specific regions" included Egypt and Persia. Japan, with its Manchurian problem, found this a relief.

The Japanese government found it imperative it prevent the treaty from becoming an obstacle to its protection of Japanese residents and interests in China, particularly in Manchuria. Thus it dispatched special envoy Uchida Kōsai to the Western capitals to explain Japan's position. Although the timing of Uchida's visits coincided with the dispatch of Japanese troops to Shandong preceding the Jinan Incident, the Western powers did not connect these Japanese actions to the treaty and simply listened to Japan's explanation. The Japanese government must have believed that it had taken all the precautions that were available to it. When Japan was defeated in World War II, however, none of the specific "reservations" that countries had made, including Japan's, were taken into consideration and Japan was accused of violating the spirit of the treaty.

The Tanaka Cabinet Resigns

Prior to these developments, the first Japanese general election with universal suffrage was held in February 1928. The Seiyūkai defeated the Minsei-tō by just one seat to become the ruling party. Taking into consideration the advantage it had as the government party—i.e., its ability to use the police to interfere with the election and its access to abundant election funds—this was a de facto defeat for the Seiyūkai, which had not yet recovered from the defection of half of its former members to the Minsei-tō. Subsequent management of the House of Representatives was stable, however, partly due to the defection of former Seiyūkai members from the Minsei-tō. But the Seiyūkai government faced a difficult situation in the House of Peers. This was especially so in that it was argued that the reference to "in the names of their respective peoples" in the Kellogg-Briand Pact violated the emperor's sovereignty, and concern over this delayed the signing of the treaty. Although the Tanaka cabinet succeeded in mobilizing its considerable political clout to overcome these problems, the Zhan Zuolin assassination turned out to be fatal for the cabinet.

At first, Tanaka did not know the truth of the incident. According to a memoir by Ugaki Kazushige, when Tanaka learned the truth, he invited

Ugaki to his private residence and repeatedly deplored, "Fools! They are like children who do not know what their father is trying to accomplish." Before this conversation took place, Saionji Kinmochi had advised Tanaka, saying,

> If it should be found the Japanese military was behind the incident you must harshly discipline those who were involved in order to tighten official discipline in the Japanese military. Even if your conduct may not be temporarily popular, it will be the only way to maintain Japan's international credibility. So far, the Imperial Army has behaved as it likes. If the Imperial Army is taught that the changing times require stricter discipline and it can no longer do as it pleases, that will improve China's perception of Japan in the long run.

This was also what Tanaka had in mind. In fact, on December 24, he reported to the emperor that, as soon as the investigation was complete, he intended to make its results public and deal severely with those involved in the scheme. However, members of his cabinet, including not only the war minister but other ministers such as Railroad Minister Ogawa Heikichi, opposed Tanaka on this, isolating him in his own government. At this point, though, those opposing Tanaka were driven not so much by their inability to control the arbitrary conduct of young officers but more by an aversion to publicizing an embarrassing truth. As Saionji had predicted, failure to disclose what had really happened was a source of regret in the subsequent history that led to the war.

In March 1929, War Minister Shirakawa, admitting it was Colonel Kōmoto who was behind the Zhang Zuolin assassination, reported to the emperor, "Because the disclosure of what really took place would be detrimental to Japan, we wish to improve military discipline in a way that will not damage Japan's credibility." In other words, what Shirakawa suggested was to leave the culprit unknown and impose an administrative penalty for negligence on the officers responsible for security. Prime Minister Tanaka thought the Emperor had approved this report by War Minister Shirakawa, but that was a misunderstanding. According to the Emperor's memoir, when Tanaka reported on the measures that the government had taken in June, "I said that is not what I remember being told would happen, and I raised my voice to request Tanaka's resignation." When Tanaka

The Tanaka Giichi Cabinet resigns en masse (photo courtesy of Kyodo News)

attempted to defend himself, the Emperor refused to hear him out. Being a loyal and faithful army officer himself, Tanaka had to resign as prime minister when he lost the confidence of the Emperor. Other members of the cabinet opposed his resignation, and when Communication Minister Kuhara Fusanosuke ran after Tanaka as far as the staircase in a last-minute attempt to dissuade him, Tanaka yelled, "Shut up" and walked away.

Genesis of the Japanese Military's Arbitrary Conduct

Zhang Zuolin's assassination was disastrous for Japan. First of all, this incident gave the military a free hand to do whatever it pleased as long as it was motivated by a pure desire to serve the country. When a member of the military is protected by his superior officers and colleagues no matter what he does, there is no military discipline to speak of. In my opinion, Yangmingism, which had been the philosophy of revolutionaries and men of virtue since the last days of the Tokugawa shogunate, is also to blame. Yangmingism dictates that you must not hesitate to do what you believe in. The only criterion for action is that it conform with the way of Heaven. The order from Heaven must take precedence over the command of a superior officer, and you have nothing to be ashamed of as long as your integrity is intact and your spirit is pure. Saigō Takamori says in his *Nanshū-Ō ikun* (The last instructions of the venerable Nanshū), "A man who does not care about life, honor, official rank, or money is difficult to control. But it takes such difficult-to-control men to share your hardships and accomplish the grand enterprise of the state."

Yangmingism encourages this kind of difficult-to-control men. While Yangmingism comes with a strict disclaimer that this person must be unconcerned about his own life, death, honor, or disgrace, this disclaimer ceases to function if a violator is never punished, leading to a rampancy of half-hearted, self-assumed heroes. Moreover, in the subsequent Shōwa history, it often happened that the very person who was directly responsible for the trouble not only stayed on the road to success but also even attained honor, nullifying the spirit of Yangmingism. As a result, a free-for-all situation emerged for those who were hungry for distinction and honor. It is, therefore, no exaggeration to say that the assassination of Zhang Zuolin presaged the military rampancy that eventually led Japan to disaster.

The other adverse effect of the assassination of Zhang impacted Emperor Shōwa. Emperor Shōwa was truly a child of the Taishō Democracy. His formative years from birth until he became twenty years old coincided with the duration of the Anglo-Japanese Alliance. When he visited Europe in 1921, he was so impressed by British culture that he later reminisced it was the most pleasant time of his life. He became the prince regent in the same year and acceded to the throne in 1926. He was about to take part in the enthronement ceremony in December 1928 when Zhang was assassinated.

Emperor Shōwa's enthusiasm for exercising imperial authority as a new emperor must have been behind the loud and clear expression of his will vis-à-vis Prime Minister Tanaka. However, he later became remorseful over his attitude and, haunted by this experience, subsequently held back from expressing himself. Even discounting his youth, Emperor Shōwa's conduct at that time was, indeed, something he would later regret. If he wanted a tightening of military discipline, he should have made it clear to War Minister Shirakawa in the beginning. Otherwise, his conduct vis-à-vis Shirakawa and Prime Minister Tanaka was contradictory. One possibility is that Emperor Shōwa was angry at himself for having been taken in by Shirakawa's bureaucratic explanation, and he might have taken this anger out on Tanaka, accusing the latter of going back on his word. Given Emperor Shōwa's inexperience at that time, this is plausible.

Although Saionji Kinmochi had long emphasized the need for stricter military discipline, his ultimate concern and duty was to protect the Imperial Family. This superseded anything else, including military discipline. The fact that the Tanaka cabinet had to step down because of Imperial non-confidence would place a political responsibility on Emperor Shōwa, which was utterly unacceptable to Saionji. The emperor, knowing full well Saionji's position, misspoke in referring to Tanaka's resignation. This slip violated the principle of British parliamentary democracy—that is, the English sovereign reigns but does not rule—that Japan's Imperial Household held up as its model. Emperor Shōwa's remorse subsequently hemmed in his willingness to restrict the arbitrary conduct of the military even though the military invoked the supreme authority of the emperor to justify its actions. Given the autonomy of military command, it was only the supreme authority of the emperor that could rein the military in. Nevertheless, Saionji strongly opposed the exercise of this authority by the emperor, and Emperor Shōwa himself deferred to Saionji's judgment and exercised self-restraint. This led to the structural tragedy of the history of the Shōwa era.

CHAPTER
13

Shidehara Diplomacy's Last Hurrah

—Shidehara Remained Unchanged in the Midst of Turmoil—

Reappointed Foreign Minister

During Tanaka Giichi's time, when Shidehara lived in seclusion at his retreat in Kotsubo near Kamakura, Saionji Kinmochi presented Shidehara with a piece of calligraphy. It contained the two letters "shū-en" (to gather from afar), Saionji's signature, and his age (seventy-nine). Saionji also christened Shidehara's retreat Shū-en Sō (Shū-en Lodge). When Shidehara visited Saionji to express his appreciation, Saionji asked what he made of the calligraphy. Shidehara said, "Because you can view Mt. Fuji and the Hakone mountains from my retreat, I thought you might have praised the spot as commanding a view of these remote sceneries together." In response, Saionji replied, "I meant to praise you, on whom all the world's hopes are focused." Saionji thought so highly of Shidehara that he always wondered out loud whether Shidehara could be given a status equivalent to elder statesman in diplomacy.

Shidehara was highly thought of not only in Japan and China but throughout the world. In 1928, an arbitration treaty was concluded between the United States and Germany with the purpose of settling all bilateral conflicts through peaceful means. This was to be accomplished by a committee of two members each from the two countries and a chairman

The Hamaguchi Osachi Cabinet takes office (photo courtesy of Kyodo News)

from a third country. The signatory countries had to agree on the chairman, who had to be neutral and impartial. The United States and Germany nominated Shidehara for this post. Because the position would require his time and labor once an incident occurred between the two countries, Shidehara accepted the nomination on the condition that he would serve only as long as doing so would not interfere with the performance of his duty as a Japanese subject. As it turned out, no incident occurred. In Germany, this was the time of the Weimarer Republik (Weimar Republic) in which Gustav Stresemann served as prime minister and foreign minister; in Japan, it was the period of the Taishō Democracy. Those were the good old days when the dream of international cooperation was still intact and people believed international disputes could be settled peacefully.

Meanwhile, Shidehara was reappointed foreign minister. In 1927, two months after the formation of the Tanaka Giichi cabinet, the Kenseikai merged with the Seiyū Hon-tō to form the Rikken Minsei-tō. Hamaguchi Osachi, a close friend of Shidehara's, was elected its first president. At this point, Japan entered a brief period known as the Seiyūkai-Rikken Minsei-tō two-party system. When Prime Minister Tanaka resigned in July 1929, Hamaguchi received an Imperial mandate to form a new cabinet the very next day; he appointed Shidehara his foreign minister.

Persuading China and Russia

As soon as Shidehara assumed the foreign ministership, he was faced with an incident that called for his internationally acclaimed abilities. Although the young Soviet Union had put up a gallant pose of abandoning all the acquisitions obtained by the Tsar's imperialistic diplomacy, it did not willingly give up its vested interests. As far as the Chinese Eastern Railway—one of those vested interests—was concerned, the Soviet Union reached an agreement with China in 1924 for joint management on a more or less equal footing. Toward the end of 1928, after flying the national flag of the Republic of China all over Manchuria, Zhang Xueliang attempted to recover China's concessions in the Chinese Eastern Railway high-handedly: He ordered a house search of the Russian consulate general in Harbin, claiming he found evidence that the railway had been used to promote Communism in China, and fired and evicted Russian railway employees. The Soviet Union retaliated by severing diplomatic relations with China and moved its military to the Soviet-Manchuria border.

The United States and France sent a strong warning, referring to the Kellogg-Briand Pact. This warning generated strong resentment from both China and the Soviet Union. Shidehara reminisced that he thought the reference to such a formal document as the Kellogg-Briand Pact would not only agitate the two parties but even potentially provoke a war between them as they sought to save face. He informally chided the Chinese side that it should have formally protested by disclosing the evidence it had found instead of resorting to the use of force without disclosing the evidence. Shidehara said he thought the Chinese act was unjustifiable. To the Soviet Union, Shidehara warned that Japan would react sharply if the Soviet army invaded Manchuria. This was not an empty threat and, in fact, the Chinese side had anticipated that Japan would support China's attempt to block the advance of Communism in China. In his post–World War II memoir, Shidehara reminisced wryly, "Today, it is utterly unthinkable for Japan to force its will on China and the Soviet Union." In retrospect, Japan was then powerful enough to do that.

Upon hearing Shidehara's warning, the Soviet army, which had already advanced to Hailar, withdrew from Mongolia. It was only after 1932 that the Soviet Union became confident with the successful completion of Stalin's first five-year plan. At that stage, the Soviet Union was not willing to go against the Japanese military. Partly because of this incident, the Chinese side welcomed Shidehara's reappointment, cheering the end of Tanaka's militarist diplomacy and the arrival of Shidehara's peaceful diplomacy. The anti-Japan movement among the Chinese people, which had intensified since the Tanaka government's dispatch of Japanese troops to Shandong, was considerably subdued. Chinese perceptions of the Japanese government also improved when Saburi Sadao, a confidant of Shidehara's, forwent his chance to become ambassador to the Soviet Union and accepted the post of Japanese minister to China.

The first things Saburi did as Japanese minister to China were to have heart-to-heart talks with Chiang Kai-shek and other Chinese leaders and to visit Manchuria to study the situation. He subsequently returned to Tokyo temporarily to secure the Hamaguchi cabinet's approval through Shidehara on future policies toward China. It was immediately before his return to China that his body was found at the Hakone Fujiya Hotel where he was staying. Although the police judged that it was a suicide, nobody could think of why Saburi would kill himself. There were a lot of suspicious points that challenged the conclusion of alleged suicide. Shidehara remained suspicious of the cause of Saburi's death until the very end of his life. If it was a murder, it could not have been accomplished without elaborate behind-the-scenes machinations by the military or the police. To this day, this incident remains a Shōwa history mystery.

We can imagine that Saburi's mysterious death was a serious psychological blow to Shidehara himself. It also placed Japan in a grave situation when China refused to agree to Obata Yūkichi as Saburi's successor on the grounds that he had earlier participated in drafting the Twenty-One Demands. When a country appoints an ambassador, it has to informally obtain an agrément from the host country, and it is not uncommon for appointments to be rejected. As a matter of fact, the Japanese government had just refused to accept the US ambassador-designate on the grounds that his prior post had been in China and he had made *non grata* remarks about Japan. Although the entire process was supposed to be carried out secretly through diplomatic channels, the Chinese side, in an expression of Chinese nationalism, disclosed the reason for the refusal at a press conference. This issue was settled, in the end, by the Japanese government's appointing Shigemitsu Mamoru acting minister on the condition that he would later be promoted to full minister. But the Chinese rudeness was inexcusable. Public opinion in Japan was infuriated and became all the more critical of Shidehara's peaceful diplomacy.

For Shidehara, who had returned to the Foreign Ministry, the top priority for Japan's China policy was the issue of Chinese tariff autonomy. At the Beijing Tariff Conference in 1925, the Japanese government, at Shidehara's initiative, was the first of the participating powers to take a favorable position on China's demand for tariff autonomy. Although the Japanese government's decision was partly motivated by the desire to institute a differential tariff schedule that would be favorable to Japan instead of the one-rate-fits-all tariff schedule, the Chinese side was nevertheless pleased with Japan's position. While the discussions at this conference came to naught due to the collapse of the Chinese regime, the situation in China underwent a drastic change in the subsequent four years. As soon as the Northern Expedition army triumphantly entered Beijing in June 1928, Chiang Kai-shek declared the abrogation of all the unequal treaties and communicated to the Japanese government that it held the treaties concluded in 1896 and 1904 to be invalid.

Change could no longer be stopped. While the United States, Britain, France, and other major powers entered into negotiations with China to recognize China's tariff autonomy, Japan lagged behind, demanding the Shandong Expedition and Jinan Incident questions be settled prior to the tariff negotiations. It was under these circumstances that Shigemitsu, who succeeded Saburi, had to negotiate with the Chinese side. He succeeded in concluding the Sino-Japanese Tariff Agreement (the Shigemitsu-Soong Tse-wen Agreement) in May 1930. Sino-Japanese relations improved somewhat and a variety of bilateral negotiations made significant progress until the Manchurian Incident. The military advisors whom Chiang Kai-shek invited from Japan numbered sixty to seventy as of July 1931, even though all of them were lieutenant colonels, majors, or lower-rank officers. Chiang even commissioned Japan to construct a naval cruiser for China, making the strains of only eighteen months earlier seem ancient history.

Taishō Democracy's Last Act

The conclusion of the London Naval Treaty in 1930 was cooperative diplomacy's last accomplishment. Japan's signing the treaty despite

The London Disarmament Conference opening ceremony (photo courtesy of Kyodo News)

resistance from the Imperial Japanese Navy General Staff signified that party politics was still functional in Japan and was still able to suppress the military. That was the last accomplishment as well as the last legacy of Taishō Democracy. But it was the London Naval Treaty's negative impact that more gravely affected Japanese history. The issue of the prerogative of supreme command was exploited as a tool of party strife, and this turned out to be the origin of the subsequent tolerance of arbitrary conduct by the military. In the following, I will briefly review the accomplishments of the London Naval Conference with special emphasis on its impact on subsequent politics in Japan.

The London Naval Treaty was an attempt to reduce the number of naval vessels, other than capital ships, each party possessed. These numbers had already been limited by the Washington Naval Treaty of 1922. Although the Washington Naval Conference also proposed capping smaller ship limits, France had adamantly rejected the proposal in London. France intended to make up for its humiliating low ratio of battleship tonnage—1.75 against 5.0 each for the United States and Britain and 3.0 for Japan—with smaller vessels. The Geneva Naval Conference of 1927 had also failed to achieve a reduction in smaller naval vessel tonnage. This failure was mainly attributable to the US rejection of the British proposal to reduce heavy cruisers carrying 8-inch guns, which excluded light cruisers with 6-inch guns from the reduction. Behind the US rejection was the fact that Britain had 42 sophisticated merchant ships that could easily be retrofitted to serve as auxiliary cruisers with 6-inch guns, whereas the United States had only four such ships. Negotiations on limiting non-capital ships were resumed in 1929, aided by the election of Herbert Hoover as US president and the appointment of James Ramsay MacDonald as British prime minister. Both men were known advocates of arms reduction.

The issue of contention for Japan during the London Naval Conference was to secure a tonnage limit ratio of 7 for non-capital ships against the US proposal, which aimed to extend the 5:5:3 ratio of capital battleships tonnage limit to non-capital ships. Japan also insisted on retaining a total of 78,000 tons for its submarines as against the British proposal calling for total abolition. Japan and the United States finally reached a compromise during the conference on Japan's tonnage limits: a ratio of 6 for its heavy cruisers against 10 for the United States and 8.1 for Britain; 69.75 percent of those of the United States and Britain for its auxiliary ships; and 52,700 tons for its submarines.

Although Navy Minister Takarabe Takeshi, Japan's chief delegate to the conference, and Deputy Minister Yamanashi Katsunoshin supported the compromise, to which not only Shidehara but also Prime Minister Hamaguchi agreed, Chief of Naval Operations Katō Haruhiro and the Imperial Japanese Navy General Staff were dissatisfied and demanded it be renegotiated. As the deadline for instructing the Japanese delegation approached, Prime Minister Hamaguchi instructed former navy minister Okada Keisuke (prime minister at the time of the February 26, 1936, Incident) to coordinate responses within the Imperial Navy. Okada, in response, replied, in the presence of Yamanashi and Katō, that "Although the Imperial Navy cannot agree with the compromise proposal from a professional viewpoint, it will make every effort to study what is best for Japan's defense in line with the proposal if it is approved by the cabinet." While Katō did not actively support the compromise proposal at this meeting, nor did he wield his veto power based on the autonomy of military command to kill it.

The cabinet meeting of April 1, 1930, decided to instruct the delegation in London to accept the compromise proposal and, subsequently, promised the Imperial Navy General Staff future cooperation to make up for the compromise, including the reinforcement of the navy air corps. Had the issue been settled at this point, it would have been an excellent precedent with the Imperial Navy General Staff respecting the decision of the cabinet. Because the Seiyūkai decided to exploit this issue for politics, however, this incident ended up creating future problems.

Seiyūkai Party Strategy

At that time, the Minsei-tō had an absolute majority in the Diet. In the general election of February 1930, the Minsei-tō won 273 seats while the Seiyūkai won only 174. In the half year since its formation, Prime Minister Hamaguchi's administration had emphasized a tight fiscal policy, including a 10 percent reduction in government officials' salaries. As a result, and compared to the Seiyūkai's loose financial policies, the party's name, Minsei-tō, became associated with recession in people's minds. This was by no means a vote-winning policy. The Minsei-tō nevertheless won a landslide victory in the election. The victory was, at least, partly attributable to the shortage of campaign funds on the part of the Seiyūkai, which had abruptly abandoned the government in 1929. Compared to former party president Tanaka Giichi, who had allegedly spent some 10 million yen in the previous election, President Inukai Tsuyoshi, who was known for his poor fundraising skills, was able to spend only 3 million yen in the 1930 election.

Perhaps more important, however, was the business sector's dissatisfaction with Tanaka's China policy, which led to a Chinese boycott of Japanese exports. Moreover, people had already become weary of the Tanaka administration. The Minsei-tō looked comparatively more reliable and trustworthy in the eyes of the Japanese people, particularly with the accessible personalities of Hamaguchi and Shidehara. Even in early Shōwa Japan, the democratic checks and balances were functioning fairly well. It would be wrong, therefore, to conclude that the Zhang Zuolin assassination decisively tilted Japan to militarism.

In an attempt to undermine Minsei-tō dominance, Inukai Tsuyoshi and Hatoyama Ichirō of the Seiyūkai attacked the Hamaguchi government for violating the autonomy of the military command. It should be recalled that it was Hara Takashi, prime minister of the first party administration under the same Seiyūkai, who had decided to control the autonomy of the military command, which was the last remaining obstruction to democratic politics. Hara had secretly waited for the chance to eliminate this obstacle after the demise of Yamagata Aritomo. Unfortunately, Hara himself was assassinated before Yamagata died. It was, therefore, truly ironical that, no sooner had a party cabinet succeeded in controlling the Imperial Navy General Staff than Hara's successors in the Seiyūkai demanded respect for the autonomy of military command as a means of attacking the government party.

This was probably due to the imprudence of politicians at the height of party politics. It must never have occurred to them that this issue would contribute to crumbling the foundation of party politics in less than ten years. When bipartisan cooperation cannot be pursued in the field of national security, there is always the danger democracy will self-destruct.

Legal Interpretation of the Autonomy of Military Command

The issue of the autonomy of military command, however, was not the only factor that killed Japan's short-lived party democracy. The subsequent arbitrary conduct by the military derived from a variety of causes, including the Great Depression and the situation in Manchuria. What happened was by no means solely attributable to the legal interpretation of the autonomy of the military command. In fact, it is highly doubtful the autonomy of the military command inevitably derived from the Meiji Constitution. In his 1919 monthly *Chūō Kōron* article, Meiji-Shōwa navy-officer-turned-military-critic Mizuno Hironori argued that there was nothing in the Meiji Constitution that explicitly endorsed the autonomy of the military command. While Article 11 did stipulate that "the Emperor has the supreme command of the Army and Navy," Mizuno stressed that this article did not preclude the prime minister's involvement because it was among other similar articles such as Article 15 which stipulates "the Emperor confers titles of nobility, rank, orders and other marks of honor" and Article 16 which reads "the Emperor orders amnesty, pardons, commutation of punishments and rehabilitation"—both of which allow involvement by the prime minister.

Mizuno's interpretation must have been legally correct. As a matter of fact, the Japanese military in those days themselves explained that the autonomy of the military command had been a long-standing practice since ancient times, endorsing the view that it derived more from common practice than from a constitutional stipulation. Earlier, the *hanbatsu* military clique led by Yamagata Aritomo had done everything possible to block the formation of a democratic government. Once it became obvious to them that a democratic government was unavoidable under the Meiji Constitution, they made the government of the time adopt a rule that only incumbent military personnel could be appointed war and navy ministers. This was their way of attempting to prevent the military command from being controlled by a party government. They also made the Imperial Japanese Army General Staff Office in Miyakezaka in central Tokyo a much more imposing building than the other government offices.

Had it not been for the many layers of intentional faits accomplis by the military, the military command issue would have remained one of military-government relations concerning only the top state leaders during such crises as might occur every few decades. The absurd scene that was repeated frequently in the early Shōwa period, with a mere soldier brandishing a naked sword to threaten civilian officials and accuse them of violating the autonomy of military command, would certainly not have taken place. Mizuno Hironori was a defense intellectual, a breed so rare in Japan that there is no appropriate Japanese term for it. Because Japan in those days had no appropriate position for this kind of a maverick, only a few in today's Japan know of Mizuno. But he was quite well known among intellectuals in the Taishō and early Shōwa eras. An elite navy officer, Mizuno was the commander of a torpedo boat during the Battle of Tsushima and participated in the bold night raid on the Baltic Fleet warships, for which he earned a letter of commendation. He was later awarded the Order of the Golden Kite for his distinguished service during this battle. Furthermore, his 1911 memoir, *Kono issen* (This battle), won him literary distinction overnight and he took a trip to Europe with the royalties. In Europe he witnessed the miseries caused by World War I. This trip transformed him into a unique critic who could discuss military affairs from a pacifist viewpoint.

On Mizuno, journalist and political commentator Baba Tsunego writes in his *Wasurerarenu tomodachi* (Unforgettable friends), "His good heart is truly pure from top to bottom. He is thoughtful and totally devoid of selfishness. He worried about state affairs as fervently as when he was a warrior. And he is completely selfless when interacting with others." As early as 1924, Mizuno predicted Japan's future in a treatise:

> In case a war should break out between Japan and the United States, Japan would have no ally in the world. This war will inevitably become a protracted struggle. It appears that it is Japan's defense policy to rely on neighboring countries for food and raw materials in case of a war with the United States, but I wonder if our neighbors will show goodwill and sympathy to Japan when we threaten to plunder their resources. Therefore, Japan will not be able to wage a war against the United States unless it is prepared to make the entire world its enemy.

> If Japan goes to war,
> it will be forsaken by everybody in the world.
> Alas, a glorious 3,000-year history
> will go to ruin.
> (poem composed circa 1934)

This indicates that Mizuno was one step more insightful than the genius Ishiwara Kanji, who had theorized about controlling Manchuria's resources in preparation for a final world war with the United States. It is truly regrettable that the intellectual climate in Japan at the time was not mature enough to discuss the issues presented by such an insightful defense intellectual.

London Naval Treaty: The Greatest Tragedy for Japan

Since the Minsei-tō had a majority in the House of Representatives, the Seiyūkai had a hard time obstructing ratification of the London Naval Treaty. In the Privy Council, however, which was dominated by conservatives, the committee responsible deliberated the treaty for nearly two months. Instead of humbly beseeching the Privy Council, both Hamaguchi and Shidehara simply talked to the committee members "candidly with a serene state of mind," to borrow Hamaguchi's phrase. In these talks, Hamaguchi delivered sound arguments such as:

Constitutionally, the military command, the determination of the size of military strength, as well as the signing of treaties are over-arching prerogatives of the Emperor. Therefore, it is in no way possible for one such prerogative to violate other prerogatives. Power struggles among administrative organizations have nothing to do with the Emperor's prerogative.

Hamaguchi also stressed, "It would be the government, including the navy minister, that shoulders the responsibility for national defense." However, the deliberations in the Privy Council remained at such a low level as "the government ignored the military," vs. "the government did not," and "Chief of Naval Operations Katō should be made to testify," vs. "No, he should not." In the end, ratification of the London Naval Treaty turned out to be a complete victory for Hamaguchi and Shidehara. Behind this success was the active involvement by Saionji Kinmochi, who was gravely apprehensive about the situation.

The first thing Saionji did was to dissuade War Minister Ugaki Kazushige, who had been hospitalized for sickness and expressed his intention to resign, from resigning. Saionji's intention was to block the simultaneous resignation of the ministers of war and navy. Taking advantage of Ugaki's sickness, the navy had schemed that the resignations would be a sign of navy-army partnership on the issue of the autonomy of military command. Upon hearing of Ugaki's change of mind, Saionji left him a message, saying, "Although I have never meddled in another's affairs so boldly before, this time I cannot thank you enough for refraining from resigning."

Next, Saionji advised Hamaguchi, saying, "If the Privy Council makes unreasonable demands, you can exercise your authority as prime minister and dismiss its president and vice president." In response, Hamaguchi expressed his resolution, declaring, "I may have to dismiss the president and vice president of the Privy Council. I may also need to remove committee chair Itō, as well as the former Chief of the Naval Operations, for leaking military secrets. These actions are tantamount to a coup d'état but I seem to have no other recourse." Even the Privy Council could not withstand Hamaguchi when he demonstrated his conviction and resolution. It was at this point that committee chairman Itō Miyoji abruptly changed his attitude and, to the surprise of all parties concerned, persuaded the committee members to ratify the London Naval Treaty.

It is not hard to imagine the despair of those who had opposed the treaty with all kinds of plots and schemes. Sure enough, Hamaguchi was assaulted by a right-wing terrorist and mortally injured a month after the treaty's ratification. This turned out to be the first of a series of terrorist activities, culminating in the May 15 Incident of 1932. Felled by a bullet, Hamaguchi told Shidehara, who rushed to him, "It is every man's dream to encounter a bullet. It happened at the right time, too, because we had just finished the cabinet meeting on the budget." Taishō-Shōwa journalist and military commentator Itō Masanori, in his book *Dai-Kaigun o omou* (The Great Navy in retrospect) called the treaty issue "the greatest tragedy for Japan," citing the chain of incidents culminating in the May 15 Incident.

Another tragic outcome Itō cited was the internal division in the Imperial Navy, which had boasted iron solidarity under the leadership of Yamamoto Gonbei and Katō Tomosaburō, into a Treaty Faction and a Fleet Faction. The Treaty Faction included, among others, Yamanashi Katsunoshin, Hori Teikichi, and Suzuki Kantarō, while Katō Hiroharu and Suetsugu Nobumasa were believed to belong to the hawkish Fleet Faction. Much more regrettable, however, was the ousting of several promising people on whom the future of the Imperial Navy should have rested, this in the navy tradition of "In a quarrel, both parties are to blame." In other words, proper personnel management was disrupted by the division within the navy. Among those dismissed was Hori, a colleague for whom Yamamoto Isoroku had the utmost respect. Yamamoto later mused to Itō Masanori, "I wonder which was more harmful to the navy, the dismissal of Hori or the 10 percent reduction in heavy cruisers. That was the most foolish personnel change the Imperial Navy ever undertook."

Domestic and International Situations at Dead Ends

Shidehara was appointed acting prime minister during Hamaguchi's hospitalization, and the Minsei-tō in time elected Wakatsuki Reijirō its president. Elder statesman Saionji chose Wakatsuki as the next prime minister. Saionji explained his choice of Wakatsuki, saying, "Because this government change was caused by a politically motivated assassination, we must

refrain from a regime change that would encourage more assassinations."
Shidehara naturally remained in the Wakatsuki cabinet as foreign minister. Shidehara's stance likewise remained unchanged. Orthodox diplomacy such as Shidehara's does not change easily. But the domestic and
international situations were hopelessly at an impasse. In order to explain
these situations, allow me to quote works by other authors.

Shigemitsu Mamoru, who became foreign minister during World War
II, left the following analysis in his memoir.

> As far as Japan's domestic politics were concerned, all the backing
> to promote Shidehara's diplomacy toward China completely disap-
> peared. At the same time, China's pursuit of its revolutionary diplo-
> macy became all the more blatant, leaving little room for Shidehara
> diplomacy to pursue its objectives.

In his *Hyōden Yoshida Shigeru* (A Yoshida Shigeru biography), political
scientist Inoki Masamichi opines:

> What was devastating for Shidehara Diplomacy and, for that matter,
> Japan's foreign policy as a whole, was that the Chinese nationalist
> movement decided to squarely challenge Japan's special interests in
> Manchuria and Mongolia. Professor Hosoya Chihiro was absolutely
> right when he said, "When the wave of Chinese nationalism was
> about to reach the region that was regarded as Japan's lifeline, the
> Washington Conference system no longer functioned."

In today's global ethic, an unequal treaty is of course evil, while nationalism that resists the unequal treaty is good. Therefore, China's revolutionary diplomacy would be considered good and the diplomacy of
international cooperation that aims at maintaining the status quo would
be considered evil. As I wrote earlier, however, to criticize leaders in an
age of imperialism for being imperialists is as meaningless as denouncing
medieval people for being medieval and pre-modern. At the time of the
International Military Tribunal for the Far East or, more precisely, when
the victors wanted to execute the defeated nation's top leaders, an unreasonable attempt was made to allow the application of laws retroactively
in order to justify the sentences as more than mere retaliation. While this

might have affected the historical view of post–World War II Japan, it should be noted that the study of history should be separated from a war or retaliation. History is an act of exploring and understanding the truth of the time and nothing else. We should particularly refrain from judging history by today's standards.

MacMurray's Memorandum

There was an American diplomat who had observed Japan as an objective third party. John MacMurray was a China specialist who participated in the Washington Naval Conference of 1921 as US Department of State director of Far Eastern affairs. Subsequently, he served as the American minister to Beijing in 1925 through 1929. An internal State Department document that he wrote in 1935 was recently elaborated upon by American historian Arthur Waldron in his book *How the Peace was Lost.*

Although only a few read this document when it was written, it nevertheless made a strong impression on Joseph Grew, US Ambassador to Japan when the Pacific War erupted. The document also became something akin to the bible of Far Eastern political analysis for George Kennan, the architect of American diplomacy during the Cold War. In particular, MacMurray's view that, "In case of need we could and doubtless would outbuild Japan to the extent that we could successfully attack her navy even with the protecting ring of islands that make the western Pacific almost a Japanese lake. . . . Nobody except perhaps Russia would gain from our victory in such a war," turned out to be a highly accurate prediction of the reality in East Asia after World War II. American leaders in the 1950s were surprised at how right MacMurray had been in the mid-1930s. It was around this time that General Douglas MacArthur, who had just been relieved of his command by President Harry Truman, testified that the Pacific War was an act of self-defense for Japan.

MacMurray observed that Japan "for almost ten years (up to the beginning of the invasion of Manchuria, in September 1931) was . . . scrupulously loyal in its adherence to the letter and the spirit of the Washington Conference." This was a perfectly accurate evaluation of Shidehara's diplomacy. MacMurray said "The issue of success or failure for the policies evolved at the Washington Conference was actually in the hands of

China herself, of Great Britain, and of the United States." He goes on to say that, while the United States should have quietly informed the Chinese that it could not condone their intentionally irresponsible behavior, it instead indulged in "a few years of experimentation with the policy of 'playing up to' the Chinese" and "within five years of the close of the Washington Conference, the ideal of cooperation in the Far East ha(s) been nullified."

MacMurray's memorandum was a retrospective analysis of the situation prior to the Manchurian Incident and explored the reasons behind the incident. It is interesting that the unbiased and moderate segment of Japanese intellectuals in those days shared a similar view. To quote Yanaihara Tadao for one:

> One reason the pursuit of Japan's special interests in Manchuria/Mongolia resulted in the establishment of Manchukuo (Manchu State) must have been the Chinese impatience to recover concessions.

And Kawai Eijirō for another:

> Even if we sympathize with the Chinese aspiration for national unity, it would take a man of super-human goodwill to consent to their demands. The Chinese began to claim our vested interests in Southern Manchuria as if they all rightfully belonged to China instead of asking for them earnestly and courteously. To begin with, our concessions in Southern Manchuria were obtained from Russia by transfer. Unlike the British and French concessions, they were not snatched directly from China.

The international common sense at the time was that it would certainly take a super-human (i.e., impossible in human society) altruism and spirit of self-sacrifice to give away concessions that Japan had earned in Manchuria/Mongolia since the Russo-Japanese War.

Voices opposing Manchukuo became almost completely extinct after the proclamation of its independence. Even advocates of international cooperation accepted the existence of Manchukuo as a fait accompli and continued to preach international cooperation. This must have been due more to a near consensus within Japan that all the other realistic alternatives had already been lost rather than a rightist/militarist trending of public opinion or a fear of terroristic attacks by the military or the rightists.

China's Revolutionary Diplomacy

What, then, was China's revolutionary diplomacy like? According to the schedule for revolutionary diplomacy announced by Republic of China Foreign Minister Wang Cheng-t'ing (C.T. Wang), China sought to accomplish the restoration of tariff autonomy in its first phase; the abrogation of extraterritoriality in the second phase; the retrieval of foreign settlements in the third phase; the return of leased territories in the fourth phase; and the restoration of the railway and other concessions in the fifth phase. When Acting Japanese Minister to China Shigemitsu Mamoru visited Wang in April 1931 before he temporarily returned to Tokyo, he asked Wang if he was serious about the announced schedule. Wang replied affirmatively and added that the leased territories included Lüshun and Dalian and the railway concessions included the South Manchuria Railway. This conversation was reported to the Tokyo government via a confidential telegram, but its content was somehow leaked, hardening Japanese public opinion.

Returning to Japan, Shigemitsu reported to Shidehara that Japan and China were on a collision course and something had to be done to avoid a confrontation. Shigemitsu said, "If it has come to a dead end no matter what, it will have to be an internationally justifiable dead end." The two men agreed to make this "internationally justifiable dead end" a touchstone of China policy and shook hands in parting. Shigemitsu later explained that in stressing an "internationally justifiable dead end" he and Shidehara agreed to "make every effort to ensure the Japanese diplomatic position was justifiable in the eyes of the world." More precisely, perhaps, they must have agreed on the need to be prepared for the dead end, i.e. Japan-China confrontation. They were determined to leave no room for international criticism of Japan's position when the confrontation, whether diplomatic or military, came.

While the Japanese government might have been confident it could successfully manage it if it were a state-to-state diplomatic or military confrontation, it had difficulty coping with the popular anti-Japanese and Japan-slighting movements in China. They were rampant—even in Manchuria under the Zhang Zuolin regime, which had grown under Japan's protection—particularly after the Tanaka Giichi government sent Japanese troops to Shandong in 1927-28. When Shigemitsu visited Manchuria in 1929, he was shocked to find a major change of atmosphere in the region and left the following observation in his *Shōwa no dōran* (Shōwa: A time of upheaval).

> The harmony between Japanese and Chinese, both official and private, that I had witnessed fifteen years ago while I was stationed in Mukden has all but vanished and is nowhere to be found. Even those Chinese with whom I had associated closely in my Mukden days had to visit me at my hotel under cover of night. Except for a few long-time residents, the Japanese residents said that it did not seem feasible to cooperate with the Zhang Xueliang government, which has recently become increasingly arrogant.

Coming back to Tokyo, Shigemitsu reported to Makino Nobuaki, Lord Keeper of the Privy Seal of Japan, on the situation in Manchuria, stressing that it was on the verge of exploding at any moment if left unattended. Surprised to hear how serious the situation was, Makino instructed Shigemitsu to report also to Saionji.

Anti-Japan movements appeared to die down temporarily when Shidehara was reappointed foreign minister. But the decisive battle erupted in early 1931 between Chiang Kai-shek's army and the anti-Chiang alliance, in which Zhang Xueliang, after carefully watching the situation, decided at the last minute to side with Chiang and contributed to his victory. Subsequently, Zhang pledged allegiance to the Kuomintang and started acting in concert with the latter's sovereignty restoration movement. His distinguished service won him control of Beijing, after which he promoted anti-Japan policies with confidence.

When the Japanese side suggested a talk on the railway issue, which had been pending since the assassination of Zhang Zuolin, Zhang Xueliang would not listen and insisted Japan should talk with the Kuomintang government in Nanjing on that matter. Zhang's position totally nullified Japan's conventional method of maintaining its concessions through negotiations with the local authority in Manchuria. Zhang Xueliang had a plan to construct a harbor in Huludao near Jinzhou from which he was contemplating building a railway parallel to the South Manchuria Railway. His intention was to pit Huludao harbor and the new railway against the ports of Dalian and Lüshun and the South Manchuria Railway. Zhang's highly vocal announcement of the harbor construction plan agitated the Japanese side.

In 1930 the South Manchuria Railway ran a record deficit—the largest since the company's launch in 1906—and had to lay off some employees and freeze pay raises. While the situation was chiefly attributable to the Great Depression of 1929, the impact of the race with Zhang's rival railway to discount fees was also undeniable, affecting the lives of tens of thousands of Japanese residents who relied upon the South Manchuria Railway.

Japanese Residents in Manchuria Revolt

What made the Japanese residents most uneasy and actually affected their lives was the anti-Japan, Japan-slighting movements. These were more political campaigns led by the Kuomintang than spontaneous expressions of nationalism. In his telegram to Japanese Minister Shigemitsu immediately after the Manchurian Incident, Foreign Minister Shidehara said:

> To begin with, the anti-Japan movements in China have been promoted both directly and indirectly by the Kuomintang, whose function is inseparable from that of the government, as a means to accomplish its policy goals. The movements, therefore, cannot be seen as an uncontrollable movement driven by individuals exercising free will.

The truth of the anti-Japan, Japan-slighting movements in China remains unknown. Although the Japanese military announcements and media reports referred to massacres of Japanese residents and sexual assaults on Japanese women, they were not backed up with concrete evidence. Most likely, the majority of them were exaggerations. This is only common sense. Wise Chinese people would not do anything reckless unless they were assured that there would be no evidence or danger of retribution. They knew that explicitly provocative behavior would give the Japanese reason to retaliate in force, and they also knew they were no match for the Japanese military, which would take something else anew from China. A more appropriate Chinese strategy in those days was to harass the Japanese residents just enough to make it uncomfortable for them to stay in China but not enough to give the Japanese an excuse to use force in retaliation. As a matter of fact, not a few Japanese residents returned home, abandoning businesses they had developed.

Imamura Hitoshi, who later became the commander of the Eighth Area Army during World War II, was chief of the operations section at the Imperial Japanese Army General Staff Office at the time of the Manchurian Incident. He reminisced, "When we heard complaints such as, 'I was struck by Manchurians again,' 'I was spit at,' 'They threw stones at my children on their way to school,' and 'They stopped selling vegetables to us,' it was only natural that we sympathized with their hardship and burned with indignation." Once they were determined to expel Japanese settlers, the most effective method available the Chinese was this indirect harassment rather than direct violence. And this provided the background for the accused at the Tokyo War Crimes Tribunal to defend their conduct as an act of self-defense. Whether this defense could be justified from the standpoint of international law or not, Manchuria in those days was in a lawless state where international laws—that is, laws that govern the relations between and among responsible states—did not apply.

In order to counter the anti-Japanese movements, the Japanese residents in Manchuria grouped together to form the All-Manchuria Japanese Association and the Manchuria Youth League. Resentful of Foreign Minister Shidehara's attitude and disillusioned with the Foreign Ministry, Association members structured the association as an autonomous non-governmental association. At the same time, its members, with the support of military personnel, demanded that the Japanese government and political parties "settle the Manchurian issue by force." This was tantamount to an open rebellion by the Japanese residents in Manchuria against Shidehara's foreign policy.

Inoki Masamichi was correct when he likened this rebellion by the Japanese residents to the role played by the French settlers in the upheavals that eventually culminated in the Algerian War (1954–62). In fact, Algerian independence would have been utterly impossible had not President Charles de Gaulle suppressed the opposition of the colon (French settlers in Algeria). Later, an organization affiliated with former colon sought to kill de Gaulle as long as he lived.

Thus it is that political historian Itō Musojirō's *Manshū mondai no rekishi* (History of the Manchurian issue) referred to the rise of not only the above two organizations but all the Japanese associations in Manchuria and concluded that the Manchurian Incident was no longer avoidable at that point. He went on to say, "It was the collective will of all the Japanese people in Manchuria that ignited the Manchurian Incident." This was the situation in the spring of 1931. Then came summer and autumn, and with them crisis.

CHAPTER
14

Epilogue: The End of Shidehara Diplomacy

—Japan Is Deprived of a Priceless Diplomatic Asset—

Prelude to the Manchurian Incident

The summer of 1931 witnessed the Nakamura Incident in June and the Wanpaoshan Incident in July. The Wanpaoshan Incident was a clash between local Chinese farmers and Korean farmers who had settled in the northwest of Changchun. Some Chinese shooting occurred and Japanese police were mobilized to suppress the dispute. In Korea, the reporting on this incident, including some misinformation, infuriated the public. Some local Chinatowns were vandalized and more than a hundred Chinese residents were killed by mobs in Pyongyang. This incident was directly attributable to the Korean migrant farmers who constructed an irrigation canal without the consent of local Chinese residents. The Japanese side, nevertheless, took it as further evidence of rampant Chinese bullying of the Japanese and Korean residents.

On June 12, Foreign Minister Shidehara Kijūrō sent a directive to Hayashi Kyūjirō, the Japanese Consul-General in Mukden. In this, he pointed out that, despite recurrent assaults on Japanese residents, the Chinese police authorities do nothing to control the riots. Some authorities in fact sided with the mobs. Shidehara severely warned the Chinese side that, "Since public opinion in Japan has hardened on this issue, unless it is settled, the Japanese government may have no recourse but to dispatch troops to China as it did to Shandong previously." While the Japanese side insisted that the treaty of 1909 granted Japanese and Korean farmers the right to lease land and engage in farming, the Chinese side took the position that all unequal treaties, including the 1909 treaty, had already been unilaterally nullified. This Chinese position undermined Shidehara's ideal of a Manchuria where Japanese, Chinese, and Koreans could participate in economic activities on an equal footing. As far as this single incident was concerned, the Chinese side backed off for fear of the Japanese military. But the Chinese side never made its position clear vis-à-vis the fundamental questions Shidehara had raised, thus ending the incident without making any guarantees for the future. Shidehara Diplomacy was evidently at an impasse.

Around the same time, Captain Nakamura Shintarō of the Imperial Japanese Army was arrested and killed by the local military authority during his tour of eastern Mongolia. It was in August 1931 that this incident became known to the Japanese side. Weary of Japan's moves in Mongolia, the Chinese side restricted foreigners visiting the region. The Japanese government had protested the restriction. Because Captain Nakamura entered a restricted area to do some geographical surveying, his conduct could have been interpreted as an act of espionage. Nevertheless, the Chinese murdering Nakamura without a proper trial, cremating his body, disposing of the remains, and hiding all of this was clearly inexcusable. The Japanese public was naturally infuriated. The daily *Asahi Shimbun* published an editorial titled "Reprimand China's Atrocious Conduct in Slaughtering Our Military Officer" to spur the Japanese government to take resolute action. The editorial said:

This unprecedentedly atrocious slaughter of Captain Nakamura by the Chinese authority was an extremely contemptuous act toward the Japanese, a result of the heightened arrogance of the Chinese toward Japan. Unless the Japanese government takes firm measures now to denounce this Chinese atrocity, we are afraid this incident will be followed by a chain of even more deplorable and horrifying incidents. This Chinese conduct is utterly inexcusable.

The Kwantung Army was inspired by the incident, interpreting it as "the best opportunity to demonstrate the authority of the Japanese military, fulfill the Japanese people's expectations, and find a way to settle the Manchuria/Mongolian issue." Nevertheless, Shidehara, in consultation with the Imperial Japanese Army, decided to settle this issue by making the Chinese side formally apologize, punish those who were responsible, indemnify for the damages, and give a guarantee for the future. In the instruction from the war minister addressed to the commander of the Kwantung Army, it was specifically stated, "We must not use this incident as an opportunity to settle the Manchuria/Mongolian issue." This was another disappointment for the Kwantung Army, as revealed in staff officer Ishiwara Kanji's lengthy letter to General Nagata Tetsuzan. The letter said, "It was truly deplorable that the central government did not adopt our views." It was most likely around this time that Ishiwara and his sympathizers made up their minds that they had to act on their own to settle the Manchuria/Mongolian issue.

Imperial Army's False Obedience

Hence the summer of 1931 was filled with an atmosphere in which something could happen at any moment. On August 4, in his instruction at a meeting of army divisional commanders, War Minister Minami Jirō pointed out that "irresponsible outsiders" were conducting a negative campaign against the military, recklessly demanding arms reductions. Although Manchuria/Mongolia was critically important for Japan's survival and development, according to Minami, the situation in the region left much to be desired. Minami concluded that the military must be fully prepared to do its duty.

Although Prime Minister Wakatsuki Reijirō requested War Minister Minami maintain military discipline on August 21, Minami deliberately dodged Wakatsuki's request and failed to deliver a sincere reply. Apprehensive about how the situation was developing, Home Minister Makino Nobuaki consulted Saionji Kinmochi and arranged for Emperor Shōwa to question the war and navy ministers directly. On September 11, one day before the scheduled inquiries by the Emperor, War Minister Minami, who must have learned about the intended imperial inquiries from the navy minister, announced his intention to tighten up military discipline.

This announcement left little space for the emperor to inquire and reprimand the war minister. Minami was reprimanded by Saionji, but he simply repeated himself, saying, "I wholeheartedly agree with everything Your Excellency has pointed out. I will take full responsibility for seeing that your will is carried out." Saionji was later heard to say talking with Minami was "like beating the air."

Perhaps Minami knew that the army had already become uncontrollable. Moreover, he might have had no intention of suppressing the movements with which he himself sympathized and decided to assume the role of bowing low to fend off interventions by the emperor or Saionji for the time being. In other words, it might have been his strategy to bide his time by pretending obedience as long as the Minsei-tō remained the government party and Shidehara the foreign minister.

Catastrophe Just a Matter of Time

Controversy exists over the historical interpretation of the Zhang Zuolin assassination and the Liutiaohu Incident. Some scholars argue that those incidents were arbitrary actions by the likes of Kōmoto Daisaku and Ishiwara Kanji, while others maintain that there had been prior instructions from the Army leadership. In 1953, before he died of illness at the war criminal camp in Taiyuan, China, Kōmoto left the following verbal confession:

> What I would like to clarify is that it was not my wish but the wish of the commander of the Kwantung Army that made me do what I did. Thus, while I may be chiefly responsible, it is the Kwantung Army that should bear all responsibility.

This might have been closest to the truth. It is quite conceivable that a consensus had already been formed among the Imperial Army elite that, sooner or later, only military might could settle the Manchuria/Mongolian issue.

A committee composed of the directors of the major departments in the Ministry of War—including Director of Military Affairs Nagata Tetsuzan and under the chairmanship of General Staff Office section chief Tatekawa Yoshitsugu—compiled an outline of measures to settle the

Manchuria/Mongolian issue in early June 1931. Anticipating that Japan would have no choice but to resort to military action if the anti-Japanese movements in China remained unattended to, the outline proposed that Japan publicize the reality of the anti-Japanese movements both domestically and internationally so that the Western powers would understand Japan's position and would not criticize or oppose Japan's military action when it became unavoidable. The outline also proposed that preparations should be made in about a year.

It so happened that around the same time Shigemitsu Mamoru predicted that Sino-Japanese relations would sooner or later reach a dead end and agreed with Shidehara that "If it has come to a dead end no matter what, it will have to be an internationally justifiable dead end." This thinking was cut from the same cloth as the military's outline. Morishima Gorō, director of the foreign ministry's First Asian Affairs Division at that time, also referred to the similarity between the committee's thinking and Shigemitsu's opinion in his memoir. At the same time, though, Morishima saw through to the army's underlying motive, saying it was quite misleading of the army to set the goal of obtaining the world's support for Japan's position within a year using PR activities, because such a thing could never be accomplished in a year or two. This one-year deadline should be interpreted as saying the Japanese military intends to undertake military action against China in a year's time no matter what. Seen from that angle, the Manchurian Incident was just a matter of time.

Shidehara Diplomacy at a Dead End

Quite unexpectedly, both the military leadership and Shigemitsu at the Foreign Ministry predicted that the Manchurian issue would come to an impasse. What, then, was Shidehara's view on this? The most useful document from which to glean Shidehara's thinking is the record of three candid talks Shidehara had with Eugene Ch'en, foreign minister for the Wang Jingwei government in Guangdong, a month before the Manchurian Incident. Shidehara shared his historical perception with Ch'en, saying:

Although the Chinese seem to believe Manchuria belongs to China, as far as I can tell it was Russian territory. After the Boxer Rebellion, the Japanese government had to obtain Russia's permission to appoint a consul in Yinkou. And it was Japan that expelled Russia from Manchuria. There is no doubt that, had nature taken its course,, Manchuria would still have been lost as Chinese territory.

Thus Shidehara stated that Manchuria had had a distinctive history. Objectively speaking, it was beyond doubt that Manchuria would have remained Soviet territory at least until the Soviet Union's demise in 1991 if Japan had not fought Russia. Shidehara also pointed out that had Japan known of the Li-Lobanov Treaty, a secret Sino-Russian military alliance, that knowledge would have given Japan good reason to pursue a different policy. Japan would have advocated for the cession of the Manchurian territory from Qing, which was Japan's formal adversary, because the treaty was still valid at the time of the Russo-Japanese War. Nevertheless, Shidehara declared that Japan would not claim territorial rights. Before Ch'en's visit to Japan, it was reported in Japan that the purpose of his visit was to sell Manchuria to Japan. What Ch'en actually proposed, instead, was to let China maintain nominal suzerainty over Manchuria with the territory being governed by a high commissioner appointed by Japan. China would give nominal approval to Japan's decision after expelling Zhang Xueliang.

In response, Shidehara replied that it was not territorial rights that Japan was after in Manchuria and said, "What Japan wishes to accomplish is to firmly establish a situation in Manchuria in which Japanese can live together with Manchurians and Koreans and participate in economic activities in mutual friendship and cooperation. We consider this morally reasonable." Concerning the railroad, Shidehara insisted that "it is self-evident from the standpoint of mutual good faith that China should not build a railroad that would diminish the value of the Japanese railroad," especially since China had guaranteed Japan it would not build a railroad to rival the South Manchurian Railway.

Was this Shidehara vision really achievable, or was it doomed from the start? Prior events had already proven that it would have been extremely difficult to achieve it considering Zhang Xueliang's feelings and policies. If Shidehara wished to make a breakthrough with his orthodox approach, his only option would be to fully utilize his diplomatic power to mobilize the United States and Britain so that the three countries together could persuade both Chiang Kai-shek and Zhang Xueliang to comply with the existing treaties and settle every confrontation through good-faith discussions, thus restraining the hasty drive for recovery of concessions and the anti-Japanese movements. This would have been tantamount to a tripartite effort to maintain the Washington Treaty regime.

It should be recalled this was exactly the policy that John MacMurray had advocated, only to be rejected by the State Department, forcing him to retire in disappointment. It would be unrealistic to expect Shidehara to be more persuasive vis-à-vis the State Department than MacMurray, who was a high-ranking official at the department. That being the case, and given the peculiar historical background of Manchuria that Shidehara himself had stressed, Shidehara had no recourse other than the kind of "special measures for settlement" proposed by Eugene Ch'en. But taking such measures would restrict China's territorial sovereignty, which was incompatible with Shidehara's determination to respect the Nine-Power Treaty. Here, too, Shidehara diplomacy came to a dead end.

Ishiwara Kanji, a Genius the Imperial Japanese Army Produced

Ishiwara Kanji arrived at the Kwantung Army Headquarters in Lüshun to take up his position as senior staff officer in 1928. Ishiwara was a genius produced by the Imperial Japanese Army. He had entered the Army War College without much preparation yet graduated second in his class with the honor of a military sword presented by the emperor. According to *Ishiwara Kanji* written by the former Kempeitai colonel Fujimoto Haruki, everyone who participated in Ishiwara's education said, "Ishiwara must be the brightest student that the Army War College has ever had."

His assignment to the Kwantung Army was by no means a promotion. According to journalist Ishibashi Tsuneyoshi's *Shōwa no hanran* (Shōwa rebellions), liberalism was still in full bloom around 1928 when soldiers were looked down on as good-for-nothings. A Kwantung Army staff officer was regarded as inferior to a South

Ishiwara Kanji (photo courtesy of Kyodo News)

Manchuria Railway section chief. Although Ishiwara had been highly respected at the Army War College as an excellent lecturer on the Napoleonic Wars, no institution was willing to offer him a post. In the end, Colonel Kōmoto Daisaku agreed to accept Ishiwara to the Kwantung Army as a staff officer.

The fact that he had been the second best student throughout his years at the Army War College itself was testimony to his genius. A genius sees things differently. Positively speaking, a genius knows how to see the big picture. While it is difficult for such a person to be number one in the Japanese educational system, which emphasizes the virtue of faithfully memorizing textbooks, he can be number two with outstanding potential. Rumor has it that Ishiwara was actually by far the brightest in his class, but he was not given the status of number-one student because he was such a maverick. Also, because a civil servant is expected to just steadily get through the day's tasks, it is difficult to accommodate an over-capable genius. Hence, nobody wanted Ishiwara. Japanese society ordinarily shunts such people off to an organization where talent is bottled up. To give Ishiwara a post in Manchuria was like letting a tiger run loose. As soon as Ishiwara assumed his post, he devoted himself to the study of the Manchurian issue. By 1929, he seemed to have worked out a definite plan to settle the issue. Itagaki Seishirō, who later became Chief of Intelligence for the Kwantung Army, arrived in Manchuria to assume his new post around this time. He immediately agreed with Ishiwara's plan, thus giving birth to the Itagaki-Ishiwara partnership. Tellingly, the Chinese characters "sei" and "ji" used in world-famous conductor Ozawa Seiji's name were taken from Itagaki *Sei*shirō and Ishiwara Kan*ji*, two of the heroes of the Manchurian Incident.

Ishiwara was a philosopher, and a philosopher, the Shōwa Japan political scientist Murakami Yasusuke observed, has to be consistent in his opinions. And in order to remain consistent, there must be a perfect coherence among his philosophy, his historical view, and his actual policies. In the case of Ishiwara, his coherence derived from the prediction based on the Lotus Sutra's *mappo* doctrine that grand pandemonium would come in the form of a US-Japan war across the Pacific. According to this prediction, Japan and the United States would survive semi-final wars with their respective rivals and become the two leading finalists of the world, and there would then be a final showdown between these two using weapons of mass destruction.

In actuality, we know that the US-Japan war took the form of World War II in which Japan was defeated. The final showdown using weapons of mass destruction that Ishiwara had predicted showed up in the form of the nuclear confrontation between the United States and the Soviet Union. Had these two countries actually fought a nuclear war, it would necessarily have been a quick showdown. As it happened, their confrontation took the form of the Cold War, a protracted struggle between two different economic regimes, from which the United States emerged victorious.

Ishiwara's Plan to Govern Manchuria

Nevertheless, it should be pointed out that Ishiwara's theory was based on his very meticulous study of military history rather than on mere divine inspiration. First, Ishiwara questioned Japan's victory in the Russo-Japanese War, paying particular attention to the high probability Japan would have lost had Russia continued to fight a little longer. After studying the Napoleonic Wars to explore the causes of the French defeat, Ishiwara concluded that the key in both cases was the ability to win a protracted struggle that required tremendous resources. It was, incidentally, Ishiwara who changed the dichotomy of war from the traditional "war of annihilation" vs. "war of attrition" to "decisive battle" vs. "protracted struggle."

The conclusion that Ishiwara drew—that World War I was not the final war that was yet to come, which would be an extraordinarily large battle requiring tremendous resources—was an extremely accurate prediction of things to come, for which he really did not need to quote Nichiren. Subsequent history proved how right he was. As for concrete strategy, Ishiwara first proposed that Japan expand its control of Manchuria to include the northern half and tighten its defense in order to block a Soviet attack on Japan, a lesson he learned from Napoleon's having been attacked from behind by Russia in the midst of its war with Britain. Subsequently, it was Ishiwara's strategy to mobilize all the resources of Manchuria/Mongolia, Korea, and Japan in order to prepare for the final war with the United States.

Actually, Ishiwara had a plan to be followed after the occupation of Manchuria in case Japan actually resorted to the use of force there. That made him different from Kōmoto at the time of the Zhang Zuolin assassination. Kōmoto simply hoped that an opportunity would emerge out of the confusion if he killed Zhang. He did not plan his next move. While the Kwantung Army and the Japanese residents had long wanted to separate Manchuria from China, it took a strategist like Ishiwara to accomplish this. Ishiwara also paid close attention to the international situation. Since controlling Manchuria would risk a confrontation with the United States, it was crucially important Japan make sure it would not be attacked from behind by the Soviet Union. The Soviet Union had not yet completed its first five-year plan and could not afford to engage a foreign adversary militarily, which Ishiwara thought a great opportunity for Japan. As a matter of fact, the Soviet Union had no intention of intervening militarily and, instead, proposed a mutual non-aggression treaty for fear of a military confrontation with Japan after Japan conquered Manchuria.

The United States was in the midst of the Great Depression and could not afford an international confrontation. Chiang Kai-shek was too busy expelling Communists, while Zhang Xueliang gathered his main forces around Beijing. Thus the situation presented a far better opportunity for Japan than Ishiwara had hoped for, and it was only a matter of time until Ishiwara and his comrades carried out their plan. Morishima Gorō, who was ordered by Shidehara to inspect the site immediately after the Manchurian Incident, made the following report to Shidehara.

> Whenever they get together for drinks, Kwantung Army staff officers boast, "We have thoroughly planned this scheme for quite some time. Now that we have succeeded in carrying out this part of it, we will go back to Japan and stage a coup to destroy all the political parties and establish a national socialist state centered around the Emperor. We will eliminate all the zaibatsu like Mitsui and Mitsubishi and distribute wealth equally among the people. Mark my words. We will do it."

In the minds of the Imperial Japanese Army leaders on the eve of the Manchurian Incident, the only real question was whether to revolutionize Japan itself first and then save the Japanese residents in Manchuria or to attend to the problems in Manchuria first and then use that leverage to reform Japan. As it turned out, coup attempts in Japan, including the March Incident (1931) and the October Incident (also known as the Imperial Colors Incident) on October 21, 1931, failed, while Ishiwara and Itagaki's Manchurian adventures succeeded.

The Liutiaohu Incident

The Nakamura Incident was at last settled in 1931 when the Chinese side acknowledged the facts on September 11 and officially apologized on September 14. Concurrent with this, the war minister reported at an intra-ministerial meeting on September 14 that he had been reprimanded by the emperor on September 12, which suddenly moderated the meeting's hitherto hard-line atmosphere. It is not hard to imagine how these developments might have exacerbated the sense of impatience Ishiwara, Itagaki, and others in Manchuria felt as their golden opportunity seemed to be slipping away.

On September 15, a secret telegram arrived from Hayashi Kyūjirō, Japanese Consul-General in Mukden, reporting that "the Kwantung Army has assembled its troops and taken out ammunition and other equipment. It appears it is going to take some kind of military action soon." This telegram was discussed by Shidehara at the cabinet meeting. Promising that he would look into it, War Minister Minami dispatched Tatekawa Yoshitsugu, Chief of the Imperial Japanese Army General Staff 4th Section, 2nd Bureau, to Manchuria with a personal letter to convey the emperor's concerns.

The news of Tatekawa's dispatch was reported confidentially to the Kwantung Army by Hashimoto Kingorō and prompted the Kwantung Army to advance the schedule for the explosion from September 28 to September 18. When Tatekawa arrived in Mukden on September 18, he was welcomed with a banquet, during which he allegedly became drunk and dozed off. It was after Tatekawa was incapacitated that the Liutiaohu Incident erupted. But Tatekawa reminisced that, when he secretly broke the seal on the war minister's letter, he found only the crisp instruction, "Take it slow." It is very doubtful Tatekawa had any genuine intention to restrict the Kwantung Army, given that he chose to travel to Manchuria by train rather than airplane despite the urgency of the situation. Considering that Tatekawa was the model for Yamanaka Minetarō's *Tekichū ōdan 300-ri* (1,200 km through enemy lines), a magazine serial immensely popular among pre–World War II Japanese boys, and that he remained a central figure in the military throughout Japan's militarist era, it is only natural to see his conduct as a charade that he put on with full knowledge of the circumstances.

The hastily implemented explosion was a clumsy affair. It destroyed

Scene of the Liutiaohu Incident where part of the South Manchuria Railway track was wrecked (photo courtesy of Kyodo News)

just 70 cm of track in one direction and 10 cm in the other direction and damaged only two ties, causing no problems for subsequent traffic. Overall, the damage was so light that international investigators later wondered how such minor damage could ignite a major incident. In those days, however, people only knew what the Japanese Army had announced and nobody knew the truth. In contrast to the shoddiness of the explosion itself, subsequent military operations and the briefings that Ishiwara had planned were thorough and expeditious in the extreme.

The first report on the incident reached Tokyo around 01:30 on the morning of September 19 and said: "At around 22:30 on the evening of September 18, riotous Chinese troops destroyed the South Manchuria Railway tracks, assaulted our garrison, and provoked armed confrontation with our forces. Receiving this report, the Second Battalion of the Mukden Independent Garrison has been dispatched to the site." Subsequent telegrams reported that the enemy continued to resist and that Senior Staff Officer Itagaki had issued orders to clear the enemy from the Chinese garrison in Beidaying and initiate an all-out attack on the city of Mukden.

Of course, the enemy attacks and resistance were all fiction. The truth was that Chinese troops in Beidaying were assaulted by the Japanese troops in their sleep. Because they were under strict non-resistance orders from Zhang Xueliang, they simply evacuated, not knowing what else to do. Because the Chinese side had no idea what was going on and the Japanese military was the sole source of information on this incident, Tokyo and the rest of the world had no choice but to believe the Kwantung Army's announcements.

The most serious obstacle for the Kwantung Army in planning operations was the lack of troops. As stated in Ishiwara's affidavit presented at the Tokyo War Crimes Tribunal, Zhang Xueliang had more than 200,000 troops and the Kwantung Army only slightly more than 10,000 spread thinly along the 1,000 kilometers of the South Manchurian Railway. The Japanese side would be no match for the Chinese side if the Chinese troops were fully resolved to fight back, and the Japanese side's only chance was to launch a pre-emptive surprise strike. Thus it was decided to take Mukden in a mid-night surprise attack. But the Japanese side still needed reinforcements from the Japanese Korean Army in order to continue to fight the Chinese side. Staff Officer Kanda Masatane of the Japanese Korean Army had been in close contact with his long-time comrades Itagaki and Ishiwara. At 08:30 on the morning of September 19, Tokyo received a communication from the Japanese Korean Army that it had dispatched a company to Manchuria and was preparing its First Mixed Brigade for dispatch. That meant the Kwantung Army had already accumulated fait accompli ahead of the cabinet meeting to be held in Tokyo at 10:00 the next morning.

It was not that the Chinese side or Japan's Foreign Ministry sat idly by and watched things unfold. The Chinese side, in fact, notified Japan's Consul-General in Mukden by phone about the incident as early as 23:00 on September 18 and announced its non-resistance policy. The consulate, for its part, remained in contact with the Chinese throughout the night and reported new developments to Tokyo. By 06:00 the next morning, the consulate had reported that the Japanese army had already taken almost all major strategic points in Mukden. Thus the cabinet meeting on September 19 was held after these fait accompli had already been created.

At this cabinet meeting, Shidehara won a firm commitment from War Minister Minami that the Japanese army would not further expand its operations and conveyed this promise as the Japanese government's intention to the League of Nations. However, as far as the dispatch of the Japanese Korean Army troops was concerned, even Shidehara had to admit that what had been done could not be undone. In the end, the matter was settled by Prime Minister Wakatsuki's apology to the emperor for having let the Japanese Korean Army troops cross the border into Manchuria without an imperial edict. By monopolizing information and by taking prompt action, Ishiwara succeeded in creating fait accompli free of outside interference.

Appeal to the League of Nations

The Japanese legation in Beijing had been apprehensive about the worsening situation prior to the Liutiaohu Incident. Japanese Minister Shigemitsu in China had been in consultation with Kuomintang Finance Minister Soong Tse-wen and planned to visit Manchuria with Soong to explore ways to settle the Manchurian issues with Uchida Kōsai, president of the South Manchuria Railway. The Liutiaohu Incident erupted one day before their scheduled departure, nullifying their plan.

The first thing the next morning, Soong proposed to Shigemitsu that a Sino-Japanese joint problem-solving committee be launched. Shigemitsu immediately relayed the suggestion to Tokyo. Two days passed with no response from Tokyo. It was only on September 21 that Foreign Minister Shidehara finally gave authorization. Meanwhile, military actions by the Kwantung Army had expanded so widely that Soong had to say, "With the Japanese army's premeditated actions, the situation in Manchuria is now out of control. China has already appealed to the League of Nations." Chang Chun, a graduate of the Japanese military academy who later became Premier of the Republic of China, was present at the September 19 meeting. Chang pressed Shigemitsu on the point of whether the Japanese government could really control the military. To keep the meeting going, Shigemitsu replied, "Now that the Japanese government has decided against expanded military action, we will just have to do our best." In retrospect, things developed exactly as Chang had feared.

Shidehara was deeply disappointed by the action taken by the Chinese side. He immediately summoned the Chinese minister and, for three hours, tried to persuade him that China should change its mind and re-enter direct negotiations with Japan. Shidehara emphasized the futility of the appeal to the League of Nations, saying that the meeting would only become an oratorical contest among countries totally ignorant of the situation in the East. No solution could be expected, he said, because the two contending sides had to make bullish speeches to save face. After this meeting, the Chinese minister did not respond to Shidehara's invitations. Once the Chinese government decided to appeal to the League of Nations, it prohibited its minister in Japan from any further contact with Shidehara.

While Shidehara believed in cooperative diplomacy, he remained consistently skeptical about the League of Nations. He was a staunch believer in international cooperation based on orthodox mutual understanding among the major powers. But, as it turned out, it was the actions of small countries, which argued for the virtue of juridical justice, that succeeded in blocking the major powers, including Britain, from settling the Manchurian issue with a realistic compromise. Here again, Shidehara Diplomacy had to face a new situation in which traditional diplomatic common sense no longer applied.

Shidehara Diplomacy Fading from the Limelight

These developments notwithstanding, international trust in Shidehara remained high. US Secretary of State Henry Stimson wrote in *The Far Eastern Crisis* that was published in 1939:

> The Japanese government had thus for ten years given an exceptional record of good citizenship in the life of the international world, Shidehara was still in office. We knew he had been laboring hard against the pressure of the army leaders in Manchuria and for moderation. We had reached the conclusion that those leaders had engineered this outbreak probably without his knowledge and certainly against his wishes. It seemed clear to us that no steps should be taken which would make his task more difficult because certainly our best chance of a successful solution of the situation lay in him.

Stimson also wrote in his diary for September 23: "My problem is to let the Japanese know that we are watching them and at the same time do it in a way which will help Shidehara who is on the right side, not play into the hands of any nationalist agitators."

It has been a tradition in American diplomacy to encourage the pro-democracy forces and doves within an adversary country. This policy has provided the theoretical justification for recent US policies toward the Soviet Union under Gorbachev and Russia under Boris Yeltsin in the 1990s. Shidehara's foreign policy might not have succeeded due to domestic politics in Japan even if Shidehara had remained in the cabinet, but his very presence and the perception that he was struggling to pursue his good neighbor diplomacy would have been a strong shield for Japan in fending off pressure from the United States.

The Kwantung Army stopped its operations only once during the Manchurian Incident. This was when the Kwantung Army arbitrarily started advancing to Jinzhou near the Great Wall, which was Zhang Xueliang's operational base after he was driven from Mukden. Told of this advance by Shidehara, the Imperial Japanese Army General Staff Office looked into it and deemed it a violation of orders. Once the case was submitted to imperial decision, all military actions were halted by imperial decree. Stimson wrote in *The Far Eastern Crisis*: "But whatever the reason, Shidehara made on this occasion a very vigorous effort and for once was temporarily successful. The Japanese troops which had actually begun their advance from Mukden towards Chinchow were stopped on November 27th apparently by orders from Tokyo and returned to Mukden." This is why, Stimson wrote, he paid close attention during the deliberations at the League of Nations so that strong measures that could undermine Shidehara's position not be adopted despite China's strong appeal. Because it was utterly impossible for Shidehara to directly order the retreat, which would have been a violation of the autonomy of military command, Stimson's description was inaccurate. After the publication of Stimson's book, however, voices became even louder in Japan, demanding the "elimination of traitor Shidehara" and the "liquidation of betrayer Shidehara."

The imperial edict notwithstanding, the Kwantung Army resumed its full-scale attack on Jinzhou in November. When Stimson learned of Shidehara's resignation as foreign minister together with other members of the Wakatsuki cabinet on December 11, he indignantly said, "it was evident that all hope for a solution of the Manchurian problem by conciliation and for a fair settlement by even-handed negotiation" was ended. From now on, the United States would aggressively pound on Japan without restraint. He immediately placed an international call to Britain's foreign secretary to convey the US government's resolve. This new US stance took the form of a note to the Japanese and Chinese governments in the so-called Stimson Doctrine of January 7, 1932. The note read in part:

> . . . the American Government deems it to be its duty to notify both the Imperial Japanese Government and the Government of the Chinese Republic that it cannot admit the legality of any situation *de facto* nor does it intend to recognize any treaty or agreement entered into between those Governments, or agents thereof, which may impair the treaty rights of the United States or its citizens in China, including those that relate to the sovereignty, the independence, or the territorial and administrative integrity of the Republic of China, or to the international policy relative to China, commonly known as the open door policy . . .

American doctrines are often only rhetoric unaccompanied by action. This doctrine, too, fell into oblivion—but only temporarily. It was resurrected as an American policy at the opening of the Pacific War when Democratic President Franklin Roosevelt appointed Republican Henry Stimson Secretary of War in his supra-party cabinet and Stanley Hornbeck chief of the State Department Division of Far Eastern Affairs. As the Japanese government immediately pointed out, it was rather uncertain how legally valid this document by Stimson was. However, the doctrine was an expression of Stimson's indignation at having had to give up on Japan's diplomacy after Shidehara's resignation

With the resignation of Foreign Minister Shidehara, Japan was deprived of an invaluable asset in its diplomacy with the United States. By that time, the Kwantung Army's arbitrary conduct in Manchuria was completely out of government control, no matter how many times the cabinet decided on non-expansion and reprimanded the army through the war minister. The Minsei-tō cabinet was seen to be totally powerless in controlling the military. Accordingly, the idea was floated in Japan that a coalition cabinet made of all the political parties might be able to control the military in the name of the "collective will of the nation." Temporarily convinced of its viability, Prime Minister Wakatsuki discussed this idea with Home Minister Adachi Kenzō, who immediately started to lay the groundwork. When Wakatsuki consulted Shidehara and Finance Minister Inoue Jun'nosuke, however, they thought it outrageous. They declared it impossible a coalition government would pursue the Minsei-tō's traditional foreign and financial policies.

It is true that merely expanding the number of government parties alone would not lead to a strengthening of the leadership. If anything, it would dilute the government policies, which would only benefit those who had been critical of Shidehara's diplomacy. As a matter of fact, Adachi was one of the voices most critical of Shidehara's foreign policy in the cabinet. After consultating Shidehara and Inoue, Wakatsuki tried to dissuade Adachi from continued criticism. Adachi stubbornly refused to change his mind. When Wakatsuki requested his resignation, Adachi refused to be the only one to resign. Thus the Wakatsuki cabinet collapsed under intra-cabinet discord. Shidehara stayed in the midst of abuses criticizing his "humiliating diplomacy" and "weak-kneed diplomacy." Shidehara then completely disappeared from the front stage of Japan's politics and diplomacy until Japan's defeat in World War II. When, returning as Japanese prime minister, he appeared at his first press conference, some reporters were heard to exclaim, "I didn't know Shidehara was still alive." That was the degree of oblivion that Shidehara enjoyed during the era of militarism.

What was Shidehara Diplomacy?

One may wonder what Shidehara Diplomacy was all about. Against a simplistic criticism of Shidehara's cooperative diplomacy, Shidehara once said that there cannot be a diplomacy that is not independent if it is to protect the national interest, nor can there be a diplomacy that is not cooperative because a nation must deal with other countries no matter what. The four diplomacies of international cooperation, independent foreign policy, peace diplomacy, and diplomacy based on use of force shared the common goal of protecting Japan's special interests in Manchuria/Mongolia. It was not that Shidehara categorically rejected the use of force; he just wished to see Japan act as much as possible in conformity with international norms.

In a nutshell, Shidehara wished to pursue diplomacy based on the same common sense and discernment as exhibited by British and American diplomats, who were the intellectuals and elites in their respective societies.

When Shidehara was at the helm of Japanese foreign policy, the Anglo-Saxon world had been the global hegemon for four centuries. It was obvious to all that, as long as Japan associated itself with the Anglo-Saxon world or, to borrow the words of Saionji Kinmochi, as long as Japan "shared the baton of command with Britain and the United States," Japan could navigate its diplomacy safely without fear of deviating from the international community mainstream or being shut out from information access. As far as his will to steadfastly maintain the Washington Conference international system was concerned, Shidehara's stance was, if anything, firmer than that of Britain and the United States. This gave Britain and the United States reason to admire Shidehara. Had Shidehara stayed in the Japanese government, it could have expected the understanding and support of Britain and the United States, which did not wish to weaken Shidehara's position, even when, facing a crisis, the Japanese government made the aggressive decision to defend its own national interest.

The question was whether domestic politics in Japan would have continued to allow this kind of diplomatic posture. It was certainly possible during the Taishō Democracy. From the beginning, Shidehara Diplomacy had a fundamental adversary—that is, Shidehara's pro-Britain/US stance was intolerable to advocates of nationalism and pan-Asianism. His Westernized sophistication was the target of repulsion by the common people. Behind-closed-doors diplomacy by a high society gentleman, who was also the son-in-law of the Mitsubishi zaibatsu, naturally provoked antipathy among ultra-rightists, ultra-leftists, and even among the average masses. Anti-elite sentiment is not a peculiarly post–World War II phenomenon. It has always been a constant in human history.

But in the predominant atmosphere of party politics, Taishō Democracy allowed Shidehara Diplomacy to be pursued for ten years, not only letting Japan coexist with its political and psychological adversaries but also utilizing these antipathies, which were born naturally in people's minds, as checks and balances.

Epilogue

Conventional perceptions of Taishō Democracy have not necessarily been favorable in Japan. Seen from the viewpoint of *hanbatsu* champions and conservatives, the political parties that accomplished Taishō Democracy after strenuous efforts beginning with the freedom and people's rights movement in the Meiji era were just a bunch of unfilial traitors who challenged the authority of the emperor. Party government was utterly out of the question while Yamagata Aritomo lived. It was only after World War II that the word "democracy" gained genuine legitimacy in Japan. Prior to that, the perception of democracy in most people's minds had been at best ambivalent. This was particularly so on the eve of World War II, when democratic government ruled by political parties was synonymous with corruption and degeneration and putting partisan interests over the national interest, and was contrasted with the patriotic political reforms led by the military. In the post–World War II leftist historical view, Taishō Democracy has gotten good reviews only as an era during which the buds of socialism and labor movements were born. Otherwise, it has been described as an era that benefited only a small, privileged segment of Japanese society while the masses were oppressed and impoverished.

Setting aside those stereotypical descriptions, if readers ask their grandparents and great-grandparents what their own memories of Taishō Democracy era are like, they will be startled to hear quite positive recollections from most of those who had first-hand experience with the era. Bad memories heard from a few are actually attributable to the hardships during the subsequent Shōwa Financial Crisis (1927). While those Japanese who lived through the days immediately before World War II are already of advanced age, those who have firsthand knowledge of Taishō Democracy are mostly over a hundred years old and on their way out one by one. It appears, though, that almost no one would disagree with the view that it was a good time.

I quoted a number of Japanese martial songs from the Meiji era in my *Komura Jutarō and His Time*, a sister volume to the current book, in order to convey the atmosphere at the time. Their equivalents in the Taishō era are children's songs that similarly, if not more vividly, convey the atmosphere of the time. Can there be any other songs that were born from such peace and mental stability as those Taishō children's songs? The peace of post–World War II Japan has not produced any work of art as moving and as lyrical as those songs. For the Japanese, peace in the Taishō era was a product of their own efforts: the winning of the First Sino-Japanese and Russo-Japanese Wars and the conclusion of the Anglo-Japanese Alliance.

It was an era when the newly emerged middle class was confident of the stability of the state and society and enjoyed the fruits of peace.

One might say those songs are of girlish taste. But it was the spirit of Taishō to rebel against Meiji's masculine samurai spirit. Unlike the Meiji era, Taishō allowed the open expression of womanly sentiments. Behind the sentiments expressed by those songs was the unshakable sense of stability and self-confidence in the society they lived in. The artistic sense of the time found its expression not only in those children's songs but also in the highly sophisticated art songs such as those composed by Yamada Kōsaku. It is these Taishō-era Japanese songs that first come to the minds of Korean and Taiwanese people of the prewar generation when they look back on the days under the Japanese colonization not without some nostalgia. Modern Japanese civilization, thus, has another spiritual genesis in the Taishō era, along with the patriotism of the Meiji era, to which the Japanese can proudly return.

Personally, I think Taishō Democracy was a peak reached in modern Japan's politics and society. It was a fulfillment that the Japanese people had created with their own hands since the Meiji Restoration. Having won the First Sino-Japanese and Russo-Japanese Wars, the military was proud to be the bulwark of the state. Diplomats were proud to have provided Japan with the unshakable foundation of peace and prosperity in the Anglo-Japanese Alliance. And the economic ministries, the business community, and the private sector were also full of self-confidence for having achieved modernization with their own hands. And finally, political parties had at last realized a democratic government in Japan after decades of strife with the *hanbatsu* starting with the formation of the Jiyū-tō in the Meiji era and then standing at the pinnacle of power, above the military and the bureaucrats in the Taishō era.

In other words, it was an era in which each of the political actors in Japan had accomplished something of its own with its own blood, sweat, and tears and, together, provided checks and balances under the supremacy of a democratic government. With the self-confidence acquired through the attainment of modernization, people freely expressed their views. As I said earlier, the spirit of Taishō allowed the open expression of womanly sentiments. It was also in the same Taishō era in which people felt no constraints in speaking of such things as liberalism, democracy, and socialism. It was an era in open rebellion against the Meiji generation.

But Taishō Democracy collapsed. Shidehara's resignation was the most symbolic event marking this collapse. Collapsed though it was, Taishō Democracy, the culmination of Japan's modernization since the Meiji Restoration, still remains the starting point for modern Japanese history to which we can always return. Edwin Reischauer recounted in his autobiography advising the occupation forces that Taishō Democracy should be restored in Japan. And indeed, Taishō Democracy was adopted as the genesis of Japan's postwar democracy. In fact, all of the reforms proposed by Shidehara as prime minister were positively approved by General MacArthur. It was the misled policies of uneducated, petty occupation bureaucrats that crafted the interpretation, and enforced it with a strict censorship, that prewar Japan had only been a militarist dark age and that the American occupation introduced democracy for the first time in Japanese history. Nothing comes from nothing. It is because Japan had a tradition of democracy that its people struggled to build for over half a century since the Meiji era, and because Japan returned to that tradition, that Japan's democratic system today has unshakable resilience no matter how severely its inherent shortcomings are criticized.

REFERENCES

Asada Sadao; *Ryō-Taisen-kan no Nichibei kankei* (US-Japan relations between the two World Wars); University of Tokyo Press; Tokyo; 1993.

Bemis, Samuel Flagg; *A Diplomatic History of the United States*; Henry Holt & Company; New York; 1936.

Brzezinski, Zbigniew; *The Grand Failure: The Birth and Death of Communism in the Twentieth Century*; Charles Schribner's Sons; New York: 1989. (in Itō Ken'ichi translation)

Chiang Kai-shek; *China's Destiny*: in translation as *Chūgoku no meiun*; Hatano Kanichi, translator; Nihon Hyōron-sha; Tokyo: 1946.

Dōdai Keizai Konwa-kai, ed; *Kindai Nihon sensō-shi* (Military history of modern Japan); Dōdai Keizai Konwa-kai; Tokyo; 1995.

Fujimoto Haruki; *Ningen Ishiwara Kanji* (Ishiwara Kanji, the man); Taisen Sangyō-sha; 1959.

Fujimura Hisao; *Kakumeika Sonbun* (Sun Yet-sen, the revolutionary); Chūō Kōron; Tokyo; 1994.

Hall, John W.; *Japan From Prehistory to Modern Times*; Delacorte Press, New York: 1970. (in Onabe Teruhiko translation)

Hara Mokuichirō, ed; *Hara Takashi nikki* (Hara Takashi diary); Kangensha; Tokyo; 1950–51.

Hara Takashi Zenshū Hakkō-kai (Committee to Publish the Complete Works of Hara Takashi), ed: Hara Takashi Zenshū (Complete Works of Hara Takashi); Hara Shobō: Tokyo: 1969.

Hirama Yōichi; *Dai-Ichiji Sekai Taisen to Nippon Kaigun* (The First World War and the Japanese Navy); Keiō University Press; Tokyo; 1998. (plus assorted treatises he wrote during his time at the National Defense Academy.)

Hosokawa Ryūgen, ed; *Nippon saishō retsuden* (Lives of the Japanese Prime Ministers); Jiji Tsūshin-sha; Tokyo; 1985–87.

Hosoya Chihiro; *Shiberia shuppei no shiteki kenkyū* (Historical study on the dispatch of troops to Siberia); Yūhikaku; Tokyo; 1955.

Ikeda Kiyoshi; *Jiyū to kiritsu* (Freedom and discipline); Iwanami Shinsho; Tokyo; 1949.

Inoki Masamichi; *Hyōden Yoshida Shigeru* (A biography of Yoshida Shigeru); Yomiuri Shimbun-sha; Tokyo; 1978–81.

Ishibashi Tsuneki; *Shōwa no hanran* (Shōwa uprisings); Takagi Shobō; Tokyo; 1979.

Ishii Kikujiro; *Gaikō yoroku* (Diplomatic commentaries); Iwanami Shoten; Tokyo; 1930.

Itō, Masanori; *Gunbatsu kōbō-shi* (Rise and fall of military cliques); Bungeishunjū; Tokyo; 1957-58.

_____; *Dai Kaigun o omou* (Remembering the Great Navy). Kōjin-sha; Tokyo; 1981.

Itō Musojirō; *Manshū mondai no rekishi* (History of the Manchurian Issue); Hara Shobō; Tokyo; 1983.

Jones, Robert L.; *History of the Foreign Policy of the United States*; G. P. Putnam's Sons; New York; 1933.

Kaigun Rekishi Hozon-kai, ed; *Nihon Kaigun-shi* (History of the Japanese Navy); Kaigun Rekishi Hozon-kai; Tokyo; 1995.

Kajima Kenkyūjo, ed; *Nihon gaikō-shi* (Diplomatic history of Japan); Kajima Kenkyūjo; Tokyo; 1970–73.

Katsuta Tatsuo; *Jūshin tachi no Shōwa-shi* (Senior statesmen in Showa history). Bungei Shunjū-sha; Tokyo; 1981

Kimura Takeshi; *Saionji Kinmochi-den* (Biography of Saionji Kinmochi); Denki Kankō-kai; Tokyo; 1938.

Kissinger, Henry A.; *Diplomacy*; Simon & Schuster; New York; 1994. (in Okazaki Hisahiko translation)

Kojima Noboru; *Tōkyō Saiban* (International Military Tribunal for the Far East); Chūō Kōron-sha; Tokyo; 1971.

Kurihara Ken; *Tai Manmō seisaku-shi no ichimen* (An aspect of Japanese policies toward Manchuria and Inner Mongolia); Hara Shobō; Tokyo; 1966.

Kuroha Shigeru; *Nichi-Bei gaikō no keifu* (Genealogy of Japan-US foreign policy); Kyōdō Shuppan; Tokyo; 1974.

_____; *Nichi-Ei dōmei no kiseki* (The history of Anglo-Japanese alliance). Bunka Shobō Hakubun-sha. Tokyo: 1987.

Maeda Renzan; *Hara Takashi-den* (Biography of Hara Takashi); Takayama Shoin; Tokyo; 1943.

Maesaka Toshiyuki, ed; *Mizuno Hironori*; Yuzankaku. Tokyo: 1993.

Mainichi Shimbun; *Nippon no hyakunen: Shashin de miru fuzoku bunka-shi* (One hundred years of Japanese customs and culture in photographs); Mainichi Shimbun-sha; Tokyo; 1995.

McKenzie, Frederick Arthur; *The Tragedy of Korea*; E. P. Dutton & Co; New York; 1908.

Mikuriya Takashi; *Baba Tsunego no menboku* (Baba Tsunego's honor); Chūō Kōron-sha; Tokyo; 1997.

Miller, Edward S.; *War Plan Orange: The U.S. Strategy to Defeat Japan, 1897–1945*; United States Naval Institute Press. Annapolis: 1991. (in Sawada Hiroshi translation)

Ministry of Foreign Affairs Research Department, translator and editor; *Sonbun zenshū* (Complete works of Sun Yat-sen); Hara Shobō; Tokyo; 1967.

Miyazaki Toten; *Sanjūsan-nen no yume* (The thirty-three year dream); Bungeishunjū-sha; Tokyo; 1943.

Murakami Keisaku, ed.; *Sensō yōron* (On war); Tokyo-to Bōei Kyōkai; Tokyo; 1968.

Oka Yoshitake; *Nippon kindai-shi taikei* (A survey of modern Japanese history); University of Tokyo Press; Tokyo; 1969.

Ōsugi Kazuo; *Nicchū 15-nen sensō-shi* (History of the 15-year Sino-Japanese war); Chūō Kōron-sha; Tokyo; 1996.

Piggott, Francis; *Broken Thread: An Autobiography*; Gale & Polden; London; 1950. (in Hasegawa Saiji translation)

Ritsumeikan Daigaku Saionji Kinmochi-den Hensan Iinkai (Ritsumeikan University Saionji Kinmochi Biography Editorial Committee); *Saionji Kinmochi-den* (Biography of Saionji Kinmochi); Iwanami Shoten; Tokyo; 1990–96.

Sankei Shimbun; *Shō Kaiseki hiroku* (Secret memoirs of Chiang Kai-shek); Sankei Shimbun; Tokyo; 1985.

Shidehara Heiwa Zaidan; *Shidehara Kijūrō*; Shidehara Heiwa Zaidan; Tokyo; 1955.

Shidehara Kijūrō; *Gaikō 50-nen* (50 years of diplomacy). Yomiuri Shimbun-sha; Tokyo; 1951.

Shigemitsu Mamoru; *Shōwa no dōran* (Showa: A time of upheaval); Chūō Kōron-sha; Tokyo; 1952.

Shinobu Seizaburō; *Nihon gaikō-shi* (Diplomatic history of Japan); Mainichi Shimbun-sha; Tokyo; 1974.

Shioda Ushio; *Saigo no gohōkō: Saishō Shidehara Kijūrō.* (Prime Minister Shidehara Kijūrō's final service); Tokyo; Bungeishunjū-sha; 1992

Stimson, Henry; *The Far Eastern Crisis*; Harper & Brothers; New York; 1936.

Tsunoda Jun, ed; *Ishiwara Kanji shiryō: Kokubō ronsaku-hen* (Ishiwara Kanji documents: Ishiwara's treatises on national defense); Hara Shobō. Tokyo; 1966.

_____; *Manshū mondai to kokubō hōshin* (Manchurian issue and national defense policy); Hara Shobō; Tokyo; 1967.

Usui Katsumi; *Manshū jihen* (Manchurian Incident); Chūō Kōron-sha; Tokyo; 1974.

Waldron, Arthur; *How the Peace was Lost*; Hoover Institution Press; Stanford; 1992. (in Kinukawa Hiroshi translation)

Wang, Yunsheng; *Nisshi gaikō 60-nen shi* (60 years of Sino-Japanese diplomacy); Kensetsu-sha; Tokyo; 1936.

Yamaura Kanichi; *Mori Kaku*; Hara Shobō; Tokyo; 1982.

Yomiuri Shimbun; "Kōmoto Daisaku Kyojutsusho wo Nyūshu" (We got hold of Komoto Daisaku's testimony); *This Is Yomiuri*; November 1997.

Yoshimura Michio; *Zōho: Nippon to Roshia* (Expanded: Japan and Russia); Nihon Keizai Hyōron-sha; Tokyo; 1991.

APPENDIX

Chronogical Table of Shidehara Kijūrō's Life and Accomplishments

CE Year	Japanese Era year	Age	Life Events	Domestic/Overseas Events
1868	Meiji 1			Meiji Restoration
				Charter Oath promulgated
1869	Meiji 2			Satsuma/Chōshū/Tosa/Higo-*han* return the *han* registers to the Emperor Meiji
1871	Meiji 4			Abolition of the *han* system and establishment of the prefecture system
1872	Meiji 5	1	Born in August in Kadoma-mura, Kawachi-gun, Osaka, as the second son of Shidehara Shinjirō. The Shideharas were a well-off agrarian landlord family.	
1874	Meiji 7	3		Japanese troops dispatched to Taiwan
1877	Meiji 10	6		Satsuma Rebellion
1881	Meiji 14	10		Imperial edict on the establishment of parliament in 23rd year of Meiji
				Ōkuma Shigenobu dismissed as the result of Political Upheaval of 1881
1886	Meiji 19	15		First conference on revision of unequal treaties
1888	Meiji 21	17		Japan-Mexico Treaty of Amity, Commerce, and Navigation (Japan's first equal treaty with a Western country) concluded
1889	Meiji 22	18		Promulgation of the Constitution of the Empire of Japan and the Imperial Household Law
1890	Meiji 23	19		First general election for House of Representatives
				First session of the Imperial Diet

CE Year	Japanese Era year	Age	Life Events	Domestic/Overseas Events
1890	Meiji 23	19		*The Influence of Sea Power upon History, 1660-1783* by Alfred Thayer Mahan published
1892	Meiji 25	21	Graduates from Third Higher School (Dai-san Kōtō Chūgakkō)	
			Enters Faculty of Law, Tokyo Imperial University	
1894	Meiji 27	23		Donghak Peasant Revolution in Korea
				Japan and Qing dispatch troops to Korea
				Japanese fleet attacks Qing fleet off Pungdo (Battle of Pungdo); Japanese army occupies Seong-hwan and Asan (Battle of Seonghwan & Battle of Asan). Japan declares war against Qing (First Sino-Japanese War)
1895	Meiji 28	24	Graduates from Faculty of Law, Tokyo Imperial University	Treaty of Shimonoseki signed (approval of Korea's independence; cession of Liaodong Peninsula, Taiwan, and Penghu Islands; and Qing to pay 200 million taels in war indemnifications)
			Enters Ministry of Agriculture and Commerce, assigned to the Bureau of Mines	Triple Intervention by Germany, France, and Russia leading to return of the Liaodong Peninsula to Qing
1896	Meiji 29	25	Passes the Foreign Service Examination	Komura-Weber Memorandum on Korean affairs signed
			Appointed deputy consul and assigned to Incheon, Korea, in October.	Yamagata-Lobanov Agreement on Korean affairs signed
1898	Meiji 31	27		Start of Spanish-American War
				United States annexes Hawaii, the Philippines, and Guam.
1899	Meiji 32	28	Appointed consul and assigned to the Japanese Consulate-General in London in May	Boxer Rebellion (until 1901)

CE Year	Japanese Era year	Age	Life Events	Domestic/Overseas Events
1899	Meiji 32	28		Anglo-Japanese Treaty of Commerce and Navigation and other revised treaties come into force
1900	Meiji 33	29	Posted to Antwerp, Belgium, in December	Qing declares war on all Western powers
				Britain requests Japan dispatch troops. Itō Hirobumi cabinet decides to dispatch mixed brigade reinforcements
1901	Meiji 34	30	Assigned to the Japanese Consul in Pusan in September	Qing court compelled to sign Boxer Protocol (Peace Agreement between the Eight-Nation Alliance and China)
1902	Meiji 35	31		Anglo-Japanese Alliance signed
				Trans-Siberian Railway completed
				Japan and Russia sign treaty on return of Manchuria to Qing
1903	Meiji 36	32	Marries Masako, daughter of Iwasaki Yatarō, in January and becomes Katō Takaaki brother-in-law	Russia occupies Manchuria
			First son, Michitarō, born in December	Russia policies decided at cabinet meeting held in Imperial presence
				Japanese Foreign Minister Komura starts negotiations with Russian minister to Japan Roman Rosen on withdrawal of troops from Manchuria
1904	Meiji 37	33	Appointed acting secretary of Ministry of Foreign Affairs. Makes the acquaintance of Henry Denison, foreign advisor to the Japanese government, who helps him brush up his English.	Russo-Japanese War (until 1905)
1905	Meiji 38	34	Appointed Director of Telecommunication, Foreign Minister's Secretariat, in November	Bloody Sunday in St. Petersburg (Russia)

CE Year	Japanese Era year	Age	Life Events	Domestic/Overseas Events
1905	Meiji 38	34		Anglo-Japanese Alliance renewed
				Japan and Russia sign Treaty of Portsmouth
				Hibiya Incendiary Incident in protest of the terms of the Treaty of Portsmouth
				Sun Yat-sen launches Tong-menghui (Chinese United League)
1906	Meiji 39	35	Second son, Shigeo, born in February	South Manchuria Railway Co. Ltd. established
				HMS *Dreadnought* launched, revolutionizing naval power
1907	Meiji 40	36		French-Japanese agreement on Vietnam signed
				Resident-General of Korea Itō Hirobumi claims Korean court's action a violation of the spirit of the Korea-Japan Protocol and threatens war, forcing the Korean emperor to resign
				Japan-Korea Treaty of 1907 (also known as the Japan-Korea Annexation Treaty) concluded expanding the jurisdiction of the Resident-General of Korea to include not only diplomacy but the entire range of domestic politics. Korean Army is disarmed.
				The Triple Entente (among Britain, France, and Russia) formed as a counterweight to the Triple Alliance of Germany, Austria-Hungary, and Italy (with which Japan and Britain intended to restrict Germany)
1908	Meiji 41	37	Appointed to serve concurrently as Director of Investigation and Director of Telecommunication, Foreign Minister's Secretariat, in October	Japan-United States Gentlemen's Agreement on Migration signed
				Imperial Rescript of 1908

CE Year	Japanese Era year	Age	Life Events	Domestic/Overseas Events
1908	Meiji 41	37		Root-Takahira Agreement signed between the United States and Japan on Pacific issues and equal commercial opportunities in China
1909	Meiji 42	38		Itō Hirobumi resigns as Resident-General of Korea
				Japanese cabinet meeting decides to annex Korea
				Japan and Qing sign Gando Convention on five issues including Japan's railroad concessions in Manchuria
				Itō Hirobumi, President of the Privy Council, assassinated by Korean nationalist/independence activist An Jung-geun at Harbin Railway Station
1910	Meiji 43	39		Japan-Korea Treaty of 1910 (on Japan's annexation of Korea) signed
1911	Meiji 44	40	Appointed Director-General of Foreign Ministry's Bureau of Investigation in July	Japan signs treaties of commerce and navigation with the United States, Britain, and Germany, achieving tariff autonomy
				Second renewal of the Anglo-Japanese Alliance (excluding the United States from target countries)
				Xinhai Revolution (in Qing China)
1912	Meiji 45 Taishō 1	41	Appointed counselor at the Japanese embassy in Washington, DC	Formation of the Republic of China
			Makes the acquaintance of the British Ambassador to the United States James Bryce	Emperor Meiji passes away at age 61
				Crown Prince Yoshihito succeeds the throne

CE Year	Japanese Era year	Age	Life Events	Domestic/Overseas Events
1912	Meiji 45 Taishō 1	41		Second Saionji cabinet resigns en masse after rejecting the Imperial Japanese Army's demand to establish two additional divisions (Taishō Political Crisis)
1913	Taishō 2	42	Appointed counselor at the Japanese embassy in London. Makes the acquaintance of British Foreign Minister Edward Grey.	Rise of movements to defend the constitution in Japan
				Amendment of the Official Rule of Appointing War/Navy Ministers
				Japanese government obtains concession rights to Manchuria/Mongolia three railways and concession priority right to two railways. Japanese government recognizes Repulic of China.
				California Alien Land Law of 1913 enacted in the United States (intensifying discrimination against Japanese immigrants)
1914	Taishō 3	43	Appointed Envoy Extraordinary to the Netherlands and, concurrently, Denmark	Siemens Scandal
				Start of World War I (1914-18)
				British government requests Japan participate in World War I to search out and destroy German armed merchant ships in the Pacific. Japanese government agrees to join the war.
				Japan declares war against Germany. Imperial Japanese Navy captures and occupies Qingdao and the German North Pacific islands.

CE Year	Japanese Era year	Age	Life Events	Domestic/Overseas Events
1915	Taishō 4	44	Returns home in October and is appointed Vice Minister for Foreign Affairs. Serves under five foreign ministers (Ishii Kikujirō, Terauchi Masatake, Motono Ichirō, Gotō Shinpei, and Uchida Kōsai) before being appointed Japanese ambassador to the United States in 1919.	Twenty-One Demands
				Japan, France, Britain, Italy, and Russia sign the declaration to ban unilateral peace agreement
				Enthronement of Emperor Taishō
1916	Taishō 5	45		Yuan Shikai passes away
				Japanese government begins to provide loans to the Duan Qirui government in China (Nishihara Loans)
				US Naval Act of 1916 ("Big Navy Act") enacted
1917	Taishō 6	46		Germany steps up its indiscriminate assaults using submarines and other means to disrupt sea traffic
				Britain requests the Japanese fleet be dispatched to the Mediterranean. Japanese government decides to send twelve destroyers, led by the antiquated cruiser *Akashi*.
				Britain, France, and Russia acknowledge Japan's succession to former German concessions in China
				United States declares war on Germany
				Lansing-Ishii Agreement on China signed by United States Secretary of State Robert Lansing and Japanese special envoy Ishii Kikujirō
1918	Taishō 7	47		October Revolution in Russia

CE Year	Japanese Era year	Age	Life Events	Domestic/Overseas Events
1918	Taishō 7	47		Japanese troops dispatched to Siberia (until 1920)
				Rice Riots
				Hara Takashi cabinet, the first party cabinet in Japan, formed
1919	Taishō 8	48	Appointed Ambassador Extraordinary and Plenipotentiary to the United States	Paris Peace Conference
				Treaty of Versailles signed (creation of the League of Nations, territorial restrictions on Germany, war reparations imposed on Germany)
				March 1st Movement (Manse Demonstrations) in Korea
				May Fourth Movement in China
1920	Taishō 9	49		League of Nations established
				Imperial Navy's 8+8 Fleet Plan passes the Diet
				1920 California Alien Land Law passes in California
1921	Taishō 10	50	Father, Shinjirō, passes away in September	Crown Prince Hirohito tours European countries
			Appointed one of the plenipotentiaries for the Japanese delegation to the Washington Conference.	Washington Conference (1921-22)
				Hara Takashi assassinated
				Japan-Britain-France-US four-country treaty in the Pacific signed. Anglo-Japanese Alliance invalidated.
1922	Taishō 11	51	Returns home in April and is relieved of post of ambassador to the United States in December	Washington Conference concluded (Washington Naval Treaty to limit naval construction, Nine-Power Treaty on the sovereignty and territorial integrity of China, treaty on China's tariffs, and several other treaties signed)
1923	Taishō 12	52		Great Kantō Earthquake

CE Year	Japanese Era year	Age	Life Events	Domestic/Overseas Events
1924	Taishō 13	53	Appointed Minister for Foreign Affairs in fiirst Katō Takaaki cabinet in June, becoming the first Japanese foreign minister who had entered the ministry by passing the Foreign Service examination	Katō Takaaki cabinet (Three-Faction Pro-Constitution cabinet) formed
			Advocates international cooperation as the essense of his diplomacy in his first speech as foreign minister in July	Immigration Act of 1924 enacted in the United States
1925	Taishō 14	54	Participates in Special Conference on the Chinese Customs Tariff in Beijing in October. Japanese government announces at the outset that it siupports in principle the restoration of China's tariff autonomy, which contributes greatly to improving Chinese attitudes toward Japan.	General Election Law and Public Security Preservation Law of 1925 enacted
1926	Taishō 15 Shōwa 1	55	Reiterates non-interference in China's domestic politics and protection of China's justifiable interests in his foreign policy speech at the 51st Diet in January	Emperor Taishō passes away (at age 48). Crown Prince Hirohito becomes emperor.
			Appointed to House of Peers in January	
1927	Shōwa 2	56	Strives for peaceful settlment of the Nanjing Incident in March	Nanjing Incident
			Controversy between Kijūrō and Itō Miyoji, counselor to the Privy Council, on handling of the Nanjing Incident in April	First dispatch of Japanese troops to Shandong
			Resigns as Minister for Foreign Affairs	
1928	Shōwa 3	57		Zhang Zuolin assassinated in explosion
				First general election carried out
				Kellogg-Briand Pact (non-belligerency pact) concluded
1929	Shōwa 4	58	Appointed Minister for Foreign Affairs in the Hamaguchi Osachi cabinet in July	Great Depression triggered by the collapse of US stock market

CE Year	Japanese Era year	Age	Life Events	Domestic/Overseas Events
1929	Shōwa 4	58	Successfully mediates Sino-Soviet conflict	
1930	Shōwa 5	59	Shidehara Diplomacy based on non-interference in domestic affairs criticized by Japanese residents in Manchuria and the military	London Naval Conference (Japan, the United States, Britain, France, and Italy) convened
			Appointed acting Prime Minister in November due to the assassination attempt on Prime Minister Hamaguchi	Prime Minister Hamaguchi shot by a sniper
1931	Shōwa 6	60	Pursues settlement of the Nakamura Incident and the Wanpaoshan Incident through diplomatic means	Outline of Measures to Settle the Manchuria/Mongolian Issue compiled by the Ministry of War and the Imperial Japanese Army General Staff Office
			Resigns as Minister for Foreign Affairs in December as the Wakatsuki cabinet steps down	Liutiaohu Incident marks the beginning of the Manchurian Incident
1932	Shōwa 7	61		January 28 Incident
				Manchu State (Manchukuo) proclaimed
				May 15 Incident. Prime Minister Inukai assassinated
1933	Shōwa 8	62		Japan withdraws from League of Nations
1936	Shōwa 11	65		February 26 Incident
1937	Shōwa 12	66		Marco Polo Bridge Incident marks the beginning of the Second Sino-Japanese War
1939	Shōwa 14	68		Britain and France declare war on Germany, marking the start of World War II
1940	Shōwa 15	69		Tripartite Pact concluded among Germany, Italy and Japan
1941	Shōwa 16	70		Attack on Pearl Harbor marks the beginning of the Pacific War

CE Year	Japanese Era year	Age	Life Events	Domestic/Overseas Events
1945	Shōwa 20	74	Appointed prime minister in October	Atomic bombs dropped on Hiroshima and Nagasaki. Soviet Union declares war on Japan.
			Humanity Declaration for Emperor Shōwa drafted	Japan surrenders unconditionally to the Allies, ending World War II
			Hospitalized for pneumonia toward the end of the year	
1946	Shōwa 21	75	Outline of draft of amended Constitution of Japan announced in March	Japanese Constitution goes into effect
			Resigns as prime minister in April	
			Nominated as president of Shimpo-tō party in April	
			Appointed minister of state in the First Yoshida Shigeru cabinet. Appointed president of the Supporters' Association for Army Veterans.	
1947	Shōwa 22	76	Elected to House of Representatives from Osaka 3rd constituency in April.	
			Resigns as minister of state in May as the first Yoshida cabinet steps down.	
			Withdraws from Minshu-tō in November and forms Dōshi Kurabu.	
1948	Shōwa 23	77	Appointed the party's executive advisor as Dōshi Kurabu merges with Jiyū-tō to form Minshu-Jiyūtō in March	
1949	Shōwa 24	78	Elected to House of Representatives for a second term in January.	
			Elected chairman of the House of Representatives in February.	
1950	Shōwa 25	79		Start of Korean War (1950-53)
1951	Shōwa 26	80	Passes away at his residence in Setagaya, Tokyo, in March. Cause of death is cardiac infarct.	Treaty of San Francisco signed. US-Japan Treaty of Mutual Cooperation and security signed concurrently.

INDEX

Note: The abbreviation 't' after page numbers refers to tables. Page numbers in *italic* refer to photographs or illustrations.

Japanese/Chinese names are written with surname first and given name last

Canada 129, 130, 145, 147, 150

Castlereagh, Viscount 73–4

Chamberlain, Austen 196

Chamberlain, Joseph 148

Chang, Chun 282

Ch'en, Eugene 273, 274, 275

Chiang, Kai-shek 64, 115, 205, 223, 234, 250, 264, 274, 278

   China in turmoil 131, 204

   May 4th movement 132, 141–2

   Nanjing Incident (1927) 160, 208–10, 211, 212, 213–15, 226, 233, 235

   Northern Expedition (first) (China) (1926) 87, 88, 132, 206, 207, 208, 225–7

   Northern Expedition (second) (China) (1927) 231–3, 235, 236, 239, 251

China 34, 39, 40, 111, 160

   Anglo-Japanese Alliance 147–8, 149, 155

   anti-Japanese movements 63, 70, 225–8, 233, 235–8, 241, 264–7, 273, 278

   Communism 106, 107, 132, 205, 206

   freedom and equality 129, 198–200, 201–2

   Germany and 91, 138–9

   Great Britain and 89, 101

   Japan's expansion into Manchuria 58–61, 102, 103, 138

   Japan's imperialistic policies 66–8

   Japan's persistent non-interference in domestic politics 194–6, 197, 206, 209, 215, 225–6, 227, 230

   Lansing-Ishii Agreement (1917) 135–8, 156

   'multiple hearts' 211–14

   nationalism 221–4, 227, 228, 260

   Nishihara Loans 132–4

   protection of Japanese residents in 225–8, 233, 235, 236, 237, 238, 241, 265–7, 273, 278

   restoration of tariff autonomy 198–202

   revolutionary diplomacy 263–5

   Shangdong Peninsula 93, 112, 126, 131–2, 138, 140, 141

   Sino-Japanese Military Treaty 110, 115

   Soviet Union and 206, 207–8, 223, 249–51

   Tanaka Cabinet's foreign policy towards 227–31, 254

   in turmoil 204–7

   United States and 58, 59, 60, 63, 67, 135,

193, 212–13, 262, 285

   Xinhai Revolution (First Revolution) (1911) 51–8, 59, 60, 62, 112, 206

   see also Twenty-One Demands

China's Destiny (Chiang) 141–2

Chinda, Ambassador Sutemi 97, 139

Chinese Communist Party 52, 106, 223

Chinese Customs Tariff, Special Conference on the (1925) 199, 200

Chinese Eastern Railway 231, 249

Chinese Exclusion Act (1882) (United States) 39

Chinese Nationalist Party 142, 204

Chūō Kōron 220, 255

Churchill, Winston 92, 140, 148, 187

Clemenceau, Georges 22, 141

Colby, Bainbridge 47

Cold War 106, 107, 165, 171, 181, 228, 230, 261, 277

collective security 147, 157–8, 240

Colombia 37, 208, 215

Comintern 105–6, 223–4, 228

Commerce and Navigation, Treaty of (1911) 43

Communism 51, 87, 105–17, 205, 207–8, 209, 222, 228, 249

Communist Party of China 132, 205, 206, 207–9, 227, 238

Constitution of Japan 239

constitutional government *see* parliamentary democracy

Conyngham Greene, Sir William 89–90, 100

court nobles 20–4

Cultural Revolution (China) 51

Curzon, George 148

Czechoslovakia 115, 121, 158

D

Dai-Kaigun o Omou (The Great Navy in retrospect) (Itō) 259

Daniels, Josephus 144

de Gaulle, Charles (President, France) 40, 267

defence policies *see* Imperial Defense Policy

democracy *see* parliamentary democracy

Deng, Xiaoping 51

Diplomacy (Kissinger) 32–3, 157, 158, 178, 239, 240

diplomats and diplomacy 13–14, 16, 70, 82,

（英文版）幣原喜重郎とその時代
Shidehara Kijuro and His Time

2020年3月27日　第1刷発行

著　者　　岡崎久彦

訳　者　　野田牧人

発行所　　一般財団法人出版文化産業振興財団
　　　　　〒101-0051 東京都千代田区神田神保町2-2-30
　　　　　電話　03-5211-7283

ホームページ　https://www.jpic.or.jp/

印刷・製本所　　大日本印刷株式会社

定価はカバーに表示してあります。
本書の無断複写（コピー）、転載は著作権法の例外を除き、禁じられています。